Heroines without Heroes

Women Make Cinema

Series Editors: Pam Cook, University of Southampton
Ginette Vincendeau, University of Warwick

Women Make Cinema is a ground-breaking series dedicated to celebrating the contribution of women to all aspects of film-making throughout the world. Until recently feminist criticism has focused on the exclusion of women from mainstream cinema, emphasizing the relatively small number of women directors and their restricted opportunities. *Women Make Cinema* assesses the historical impact of women as both producers and consumers of cinematic images. As stars, directors, scriptwriters, editors, producers, designers, critics and audiences, they have exerted a powerful influence on world cinema. This series opens up this hidden history, giving women a central place in the development of cinema.

Heroines without Heroes

Reconstructing Female and National Identities in European Cinema 1945–51

Edited by Ulrike Sieglohr

CASSELL
London and New York

Cassell
Wellington House, 125 Strand, London WC2R 0BB
370 Lexington Avenue, New York, NY 10017–6550

First published 2000

British Library Cataloguing-in-Publication Data

A catalogue record for this book is available from the British Library.

ISBN 0-304-70249-8 (hardback)
0-304-70250-1 (paperback)

Library of Congress Cataloging-in-Publication Data

Heroines without heroes : reconstructing female and national identities in European cinema, 1945–51 / edited by Ulrike Sieglohr.
p. cm.
Includes bibliographical references and index.
ISBN 0-304-70249-8 (hb.). – ISBN 0-304-70250-1 (pb)
1. Women in motion pictures. 2. Motion pictures—Europe—History.
I. Sieglohr, Ulrike.
PN1995.9.W6H47 2000
791.43'652042'09045—dc21

99-27573
CIP

Designed and typeset by Ben Cracknell Studios

Printed and bound in Great Britain by TJ International Ltd, Padstow, Cornwall

Contents

Note: For foreign-language films, a translation of the title is given at first occurrence and the original title alone is used thereafter. If the film has not been distributed with an English title, the translation is by the author of the chapter.

Illustrations

Contributors

Noël Burch is a film-maker and Professor of Film Studies, University of Lille III. He is the author of *Praxis du cinéma* (1969), *To the Distant Observer* (Scolar Press, 1979), *Life to Those Shadows* (British Film Institute, 1980), *In and out of Synch: The Awakening of a Cine-Dreamer* (Scolar Press, 1988); editor of *Revoir Hollywood* (Nathan, 1993); co-author with Thom Andersen of *Les Communistes de Hollywood* (Presses de la Sorbonne, 1994); and with Geneviève Sellier of *La Drôle de guerre des sexes du cinéma français 1930–1956* (Nathan, 1996).

Lesley Caldwell is Senior Lecturer in Sociology, University of Greenwich. She is the author of *Italian Family Matters* (Macmillan, 1991) and wrote the chapter 'The national dimension? Verdi and Bernardo Bertolucci', in Jeremy Tambling (ed.), *A Night in at the Opera: Media Representation of Opera* (John Libbey/The Arts Council, 1994).

Erica Carter, Research Fellow in German Studies at the University of Warwick, is the author of *How German Is She? Post-War West German Reconstruction and the Consuming Woman* (University of Michigan Press, 1997); she co-edited with James Donald and Judith Squires, *Cultural Remix: Theories of Politics and the Popular* (Lawrence & Wishart, 1996); and was Managing Editor of *New Formations* between 1988 and 1991.

Susan Hayward is Chair of French at the University of Exeter. She has written extensively on French cinema – *French Film: Texts and Contexts*, co-edited with Ginette Vincendeau (Routledge, 1990), *French National Cinema* (Routledge, 1993), *Key Concepts in Cinema Studies* (Routledge, 1996) and *Luc Besson* (Manchester University Press, 1998). She is currently co-editing with Ginette Vincendeau a new edition of *French Film: Texts and Contexts*.

Christine Geraghty is Senior Lecturer in Media and Communication at Goldsmiths College, University of London. She is the author of *Women and Soap Opera* (Polity, 1991), co-editor of *The Television Studies Book* (Arnold, 1998) and has written extensively on British cinema. She is currently working on a book on British film and society in the 1950s.

Jo Labanyi is Professor of Modern Spanish Literature and Cultural Studies, Birkbeck College, University of London, and Director of the Institute of Romance Studies, University of London. She has published books and articles on nineteenth- and twentieth-century Spanish and Spanish-American fiction, including the co-edited volumes *Culture and Gender in Nineteenth-Century Spain* (Oxford University Press, 1995) and *Spanish Cultural Studies: An Introduction* (Oxford University Press, 1995). Her publications on film include 'Race, gender and disavowal in Spanish cinema of the early Franco period: the missionary film and the folkloric musical', *Screen*, Vol. 38, No. 3 (1997), and 'Fetishism and the problem of sexual difference in Buñuel's *Tristana*', in Peter W. Evans (ed.), *Spanish Film Classics* (Oxford University Press, 1999). She is currently writing a book on early Francoist cinema and preparing a collaborative research project with colleagues in Spain and the USA on *An Oral History of Cinema-going in 1940s and 1950s Spain.*

Sarah Leahy is a postgraduate student at the University of Exeter. She is currently researching and preparing her doctoral dissertation on Simone Signoret and Brigitte Bardot.

Geneviève Sellier is Maîtresse de Conférences (Assistant Professor), Department of Arts du Spectacle, Université de Caen. She is author of *Jean Grémillon: le cinéma est à vous* (Meridiens-Klincksieck, 1989), *Les Enfants du paradis: étude critique* (Nathan, 1992) and co-author with Noël Burch of *La Drôle de guerre des sexes du cinéma français 1930–1956* (Nathan, 1996). She was guest editor of 'Jean Grémillon', Special issue of *1895 Journal of Film History* (1997) and of 'Cultural studies, gender studies and film studies', *Iris*, No. 26 (1998).

Ulrike Sieglohr is Senior Lecturer in Media Studies at Staffordshire University. Her publications include *Focus on the Maternal: Female Subjectivity and Images of Motherhood* (Scarlet Press, 1998), 'Why drag the diva into it? Werner Schroeter's gay representation of femininity', in Marjorie O'Sickey and Ingeborg von Zadow (eds), *Triangulated Visions* (SUNY Press, 1998). She has also published essays on women film-makers and on various aspects of New German Cinema.

Sarah Street is a Senior Lecturer in the Department of Drama: Theatre, Film, Television, at the University of Bristol. She has published widely on British cinema; her latest book is *British National Cinema* (Routledge, 1997) and she is currently completing a book on the distribution and exhibition of British films in the USA.

Carrie Tarr is a Senior Research Fellow at Thames Valley University, London. Her work on gender, sexuality and ethnicity in classic and contemporary French cinema has been widely published in journals such as *Screen*, *Iris*, *Modern & Contemporary France* and *Contemporary French Civilization*. Her most recent publication is *Diane Kurys* (Manchester University Press, 1999), and she is currently researching a book on women's cinema in France 1980–1999.

Núria Triana-Toribio lectures in Spanish film and history at the University of Liverpool. She was awarded a doctorate for *Subculture and Popular Culture in the Films of Pedro Almodóvar* in 1994 by the University of Newcastle upon Tyne. Her publications include articles in *Film History* and *Bulletin of Hispanic Studies*, and a forthcoming chapter on *What Have I Done to Deserve This?* (Pedro Almodóvar, 1984) for a collection entitled *Spanish Cinema: The Auteurist Tradition* (edited by Peter Evans, Oxford University Press, 1999). She has also contributed to the forthcoming encyclopaedias of *Contemporary Spanish Culture* and *Contemporary Spanish Cultural Studies* (Oxford University Press).

Mary P. Wood is Senior Lecturer in Media Studies, Faculty of Continuing Education, Birkbeck College, University of London. She is responsible for an extensive programme of undergraduate and diploma classes in aspects of the media. Her research field is Italian cinema, and her most recent publications are 'Francesco Rosi: heightened realism', in John Boorman and Walter Donohue (eds), *Projections 8* (Faber, 1998) and 'Pirandello and Pirandellism in film', *Journal of the Society for Pirandello Studies* (1999).

Acknowledgements

My first debt is to the contributors. They remained patient with me even when they may have thought that my requests for revisions were excessive. Mary Wood needs to be singled out among the contributors for organizing a related conference 'Heroines without Heroes', which facilitated a lively exchange of ideas while the essays were still being written.

The idea for this book originated in a stimulating conference, 'Wayward Women and Wounded Men in Early Post-war Cinema', organized in June 1995 by Margaret Dériaz at the Goethe Institut in London. This event explored representations of gender in the years following the Second World War in the cinemas of Britain, France, Germany and the United States. Not only did Margaret spark the idea but she has always been a supportive friend.

I would like to thank both Cassell's editor Janet Joyce and the series editors Pam Cook and Ginette Vincendeau for making this anthology possible. Special thanks to Ginette for helping out on many occasions and for patiently clarifying some issues concerning French cinema.

At an institutional level I should like to thank Staffordshire University for financial and other support, in particular Professor Derek Longhurst. For personal support, sincere thanks go to to my colleagues and friends Christine Gledhill and Martin Shingler.

Thanks also to Martin Brady, Helen Hughes, Brigitte Jacobi and Hildegard Krause – the music they tracked down by Hildegard Knef kept me going throughout a summer of editing.

Finally, my deepest gratitude goes to Jim Cook, who generously offered extensive advice and assistance during the editing of this anthology.

Ulrike Sieglohr
London, 1999

To all the women who enjoyed going to the pictures after the war

Introduction

ULRIKE SIEGLOHR

The eleven essays in this anthology explore the early post-war years of European cinema (1945–51) by refiguring issues of national identity in terms of gender representation. In the aftermath of the Second World War and its social and psychic upheavals, reconstructing femininity was inextricably linked to reconstructing an official and dominant national identity. Given the extraordinary nature of women's experience during the war years, however, an unproblematic return to the traditional pre-war confines of gender and class was impossible. In addition countervailing and potentially more radical tendencies were present, eager to urge new components in the construction of national identities. In this context representations of women in the European cinemas considered here are consonant with each country's role during the war, and its victorious, vanquished or compromised post-liberation status. These representations reflect the tensions within the contemporary discourses around national identity, with the female figures not simply challenging older fixed notions of gender identity but also actively constituting expressions of new identities still in flux and contestation.

Thinking through a period of reconstruction

To argue that the years immediately following the Second World War were a period of reconstruction and cultural renewal suggests both the continuities of old structures as well as new beginnings:

> The postwar period in Europe began politically and culturally with faith in 'rebirth'. . . . Within a few years, however, it became clear that what Europe was witnessing was rather a process of 'Reconstruction', a more complex and more ambiguous process in which the rebuilding of the past was inextricably mixed with the search for the new. (Hewitt, 1989: 11)

To consider cinema's role in this period as an indicator of both social change and retrenchment, certain critical and discursive procedures are necessary. Traditionally European cinema has been discussed as 'art' in opposition to Hollywood as 'entertainment', thus foregrounding individual auteurs and national cinema movements such as Italian neo-realism, the French New Wave and the New German Cinema. While this dominant approach successfully evaluated films aesthetically and established canons according to these criteria, more recent critical developments have widened the debate by turning to previously marginalized areas, such as popular European cinema (Dyer and Vincendeau, 1992), and to the relationship between society and cinema (Sorlin, 1991). Crucially, as part of the argument that popular culture matters, this relationship between artefact and culture '[has] to be considered "not simply as evidence of social change but as an actual part of social change"' (Arthur Marwick, cited by Sorlin, 1991: 20).

Thus, writers on British cinema have noted how after the war it was felt that the national cinema should continue to project the ideals fought for during the war and strive to convey the idea of a national community, overriding differences of class, region and gender (see, for example, Higson, 1994, Chapter 5). As Michael Balcon's policy for Ealing Studios expressed it, films should be 'projecting Britain and the British character' (cited by Nowell-Smith, 1996: 436). In studies of French cinema it has been noted that the industry had prospered under the German occupation and that after the war not only were some film personnel punished for having fraternized with the Germans[1] but also, for a short period, a range of films was produced which consciously tried to compensate by glorifying the Resistance movement (see also Vincendeau, 1995: 156). In Spain, along with deprivation and political repression, the years from the mid-1940s to early 1950s were also a period in which Franco's regime attempted a national reconciliation through depoliticization, and films turned from exalting military values towards the world of romance, shifting from explicit propaganda to popular entertainment.

To conceive of cinema as a cultural tool for effecting social change was, of course, one of the most important considerations that underpinned the film policies of the Allies for political re-education in the former fascist countries:

> If there were a cultural issue around which, in 1945 itself, a large measure of agreement existed, it was that the new cinema in Europe should be democratic and the cinema should never again be allowed to be used, as it had been in Nazi Germany and to a lesser extent Fascist Italy, as an instrument of totalitarian ideology. (Nowell-Smith, 1998: 5)

Reconstructing the devastated film industries in Germany and Italy was controlled by political and economic interests, in so far as the Allied Film

Commissions (whose task it was to help rebuild the industries in the defeated countries) involved both military personnel and Hollywood executives, some of whom held military rank. Crucially, while the Commissions' rhetoric promoted democratic re-education, effectively they allowed the Americans to offload a six-year backlog of films and to restore Hollywood's hegemony in Western Europe.[2]

From a cultural studies perspective, a fruitful mapping of the interconnections between cultural productions and social experience during this period of reconstruction has been made (see, for example, Hewitt, 1989). On the other hand, from a feminist perspective studies of the roles of women in various post-war societies discuss how women, who had worked during the war in traditional male occupations, had in the post-war situation to negotiate between conflicting notions of femininity. (See, for example, Wilson, 1980, and Myrdal and Klein, 1956, on Britain; Kuhn, 1984, on Germany; Duchen, 1994, on France; Graham, 1995, on post-Civil War Spain.) Another significant body of work (exemplified by books such as Durgnat, 1970, and Higson, 1994, on British cinema; Kinder, 1993,[3] on Spanish cinema; Hoffman and Schobert, 1989, on West German cinema) takes the form of studies of national cinemas which tend to be framed in terms of reconstructing national identity. Finally, there is a smaller body of work specifically on women in particular national cinemas: Britain (Gledhill and Swanson, 1996a); France (Burch and Sellier, 1996);[4] Germany (Fehrenbach, 1995).

Each of these three broad types of study takes as its implicit rationale an equivalence between the immense popularity of cinema and its cultural significance as 'a site where issues of femininity, sexuality and nation are vividly dramatised' (Gledhill and Swanson, 1996b: 6): in Britain cinema audiences peaked in 1946 with 31.4 million per week (*ibid.*), while in 1947 in France 430 million and in Italy 500 million spectators went to the cinema (Sorlin, 1989: 89).

This anthology draws on and benefits from all of these studies and their perspectives of femininist theory, film history and star studies in order to offer the first single volume that examines representations of femininity *across* the major West European national cinemas during this period of reconstruction. To understand more clearly the varying roles played by cinema during this period of possibilities for women (women only gained the vote in France in 1944, and in Italy in 1946) this anthology offers a comparative study across five national cinemas and of their emblematic female stars. By analysing the appeal of these major European stars in terms of the post-war conditions which were the making of many of them, the essays also allow us, for the first time, to make film and cultural critical comparisons between them.

Structure and methodology

The essays prove fascinating equally for their revelation of the extent to which the same social/gender issues are negotiated as for their analyses of the different cinematic articulations of these concerns. A common characteristic that emerges is the resourcefulness and independence of the female protagonists: the women – ranging from treacherous *femme fatales* to practical 'rubble women' rebuilding their homes – are usually more decisive than the male characters, hence the title *Heroines without Heroes*.

The anthology is organized by country, and each overview chapter is complemented by a case study of a female star. The choice of star was determined less by their contemporary popularity, or lasting fame, than by their emblematic function. My broad rationale is a belief that in both film and 'real life' stars are important for the function they play in the social imaginary and a study of them can further our cultural understanding of a historical period. As Richard Dyer (1979: 38) points out, 'star images function crucially in relation to contradictions within and between ideologies, which they seek variously to "manage" or resolve.' The stars examined are composite structures comprising the 'real person', the roles/characters played and the star persona: 'The persona . . . forms the private life into a public and emblematic shape, drawing on general social types and film roles, while deriving authenticity from the unpredictability of the real person' (Gledhill, 1991: 215). Unlike popular discussions of stars, glamour is only of interest here in so far as it illuminates the socio-historical context. Although made specifically in relation to Italian stars, the following point by Stephen Gundle (1996: 316) seems equally applicable to other domestic European stars:

> there were also many stars who bore no relation at all to American [glamour] models, who could only be understood in the context of Italian society, and who in no sense formed vehicles of dreams and fantasy, whether imported or home-grown.

The selected case studies of stars should, in other words, promote 'an understanding of their relationship with social, historical, and ideological values' (Vincendeau, 1998: 447).

Specifically commissioned from scholars of the five national cinemas, the essays are at pains to put 'herstory' back into history by examining the specific historical contexts out of which representations of women in the immediate post-war period emerged. All the essays were written in the knowledge that they would appear in this *comparative* anthology. Comparison within and between the five countries is the overarching rationale for the organization of the chapters. In practice, although the chapters on each country are interrelated, they were written independently and there is inevitably some overlap between the overview and the individual case study.

It should also be noted that whereas the overview chapters tend to be weighted towards history, and the specific star studies towards representation, the crucial difference is one of emphasis and varies from section to section. Lesley Caldwell, for example, in her general survey of Italian cinema is explicit about the contradictory nature of representation when she notes that there is no simple link between an artefact and its surrounding culture, nor between minority film culture's ideological 'meaning' and the readings assumed or inferred to have been made by contemporary audiences. Similarly, in individual star case studies Núria Triana-Toribio, Sarah Leahy and Susan Hayward, and I all explicitly discuss the late-1990s implications of our studies, and Mary Wood specifically mentions the continuing contemporary relevance of Anna Magnani's star image.

It is also important to note that the current critical debate on contexts and national cinemas explicitly or implicitly informs the approaches. For instance, Noël Burch and Geneviève Sellier's polemical stance needs to be read in the context of a reaction against the traditional concern of French film criticism with aesthetic issues at the expense of the ideological, especially gender roles. Similarly, Jo Labanyi and Núria Triana-Toribio are writing about a period of Spanish cinema not only critically dismissed in general but one where discussion of gender issues in particular is almost entirely absent.

Not all of the national cinemas under consideration fit unproblematically into the designated period and indeed Spain may appear at first sight to be an anomaly since it did not participate in the Second World War. Yet, as Jo Labanyi shows, not only was the country significantly affected by the demise of fascism in Germany and Italy but, more importantly for the concerns of this volume, the Spanish Civil War, which had ended in 1939, also created similar gender upheavals. Arguably the years 1945 to 1951 offer us more issues for comparison than the immediate post-Civil War period, which was dominated by masculine values. In other words, despite some slight chronological variants, for all of the contributors the interval between the end of the Second World War and the beginning of the 1950s is seen, in Erica Carter's phrase, as an 'interregnum' for gender politics, a period during which the restabilization of national identities is attempted through various recastings of emancipated femininity in order to fit it back again into patriarchal institutions and priorities.

One of the consequences of studying single national cinemas is an undeniable exclusivity of concerns, and in attempting to confront this situation I am very aware of the sad irony that this volume may inadvertently create a larger exclusivity. Crudely put, the countries selected for inclusion are western Eurocentric. This choice may consolidate further the already marginalized study status of eastern and northern European cinemas at this (or indeed any other) time. My only justifications for producing a selective volume are pragmatism and gradualism. Pragmatically, since a relevant and varied body of work was known to me it seemed better to produce something comparative rather than nothing at all. From a gradualist point of view, and beyond its intrinsic interest, the inclusion of the Spanish studies at least starts to decentre and make a little strange the better-known national cinemas. Of course, their inclusion also highlights another ongoing problem for serious comparative research: the inaccessibility of many of the films discussed and their unfamiliarity for non-Spanish readers.

Key issues

Allowing for diversity of methodology and style, all of the essays link text and social context and are concerned with two underlying questions: What kind of femininity was promoted to serve the preferred vision(s) of national identity? To what extent were these gender identities shaped by continuing pre-war cultural and cinematic traditions and to what extent were they markedly different and new?

Negotiations of femininity

During this period of transition the five national cinemas negotiate female identity and the stabilization of national identity in rather different ways. Christine Geraghty shows how victorious Britain represented women in terms which recognized the changes from the past and the difficulties attendant on adapting to new circumstances: thus in British cinema the personal choices the women have to make between the traditional and the new are metaphors for the choices facing the nation as a whole. Similarly, as Sarah Street implies, Margaret Lockwood's characters, (frequently split between repression and sexual desire) can be read symptomatically through the contradictory femininities on offer as representations of women torn between different kinds of choice.

In contrast to British cinema produced in a country which did not have to come to terms with the past but only with post-war social changes, the cinema of a politically compromised country, such as France, stresses repression of the past and a traumatic rewriting of history by assigning shame and guilt on a division of gender. As Noël Burch and Geneviève Sellier argue, in a range of French films the historical cross-gender shame over collaboration with the Nazis was progressively recast in representations as female *collaboration horizontale*. Thus, as Carrie Tarr shows, although in the immediate post-war cinema, Micheline Presle can be seen initially as emblematic of the 'New Woman' and her subsequent containment, her sophisticated femininity was eclipsed a little later by more virulent misogynistic representations of *femmes fatales*, as, for example, those of Simone Signoret discussed by Sarah Leahy and Susan Hayward.[5] Conversely, in German cinema, as Erica Carter and I note, male directors constructed heroines as guiltless in order to allow them the function of redeemer of male guilt: the role of women, epitomized by Hildegard Knef, was to heal male pride and to restore spiritual and material order to a nation in ruins.

However, in Italy, a gender perspective on guilt does not seem to exist. In this country, where the last years of the war (1943–5) had been marked by civil war between fascists and liberal left alliances, Lesley Caldwell notes that neo-realist cinema was 'progressive' in the way it represented aspects of Italian society which were at odds with official accounts of a unified national identity. It is important also to recognize that neo-realist films were lacking popular appeal and their cultural impact was limited to a minority audience (see, for instance, Wagstaff, 1989; and Sorlin, 1989). However, although women have a more active role – at least in the neo-realist films – than in the pre-1945 films, they are usually still located exclusively within the family. In this context it is interesting that in Mary Wood's discussion of the more popular Anna Magnani – strong, erotic, maternal and embodying the experience of working-class women – she points out that the ideological drive to containment through the narrative is frequently problematized by the emotional force of the performances.

Paradoxically, the most politically oppressed society, Spain, also created the most dynamic female protagonists. Jo Labanyi demonstrates that early Francoist cinema, usually perceived as a period of high censorship and anti-women sentiment, was much more contradictory and 'not a straightforward reflection of the regime's ideology'. Although the plot structures are often traditional, as with Magnani the flamboyant performances of the female stars often go beyond them and the confines of Francoist ideology. Specifically, Núria Triana-Toribio's star study of Ana Mariscal demonstrates that although this Francoist star was in real life an arch conservative, nonetheless the roles she played were capable of generating contradictory meanings at variance with the assumed dominant ideology.

Constructing social and ideological meanings

All five national cinemas 'reflected' and responded to external events – the post-Second World War situation and the post-Civil War dictatorship in Spain – and all the essays turn to textual analysis to identify a number of recurring formal characteristics in the films' ascriptions of social and ideological 'meanings' to these events. Each cinema drew on an indigenous pre-war cinematic tradition, such as Poetic and *noir* Realism in France and Expressionism in Germany, and at the same time was inevitably influenced by Hollywood. This influence took the form either of reworking its dominant narrative conventions and gender politics (as in Germany, France and Spain) or of reacting against Hollywood dominance through the promotion and, if not always or exclusively, the practice of a more 'authentic' (neo)realism, as in Italy and Britain.

Film noir in particular and the concomitant figure of the *femme fatale* became an important mode of narration for negotiating the uncertainties of the post-war period in France. Burch and Sellier's, and Leahy and Hayward's essays offer insightful analyses of the ways in which *film noir* conventions block the articulation of a female perspective by enabling expressions of male anxieties through flashback structures usually from a male point of view. Carrie Tarr's analysis of *Le Diable au corps*, provides a further pertinent example. In the early post-war German cinema a male point of view is also privileged through flashback and Erica Carter notes specifically that in a film such as *Die Mörder sind unter uns* this is achieved through drawing on the visual and narrative rhetorics of German Expressionism. However, what is different here from the French films is that the flashbacks specifically signify the instability of the male psyche which disrupts the narrative with the guilt of repressed memories of Nazi war atrocities. Male redemption in these German films becomes possible only through female innocence – as figured by Knef – and what is at stake in the rehabilitation of men is the suppression not just of female subjectivity but of female historical agency as well – women's own complicity in the Nazi regime.

This is, of course, the absolute reversal of the French construction, as described by Burch and Sellier: it is the guilty *femme fatale*, epitomized by Signoret in *Manèges*, who figures as the scapegoat for collaboration with the Germans. Interestingly, once again issues of performance come into play here. In a nuanced disagreement with Burch and Sellier's reading, Leahy and Hayward suggest that, for example, in *Manèges* Signoret's powerful performance *expresses* female desire and thereby undermines unambiguous identification with the male point of view.

Of course, it is precisely in their adaptation from one cinematic culture to another that formal devices fuse with indigenous cinematic and cultural elements, and are modified through ideological pressures. In Spanish cinema, the *mise-en-scène* and other generic conventions of *film noir* are harnessed to domestic melodrama with the result that in one instance, *La vida en un hilo*, as Jo Labanyi shows, the investigative structure is reworked as a gender reversal when two women examine negative and positive models of masculinity and explore, not anxieties about their own sexuality, but female pleasure. Similarly, in my discussion of Knef I show how, in another generic twist, in the German film *Die Sünderin* the *film noir* voice-over and flashback structures promote female subjectivity, but only in order to realize the heroine's self-sacrifice at the end of the film.

Finally, of course, there can be productive combinations of elements from within a film culture hitherto deemed incompatible by critical orthodoxy. We have already seen how concerns of neo-realism were at some distance from state ideologies and, as Geraghty convincingly demonstrates, social issues and gender politics in Britain are addressed symbolically in a group of Ealing Studios' films which systematically fuse melodrama with realism.

In all of the cinemas considered, stars and their roles are particularly significant in so far as they embody literally contemporary social contradictions and, as my analysis of Knef shows, not just the roles but also the historical discursive construction of a star persona are inextricably linked to cinematic and social changes. Not surprisingly, therefore, it is through the detailed considerations of individual stars that the most striking differences and distinct concerns appear:

- Signoret's move from victim to 'bitch' in a period of only two years signifies a progressive structural misogyny, even if, thanks to her performance skills, these roles can be read against the grain.
- Mariscal, who was Franco's favourite star and therefore suppressed in post-Francoist accounts of the national cinema, becomes emblematic precisely because she seems unrecuperable.
- A popular British star such as Lockwood offers interesting distinctions between Hollywood and British notions of stardom. In Hollywood it was typecasting, in Britain it was a showcase for acting ability.
- Unlike Lockwood, whose star image as a 'lady' differentiated her from her fans, Magnani was a woman of the people. She embodied the aspirations of working-class women, authenticating and giving dignity to their desires.
- Finally both Presle and Knef, at the height of their success, were drawn to Hollywood in the late 1940s, albeit for different reasons, and they returned to their indigenous cinemas without having succeeded there.

While the reasons for success and failure in Hollywood are more complex than I can offer here – and Knef did enjoy a number of Hollywood successes in the 1950s – one could suggest that perhaps, apart from timing, some European stars' national emblematic qualities not only differed from Hollywood's idealized standards but also were subject to local pressures and changes. Certainly Tarr's study of Presle's star image as the 'New Woman' shows that not only were the glamour and sophisticated fashion she connoted for French audiences not sufficient in themselves to make her a Hollywood star but they were also not flexible enough to fit the changed *Zeitgeist* on her return to France. More generally, as Hollywood re-secured its hold on Europe, around 1951 the essays note a shift in all of the cinemas' representations of femininity. With the interesting exception of Spain, which came to be dominated by neo-realist art cinema representations, everywhere else new popular stars like Diana Dors,

Gina Lollobrigida and Martine Carol came to incarnate an increasingly sexualized and eroticized female body that arguably owed as much to the Hollywood international standard of glamour as to any national tradition of feminine beauty and representation.

Conclusion

Underpinning the arguments in the eleven essays, and indeed generating them, is the current conjuncture between feminist film theory and the new film history. In so far as the 'insights' of theory help order the 'facts' of history this is a methodological alliance with great potential, but history and theory are never unproblematically conjoined and a certain tension between them is perhaps symptomatic of cinema studies as currently constituted. Certainly very different readings are produced when films made half a century ago are considered from the contemporary viewpoint of radically changed but traceable histories and then from the more static and ahistorical viewpoint of representations under patriarchy. Put simply, since the present 'real' in both its cultural and cinematic manifestations bears little resemblance to the early post-war period, we have to guard against interpreting stars and narratives too readily from a present feminist consciousness whereby audience affect and understanding are inferred ahistorically.

What the theory/history interface allows us to perceive is that while any raw ideological material undergoes processes of displacement and revision during the inevitable transformation into pleasurable fiction, what is displaced or revised, and how, is governed by specific cultural agendas and imperatives. So, while narrativization generally tends to displace politics in favour of gender in all of the cinemas under consideration, it is noticeable that, for instance, in British cinema a correspondence between ideas of femininity and national needs is discernible, whereas in the cinemas of defeated or politically compromised nations politics are effectively repressed through more substantial displacements onto gender. In French cinema women are constructed increasingly as scapegoats; in German cinema female complicity is repressed so that men can be exonerated; and Italian cinema, while offering a range of images of women, is less obviously concerned with sexual politics and more with social politics in general and the conflicting notions of a Communist versus Christian identity. Perhaps most intriguingly of all, in Spanish cinema representations of femininity are put to the service of feminizing and domesticating men in order to facilitate the transition from a military ideology to one more suited to a peaceful, albeit politically reactionary, society.

I hope that conclusions like these – both provocative and provisional – will encourage us all (writers and readers alike) not only to look again at the films we know but also to seek out those we have previously been unaware of. By moving out from our national specialisms, by refining our theories with histories and, perhaps most urgently of all, by trying to develop adequate terms to describe performance and effect, we may contribute to the production of a more historically broad-based and theoretically flexible cinema studies than is often currently the case. This anthology has been produced as a contribution to such a project.

Notes

1. Famous examples to undergo *épuration* (purification) were the star Arletty and the director Henri-Georges Clouzot.
2. Although a number of governments, Britain and France in particular, were eager to regulate the flow, in fact the number of imported American films in many Western European countries led to a conflict between satisfying the audience's demand for Hollywood films and establishing 'a new cinema in the climate of cultural renewal' (Nowell-Smith, 1996: 436).
3. Although Kinder's magisterial book starts only with the 1950s, it is, nevertheless, illuminating by inference about the period under consideration.
4. Burch and Sellier's chapter in this anthology is based on their book.
5. However, Burch and Sellier note as well that in opposition to this paranoid mainstream, a few remarkable films tried 'to look at the "new deal" of equality between men and women [and] proposed gender roles and relations owing little to pre-war cinema but much to patterns developed under the Occupation'.

Britain

CHAPTER ONE

Post-war Choices and Feminine Possibilities

CHRISTINE GERAGHTY

This essay examines the symbolic positioning of women at the crossroads in British cinema between the end of the war and the early 1950s. It argues that a focus on women's choices was a significant feature of post-war British films and that the choices which women make in these films are metaphors for the choices which the nation as a whole faced in this period. Women could assume this representative role because of the social changes which had affected them during the war, particularly mobilization, and because the key issues of post-war reconstruction were strongly associated with the more traditional feminine roles – national arrangements for childcare, health, welfare and the family. Concentrating on the role of women in films of the immediate post-war period (1945–51) the essay focuses on heroines who have to choose between competing ideas about what society might be like and looks at how the consequences of such choices were represented. The problems and dilemmas posed in these films make it possible to see how apparently individual romantic choices in the films act as a metaphor for the issues of reconstruction and social choice which were crucial to post-war Britain.

I shall look primarily at three films: *It Always Rains on Sunday* (Robert Hamer, 1947), *Cage of Gold* (Basil Dearden, 1950) and *Dance Hall* (Charles Crichton, 1950). They were made at Ealing Studios, still in this period run by Michael Balcon who had established such a strong studio identity during the war. Although Ealing is now most strongly associated with its comedies, I want to draw attention to three social melodramas which combine a naturalist attention to the details of everyday life with a set of realist conventions about the capacity of an individual life to represent a social condition and with a melodramatic emphasis on women's ability to live out a fuller and more intense emotional life. Although Ealing handles its central female protagonists in a distinctive way, it was not unique in focusing on women in this period. Gainsborough Studios were notorious for portraying heroines who were frequently caught between two worlds, while quality films such as *Brief*

Encounter (David Lean, 1945) also centred on the heroine's choice between two men.[1] Ealing's overt interest in realism and social issues, however, means that its films offer particularly telling examples of this polarized narrative structure centring on women and, I would suggest, calls into question the common association between the realist emphasis of many Ealing films and what Cook (1996: 5) identifies as its 'cosy, parochial Englishness'.

The war had, it was generally recognized, given British cinema a role. In an environment curtailed by the blackout, rationing, travel restrictions and air raids, cinema was seen as a crucial source of leisure entertainment. The availability of films of all kinds was regarded as an important way of keeping up morale and mobilizing consent, particularly of civilians and most particularly of women (Thumim, 1996: 243). Cinema-going as a regular activity continued after the war. The peak year was 1946, with the massive decline not really beginning until the 1950s (Laing, 1986). In addition, it was argued in the film industry and in government that British films should have the explicit function of maintaining an idea of what was being fought for, of presenting the nation to itself, and of creating a community and unity out of the different interests and intentions of those involved (Higson, 1994: Chapter 5). Michael Balcon was one of the prime exponents of this policy, which was by no means welcomed by everyone in the industry. At the beginning of the war, he was one of the first to call for cinema to be put to the services of the war effort, and in 1945 he continued to argue the need for films which reflected Britain in a way that would encourage social responsibility within the nation and project what he called the 'true Briton to the rest of the world' (quoted in Barr, 1977: 7). There is therefore a continuity between wartime and post-war cinema as a popular source of entertainment and, at Ealing at least, a desire to reflect in some way the social changes taking place in post-war Britain.

The second important legacy of the war was that the question of women was seen as a potential source of difficulty in the post-war construction. Women had experienced profound and contradictory change and it was recognized that the demands made of them had affected their traditional pre-war roles in the family and in the labour market. In 1945 it was unclear what demands the state should make of women, how they might contribute to post-war reconstruction and to what extent they wanted to return to more traditional roles. While the war in some ways only continued the trend for women to undertake paid work, the fact of female conscription and the high-profile (if limited) shift from traditional female work to the services and 'male' work in engineering and munitions had a considerable impact. Women were better paid than they had been and certainly single women were more mobile (Summerfield, 1993, 1996; Calder, 1969). Mass-Observation diaries of the period reveal women who were often worn out by the difficulties of combining war work with running a wartime home but who welcomed the opportunity to be 'useful' and who relished the sense of freedom and the capacity to earn money themselves (Haste, 1992: 104). 'I have not enough to do to occupy me intelligently in the house,' wrote one such woman who was working temporarily as a radio valve maker, 'and . . . a small regular pay packet is very welcome' (Sheridan, 1991: 215).

But if women were expected to be workers during the war, they were also expected to be feminine. The government used women's magazines to impress on women the importance of keeping up appearances as a way of maintaining morale, even though rationing made this difficult. Beauty advertisements used the slogan 'Beauty as Duty' and munitions workers were allocated the best grades of makeup; as Kirkham (1996: 154) argues, the desire to be glamorous did not disappear even in these difficult circumstances. There is also evidence of a surge of sexual activity during the war. The family was destabilized through conscription and evacuation; there was considerable official concern from both Church and government about how women were using their increased independence (Smith, 1996). The marriage rate increased but the notion of marriage as a career seemed to be under threat as evidenced by a dramatic rise in the divorce rate (Smart, 1996). A survey in Birmingham found that illegitimate births trebled between 1940 and 1945 and in the last two years of the war almost a third were to married women (Haste, 1992: 109).

The end of the war in Europe was followed by a general election in Britain in July 1945, an election won overwhelmingly by the Labour Party, which formed the first effective Labour government. Peter Hennessy (1993) describes people at the end of the war as being in a state of exalted exhaustion – exhausted because of the demands of the war but elated because of the sense that a reward was to come, that the 'people's war' had in part been fought for social justice. The wartime cabinet contained a Minister in charge of Post-war Reconstruction and, even as the war was being fought, there was debate about what changes should be made to ensure that there could be no return to the unemployment and poverty which had characterized the 1930s. The Education Act of 1944 which 'nationalized' schooling was passed before the war ended. The Beveridge Report, which laid down plans for the social insurance system, used a rhetoric of profound change to present its proposals for a system of pensions, and sickness and unemployment payments. It proclaimed that 'a revolutionary moment in the world's history is a time for revolutions, not patching' (quoted in Timmins, 1996: 23). The war years were characterized by a demand for social change, debate about what should happen and indeed some cynicism about whether things could be changed (Turner and Rennell, 1995).

British historians disagree about how quickly changes actually occurred and whether they presaged Britain's decline rather than the rewards of victory. Nevertheless, the late 1940s represented a period of great social reform, with the establishment of new institutions for health, welfare and education. Of these the most dramatic, and arguably the most effective, was the establishment of the National Health Service in 1948, founded on the basis of free treatment regardless of the ability to pay. It is also to this period that we can date the provision of universal national insurance schemes to cover unemployment and sickness benefits, the state pension, universal secondary education and the expansion of the university and college education to accommodate service men and women returning to civilian life.

The period was also one of extremely difficult economic circumstances. The country was bankrupt. American loans which had made the war possible ended with the war and had to be renegotiated, and sterling, which was reintroduced into the currency market in 1947, fell rapidly, culminating in a massive devaluation in 1949. For women who were responsible for the organization of the domestic economy, this had particularly serious consequences. Food and clothing rationing which had begun during the war continued into the peace and indeed, in some respects, worsened: potatoes and bread were both rationed between 1946 and 1948. Bread rationing was a particularly severe blow to morale. A thriving black market operated alongside rationing, offering meat under the counter and stockings on the side. The winter of 1946–47 was bitterly cold and the fuel crisis led to frequent power failures and bans on the use of electricity for cooking. Housing quality was generally poor in dense urban neighbourhoods. In these physically difficult circumstances, families had to cope with re-establishing relationships with husbands and fathers (Turner and Rennell, 1995). Historians of the period such as Addison and Hennessy warn against painting too grim a view of day-to-day life in post-war Britain, citing a 'post-war boom in leisure' (Addison, 1985: 114) which included a record level of cinema-going, huge crowds at sporting events, the success of Butlin's holiday camps and large audiences for the dance music and comedy on the BBC's new Light Programme. But it is clear that the availability of such leisure activities varied. The practical burden of the economic difficulties of the period would be felt most vividly by women responsible for bringing up children and maintaining the physical fabric of home. For them, the leisure boom may have been less of a compensation for post-war privation than for their husbands and children. The Denning Committee Report on Procedure in Matrimonial Causes (February 1947) on divorce law reform was clear about the burdens of married women: 'the mere mechanics of everyday life have become so exhausting for women as to have an immeasurable effect, through sheer weariness, on married happiness' (quoted in Turner and Rennell, 1995: 46). In telling stories of women, marriage and the home, the films discussed in this chapter dealt with women specifically positioned in the day-to-day life of post-war Britain.

Certainly, post-war debates focused on issues which were central to the role of women in society. How was the family to be reconstructed? Would women be satisfied to return to the home and to their husbands? How could the newly developing welfare systems support women without taking over their role at the heart of the family? Should women count as part of the workforce? Would the state continue to need women's labour outside the home? These were questions which official discourses puzzled over in the post-war period. The Beveridge Report (1942: 52) had put a 'a premium on marrriage . . . in the next thirty years housewives and mothers have vital work to do in ensuring the adequate continuance of the British race and of British ideals in the world'. But anxieties were expressed about how women might undertake this task. The Women's Voluntary Service (WVS) advised about the difficulties of reunion between women who had had to become more independent during the war and men who had got used to the all-male hierarchies and companionships of the services (Turner and Rennell, 1995: 125–6); a predicted decline in the birth rate was blamed in part on women's 'selfishness' (Wilson, 1980: 27); there was concern about how disrupted family life had affected children and the start of an ongoing debate about how far working mothers were the cause of neglected and delinquent children (Lewis, 1992: 18). Additionally, while the general emphasis was on women returning to the family and making marriage their career, there were contradictory emphases in, for example, the initiative on divorce law reform and the Ministry of Labour appeal in 1947 for women to re-enter the workforce. Ironically, by late 1946, more women were rejoining the women's services than were leaving, partly, the Soldiers', Sailors' and Airmen's Families Association conjectured, because of 'the disappointments of civilian life' (Turner and Rennell, 1995: 112). Considerable ambivalence was felt by the women who did return to the home, and this was sometimes recognized by those trying to formulate policy: 'many [women] will also feel that they are going back to a prison' advised one leaflet baldly, 'unless they have some life away from sinks and brooms and washtubs' (quoted in Haste, 1992: 141).

We should not necessarily expect to see such debates and worries directly reflected in the films of the period. Films are cultural artefacts in which all sorts of economic, cultural, social and artistic pressures combine to make a specific product and they do not reflect unproblematically the social changes which women experienced. The British director Lindsay Anderson wrote, more than ten years after the end of the war, of British cinema's failure to address the post-war revolution:

> In 1945, it is often said, we had our revolution . . . According to British cinema, however, nothing happened at all. The nationalisation of the coalfields, the Health Service, nationalised railways, compulsory education – events like these which cry out to be interpreted in human terms – have produced no films. (Anderson, quoted in Murphy, 1992: 95)

More recently, feminist critics such as Sue Aspinall (1983: 282) have complained that realist British films of the early 1940s failed to represent 'the most painful experiences of women', while Sue Harper (1996: 103) has specifically castigated post-war Ealing and Balcon for misrepresenting women's choices by offering a 'horrid set of alternatives to the female audience. The only ratified conditions were virginity or respectable conjugality.'

Despite these criticisms, we can see in the films of 1945–51 that social issues of concern to women *were* being addressed, perhaps not in the direct manner which Anderson called for but in oblique and symbolic ways. The films do not, for instance, take up overtly the question of whether married women should work, which was a major social issue at the time. We can see, however, that choices are being set up for women and that the problematic split between their social role and individual needs is being given some kind of expression. In analysing the three Ealing films – *It Always Rains on Sunday*, *Cage of Gold* and *Dance Hall* – we shall see how women in films of this period stand for the nation. They must make a choice: are they willing to continue to make sacrifices for the community and the nation? are they willing to reject excitement and sensation in the interests of the national good? do their longings for luxury, sexual excitement and entertainment indicate a genuine need for self-expression and fulfilment which the government and the state ignore at their peril? In addition, I want to query Harper's characterization of that choice and to suggest that we need a rather more nuanced approach to understanding how women's choices could be represented and understood. In trying to develop such an approach, I follow Christine Gledhill's (1996: 218) argument that the polarization of melodramatic and documentary modes in critical work on British cinema is unhelpful and that it is more illuminating to examine specific films through what she calls the 'tense' interaction between melodrama and realism.

Before analysing what these films have in common, it must be acknowledged that there are several quite important differences between them. In particular, *Cage of Gold* is set in a middle to upper middle-class milieu in which Jean Simmons plays Judith, a young painter whose well-to-do family have fallen on hard times; she marries into a professional family in which both father and son are doctors. *It Always Rains on Sunday*, by contrast, focuses on a working-class woman, Rose, played by Googie Withers. When the film opens she is living in a house in London's East End with her husband George, her two teenage step-daughters and Alfie, her son by George. *Dance Hall* also portrays working-class life, but instead of focusing on a single character it uses an interweaving format to follow the lives of four girls who work together in a factory and go to dances at the local palais. (For the purposes of this essay, I am going to concentrate on the story of Eve, played by a young newcomer, Natasha Parry.) Overall, though, the films have much in common and looking at them together does, I hope, illuminate the interaction of ideas of femininity and national identity in this period.

In each film, the narrative viewpoint is almost entirely that of the women characters. This concentration on the women, allowing the audience access to their thoughts and feelings, means that the heroines lack the distance which gives an enigmatic quality and a desirability to the more wayward women of some European cinemas of the period, which are discussed elsewhere in this volume, and to post-war *film noir* heroines of Hollywood cinema. The women characters may sometimes behave badly or foolishly (Rose, in particular, is viciously acerbic on occasion), but the audience is positioned with them – we know why they do what they do. This transparency is a feature of the films' claims to realism – the heroines' plausibility makes them representative – but these heroines are placed in a narrative structure which specifically sets individual desires and needs against those of the common good. All the films are structured around a polarized choice, characteristic of melodrama, in which different men stand for different lifestyles and the heroine has to choose between her own feelings and her family responsibilities. In *It Always Rains on Sunday*, Rose has to choose between her ex-lover Tommy, now a criminal on the run, and her husband George who is stolid and unimaginative but is, as Rose says, 'decent'. Her step-daughters exemplify a similar choice for the next generation of women, as the film follows the ups and downs of relationships between brown-haired Doris and her respectable boyfriend and blonde Vi's entanglement with a married man.[2] In *Cage of Gold*, the choice to be made by Judy is between two men who represent different lifestyles: Alan is a responsible, caring and kind doctor; Bill is an ex-RAF pilot who is exciting, glamorous, irresponsible and out to give her a good time. Judy paints Bill in his uniform and the *mise-en-scène* literally positions this portrait between Judy and Alan when he criticizes her for selfishly wanting what Bill appears to offer – pink roses, champagne and 'a wonderful time'. In *Dance Hall*, Eve has to choose between her steady boyfriend, the clumsy non-dancer Phil, and Alec with his smart suits, fast lifestyle and fleet-footed dancing skills.

In each case, Ealing's emphasis on social context means that the choice between the two men has a clear social dimension which suggests that the woman's decision has a symbolic significance in relation to post-war society. Tommy's criminality is set in the broader context of the spivs who are trying to sell stolen goods and the underhand trade of the black market. His violence lies at the extreme end of a spectrum of criminal disorder which is threatening to undermine the traditional community. Bill and Alan stand for two different outcomes of the war: Bill's amorality has its roots in the fighter pilot's careless disregard for personal security, whereas Alan's decision to work in the NHS and the care he exhibits for his working class patients associate him with the new welfare systems brought in after the war. In *Dance Hall*, Eve has to choose between the British Phil, who represents the skilled working class employed in modern industry, and the American Alec, who is associated with consumption and leisure activities. The heroines have to choose between men who stand for particular social qualities and who are associated with different forms of society.

In each film it is the woman who moves between fixed male positions. The women's strength lies in their capacity to reflect on choices and to change their minds. Such a structure reinforces the sense that, during a time of social upheaval, the stability of post-war society depends on women's choices; men are what they are but women can change, and their choices both reflect and contribute to the post-war national settlement. The significance of the women's decisions is such that the films try to load the choices and make it clear how the women must act in order to make socially responsible decisions. In *It Always Rains on Sundays*, Tommy uses Rose's love to get her to hide him, but does not share her intense memories of their affair and fails to recognize the engagement ring he gave her ten years before. In *Cage of Gold*, Bill marries Judy for her money, only to disappear the following day when he discovers that she is penniless, leaving her pregnant with only Alan to turn to. Alec, Eve's lover in *Dance Hall*, dabbles in the black market and deliberately provokes trouble between her and Phil; after she has slept with him, he drops her for fear of becoming over-committed. The films try to associate the alternative good choices with the future (Alan, in *Cage of Gold*, is associated with the communal values of the new National Health Service, while Phil, in *Dance Hall*, represents the modernity of aviation and flying). But in the end they have to use excessively melodramatic devices to render the good choice as the only alternative: Tommy punches Rose and refuses her pleas to give himself up to the police; Bill is shot by his French mistress in a manner which places Judy and Alan under suspicion; after a quarrel caused by Alec's maliciousness and Phil's jealousy, Eve is reconciled with her husband in a dramatic thunderstorm with the kind of romantic clinch which we have already seen as failing to resolve an earlier disagreement. In each case, the good choice becomes the only alternative by default.

Given these over-determined narratives, it is significant that the sexuality and glamour which the heroines are seeking in their bad choices are represented most convincingly through visual style. Leisure was a strong feature of post-war life and could have been presented realistically in the narrative, as in *Holiday Camp* (Ken Annakin, 1947), which follows the experiences of a number of holiday-makers in a down-to-earth and humorous manner. Parts of *Dance Hall* also take this approach, particularly in the handling of Georgie's story, but generally these films use a different mode to express the pleasures of consumption. In all three films, the visual expression of the choice contrasts the naturalist emphasis on the rhythms of day-to-day life with the expressive effects needed to represent the more glamorous alternatives. The films represent women's work in the home in a naturalist manner – we see Rose peeling the potatoes and making pastry, Eve doing the ironing and even Judy has to look after her invalid father-in-law – but other devices are needed to express the excitement of less mundane possibilities. In all three films, this choice between men is expressed through the appearance of the women themselves. When Rose first meets Tommy she is a blonde, flirtatious barmaid; married, she is dark-haired, harassed and tired. On the dance floor Eve wears swirling skirts and low necklines; married, she wears high-necked jumpers and dresses even at the palais (Kirkham, 1995). Even the middle-class Judy is subject to such transformations: the off-the-shoulder, full-skirted evening dresses of her affair with Bill change after her marriage to high necklines and long sleeves. In addition, dissolves and editing are used to create visual transformations. In the bedroom mirror in *It Always Rains on Sunday*, Rose becomes blonde and Tommy handsome, as a flashback sequence takes them out of London into a highly stylized countryside for a love-making scene; the montage sequence of dancing, fair rides, aeroplane displays and boxing matches represents the good time Bill appears to offer Judy in *Cage of Gold*; the palais sequences in *Dance Hall* are characterized by quick editing, montages, striking close-ups and, ultimately, dissembling costumes and grotesque masks. Such devices indicate the difficulty of containing certain feelings, emotions and ideas within the documentary style which characterizes the domestic scenes in all three films.

Seduced by this sensuality, all three heroines initially make the wrong choice: each sleeps with the wrong man outside marriage. This is explicit in *Cage of Gold* and *Dance Hall* and heavily signalled in *It Always Rains on Sunday*. The films condemn not so much the act itself but the choice that it represents, since the visual and narrative split makes it virtually impossible for the women to follow these individual desires for sexuality and glamour without colluding with the dubious morals of the men who represent such positions and thus failing to live up to ethos of community and responsibility most clearly exemplified by Alan's commitment to the NHS. Conversely, Anderson's social revolution, which is associated with the good choice, loses any sense of danger and is here presented as a kind of benign common feeling which specifically excludes excitement and desire.

In making their choice, the women appear to stand outside the social structures which might offer some support. Indeed, it is precisely because the protagonists are choosing not just between men but between different forms of society that they seem so alone. The younger Rose appears to have no friends or family and she makes her home in the pub where she works; Judy's family have emigrated to Canada after the war and her romance with Bill isolates her not only from Alec but also the family servant, Waddy, who, though initially delighted to see Bill again, is deeply suspicious of his motives; Eve's mother is unsympathetic and Eve does not tell her friends about her feelings for Alec or, later, confide in them about the loneliness of her marriage. The men themselves, even the good ones, are weak and lack sympathetic understanding: 'You're thick-headed and smug', Eve's friend, Mary, tells Phil. The weakness of the men lies not in vacillation or indecision but in the stubborn way they occupy the fixed positions determined by the narratives; they cannot accommodate change, otherwise the point of the stories would be lost. Since the films share the viewpoint of the heroine, any understanding offered by their husbands can only occur retrospectively, as it does in *It Always Rains on Sunday* and *Cage of Gold*, making the men appear, for the bulk of the films, to be obstinate or unseeing. The woman's isolation is underlined by the fact that in none of the films do we see the marriage ceremony in which the heroine confirms the good choice which will bind her into post-war society. The films leave us in no doubt that the correct choice has been made but they do not celebrate it.

If the films are read by presenting an opposition between the polarized narratives and the more openly expressive visual elements, it is difficult to disagree with Thumim's (1996: 253) identification of post-war films such as *It Always Rains on Sunday* with 'the punishment of the transgressive female', films in which it is demonstrated that 'women cannot be permitted to act autonomously but must be secured in the heterosexual couple, the prelude to the nuclear familial unit, for their own protection'. Feminist criticism has tended to value other films of the period, particularly Gainsborough melodramas, which, despite the punishing endings, are thought to have offered women the more liberating possibilities of fantasy and identification and to have 'celebrated female desire' (Harper, 1996: 105). I would argue that the realist and melodramatic elements can be understood as working together to offer an account which is both emotional and analytical. The realism of these Ealing films, far from being unsympathetic to the heroines' dilemmas, offers a recognition of the bleakness of their position in post-war society which cannot be acknowledged in more positive representations. In their realist mode, for instance, the films force their narratives on beyond the point of marriage (the conventional ending of most romances and the point at which the choice might be deemed to have been made) to explore the consequences of choice. This narrative emphasis on what happens after the symbolic moment of choosing reinforces both the sense that hard decisions are being made and that the women, in making such choices, can be understood to be taking on a national function.

The view of the marriage which results from this choice is a bleak one which is entirely in accord with the pressures on women within marriage described in the 1947 report on divorce law. Post-war rhetoric about women emphasized the importance of supporting them in the family and the home. There was concern that women were exhausted by the war effort. Beveridge had asserted that 'the housewife's job with a large family is frankly impossible' (quoted in Wilson, 1980: 19). There was some agreement, in theory, that it was important for women to receive a certain amount of support if they were to play their part in national reconstruction. This was seen to be a familial role, and anxiety about mothers working outside the home was accompanied by some interest in supporting their work in the home. A report on 'The Neglected Child and His Family' argued that since the nature of the family depended on 'the capacity of the mother' (Priestley, 1948: 22) she needed to be supported in her task; the 1948 Newsom Report, 'The Education of Girls', concluded that girls need to be educated in their roles as wives and mothers (Wilson, 1980: 33).

Very little of this apparent concern appears in these films, which present their heroines, rather more realistically, as isolated in the home, receiving little support from their husbands and none from outside agencies. The isolation of the woman's initial choice is underlined in each film by her continuing isolation within the family and the home. *It Always Rains on Sunday* stresses the cramped house which makes it difficult for Rose to keep her lover out of the communal household areas such as the kitchen and stairs; Rose is frequently isolated in watchful close-up as she tries to work out how the different family members are moving behind her and hence how near they are to discovering the hidden Tommy. In the more spacious home of Judy and Alan, Judy's isolation is also expressed through the geography of the house through the use of the central stairway and hall. She is on the stairs when she first hears Bill's voice at the front door as he pays her a visit on his return from Paris and she moves out of the Christmas party into the isolation of the hall when the full implication of his return hits her. It is in the hall that she takes the phone call from Bill which leads to her assignation with him, and as she walks down the stairs she ignores the phone call from Alan which might have held her back. Most striking though is the rapidity with which *Dance Hall* moves from Eve leaving for her honeymoon with Phil (the car drives past the closed palais) to a scene which is clearly representative of their married life – Eve is trapped in their small flat, doing the ironing and waiting for Phil's late return from work. The rented flat is dark and cramped; Eve trips over and is clumsy in dealing with the housework, lacking the physical grace she shows on the dance floor. Phil, in contrast, easily falls into the married man's role: his sulkiness, his heedless disregard for the difficulties of rationing and shopping, his assumption that Eve's interests should be governed by his. His jealousy and violence could hardly be represented in a bleaker or more direct fashion. Eve later tries to convince Alec and herself about her happiness at home – 'it's silly really to keep going out when you've got a nice home of your own' – but the irony is apparent to the audience. If Ealing films are backing 'respectable conjugality' as Harper (1996: 103) suggests, they do far less than some of the Gainsborough melodramas to make it seem an attractive possibility.

This isolation within marriage is the more striking because marriage means that women are removed from the community. At one level, this is a consequence of the reliance on the romance model which tends to privilege individual rather than communal choices. Even in *Dance Hall*, although working together is clearly the basis for the group of friends at the heart of the film, the emphasis on romance sends them on to the dance floor separately and even sets them up as potential rivals. Once married, Rose and Eve give up their jobs and although Judy is referred to as a successful painter we never see her working as an artist after her marriage. This emphasis on women in the home, rather than the working women of some realist films of the war, further reinforces an emphasis on individual rather than communal possibilities. Rose's angry denunciation of her step-daughters and her wariness with her neighbours leaves her with no allies and she never leaves the house to join in the communal scenes in the pub or the market. Judy too, as Barr (1977: 151) indicates, appears to be trapped in 'a large, enveloping dark house', while Eve tells her friends, 'We don't go out much', and her return to the palais is unsuccessful: the music stops as she finally gets back on to the dance floor.

The isolation of married women from the community is backed up by the films' more general refusal to offer the traditionally cosy view of community, and hence of nation, with which Ealing is often associated (Cook, 1996). Closely bound up with the choice in favour of the community which the women have to make is an unease about what the communal now represents. In contrast to some of the Ealing comedies, these social melodramas seem to indicate that wartime versions of the nation pulling together no longer provide a rationale for communal support. The war is hardly referred to and interestingly, when it is (in *Cage of Gold*), the wartime experience invoked is not the traditional one of the community pulling together but of the unleashing of forces associated with masculine aggression which are actually a threat in peacetime. Post-war modes of community, particularly around the social spheres of health and education, find little expression in these films. Alan, Judy's good choice in *Cage of Gold*, decides to work in the NHS rather than go into private practice, but even here there is little sense of reward or thanks from his patients: one of them harks back to Alan's father as 'the Doctor' and insists that 'You can't beat the old ones'.

Unexpectedly for Ealing perhaps, the social sphere is associated with the market rather than with the community. When women do venture into social spaces outside the home, they enter the places of leisure or consumption associated with the post-war boom. Such spaces are ambivalent sites because the market is tied up with the glamour which the heroines are structured to reject. Excitement is tied to consumption, with the desire for food, clothes and luxuries, and such desires are thus positioned in opposition to the need for social responsibility. The social spaces of the films – the markets, the dance halls, the clubs – are places of exploitation as well as pleasure, where middlemen and racketeers conspire to make women want something. In *It Always Rains on Sunday*, there is a continual association between desirable goods and, at the very least, sharp practices: 'I've got another last one,' cries a stallholder in bustling Petticoat Lane market while a woman stallholder ironically offers nylons to a policeman: 'guaranteed stolen goods'. In *Cage of Gold*, the nightclub where Bill works in Paris is a place of exchange – 'diamonds, dollars, gold'. Even the dance hall, the most benign of these spaces, is run by a con man (played significantly by Sydney Tafler who was Vi's married man in *It Always Rains on Sunday*), and the film works to expose the way in which the fun and glamour is a façade, dependent on people pretending to be something they are not: the glamorous Continental dance team, Chicita and Juan, turn out to have London accents and the masks at the New Year dance take on a cruel aspect as the revellers ignore Eve's distress.

Such a glossing over of reality is associated with the Americanization of popular culture and leisure pursuits. Morrie, the married lover of Rose's step-daughter, runs a record shop and plays the saxophone, while Vi herself dreams of becoming a singer and is seduced by promises that she can win a crooning competition. Melinda Mash (1996: 260) points to the way in which in *Dance Hall* 'the danger and promise of "Americanness" is located in the palais itself, with its promises of riches and success', as well as in Eve's American boyfriend Alec, whose attractions, in marked contrast to Phil, are associated with skills on the dance floor and access to material possessions including a sports car, a record-player and his own flat. Americanness is associated with all the things the women cannot have – romantic love, material goods and fun – and the films are entirely typical of much of British post-war culture in their ambivalent exploration and ultimate rejection of such possibilities.

While cultural studies writers have commented on the antagonism to American culture expressed in many British cultural products of the 1950s (Webster, 1988), less attention has been paid to the way in which other cultures were viewed. Of the three films, *Cage of Gold* is the most crude in its representations of European cultures. Its site of entertainment, the nightclub, is not only run by foreigners but is in Paris, off British soil altogether, and a clear association is drawn between foreignness, corruption and national identity: the American soldiers in the bar expect to be ripped off; it is in the nightclub that Bill can sell his passport and his nationality; and Marie, the French singer and nightclub owner, provides a convenient and stereotypical murderess. The other films, though, both acknowledge and are doubtful about the role of other cultures in everyday British life. In *It Always Rains on Sunday*, the Jewish brothers Morrie and Lou Hyams are implicated in the dubious practices of Americanized sources of entertainment (dance halls, amusement arcades, records, the sax and the harmonica), while Lou is also able to fix more British forms of entertainment such as boxing matches. But there is also a sense of the life and energy brought about by a mix of different cultures: there are black faces in the crowds at the market and the cockney market cries give way to those of a Jewish woman crying 'Mazeltov'; Lou is clearly a member of the

East End community, having known the respectable George 'since I was in short pants', and his quick wit contributes to the market repartee; Bessie, the Hyams' sister, produces, in the youth club, the closest the film ever gets to a model Ealing community; and the only moment of harmony in the Sandigate home occurs when, in a touching scene, George skilfully plays Morrie's harmonica to his son Alfie. In *Dance Hall*, similarly, sites of entertainment offer a mingling of British and other cultures. The palais, of course, has Continental associations, is run by a Jewish manager and is the place where fantasies of foreignness can be acted out in dance whether it be the jive or the tango. In this context, the rather stuffy Britishness of the winners of the competition contrasts with the liveliness of the untutored teenage dancers. The ending, though, once again emphasizes the potential dangers of popular culture becoming too foreign. The New Year dance, with its Mardi Gras masks and streamers, shows how easily the excitement of difference can turn the communal crowd into an uncaring mob.

It is certainly possible to argue that the films exhibit a failure of nerve over their representation of popular culture and the dangers posed by its separation from the traditional communal values which Ealing associates with the war. Part of the bleakness of the films' handling of women's post-war possibilities is their inability to counter the heroines' dreams of a different form of a feminine self offered by other cultures, particularly that of America. But as we have seen, it is worth noting that these social melodramas centred on women cannot fall back, as comedies such as *Passport to Pimlico* (Henry Cornelius, 1949) do, on an ideal of a communal culture in which women tend to be ignored. Their concentration on the viewpoint of married women, on the minutiae of their day-to-day lives in post-war Britain, blocks them off from these communal solutions. In particular, the reworking of the experience of rationing and imposed economic restraint into an acknowledgement of the sheer hard work of domestic life and the lack of warmth in marriage may have been unexpectedly prescient, particularly in its construction of women at the heart of this dilemma. The suggestion that consumption and fantasy cannot fill this lack surely needs to be given some credence rather than condemned as British middle-class puritanism. For if the films cannot offer hopeful fantasies of traditional community or new consumption, they also find it difficult to represent any hopefulness in the right choices forced on the heroines. If the women are sacrificing their own needs for the common good, as the narratives suggest, the films' inability to represent the virtues of this common good reinforces the bleakness of the choices the heroines face. John Hill (1986: 71) argues that *It Always Rains on Sunday* and *Cage of Gold* work towards 'the construction of a new stability in which the woman will accept her proper place', but the films go some way to acknowledging that the 'proper place' which is being chosen may be more like the 'prison' warned against in the post-war pamphlet quoted earlier (Haste, 1992: 141). At the end of *It Always Rains on Sunday*, when Rose tries to gas herself, she walks round the kitchen, touching each door as if measuring out a cell and locks herself in her own kitchen.

Googie Withers's use of this physical action to represent her character's despair is typical of the contribution her performance makes to our understanding of the tensions embodied in Rose. Alan Lovell (1997: 239) has argued that 'British cinema is often at its most exciting when restraint and excess work together' and cites Withers's acting as an example of this. In all three films, the central performance depends on the way in which ordinary behaviour can be disrupted by deep emotion which has then to be reined back. In *It Always Rains on Sunday*, Rose's excitement and fear at hearing of Tommy's escape is marked only by a brief pause and a clenching of the comb as she continues to do her hair. The sense of pent-up emotion is clearly expressed in the scene in which Rose attacks Vi for trying to get into the bedroom where Tommy is hiding. Withers breaches the distance which she usually puts between herself and the other characters as she seizes Vi's shoulder and pulls her hair; at the end of the scene, Withers physically resumes her normal composure as she shifts her shoulders and walks straight-backed down the stairs, her face blank again. This refusal of expression at key moments, particularly through facial movement, is characteristic of all three films. In a key scene in *Cage of Gold* in which Judy talks first to Alan and then to Bill about 'the wonderful life' she is enjoying, Simmons's expression is frequently hidden, as she is positioned with her back to the camera and the two men. At the end of the scene, when Bill says 'You're going to have a baby', her face remains still, and when he announces 'We're going to get married,' nothing in her face betrays her relief and pleasure except a sideways movement of the eyes. Parry's performance in *Dance Hall* is similarly marked by the restrained play of emotions across a calm demeanour, occasionally switching to moments of extreme emotional expressiveness. Eve's decision to 'go with' Alec occurs in a wordless scene and is registered through Parry's blank face and averted gaze. A movement in the throat and a parting of the lips indicate desire, until finally she turns her head towards him to indicate acceptance. Later on, though, during a row with Phil, she expresses emotion more fully, both verbally and physically through clenching her fists, a gesture she repeats in frustration at the end when she is locked out of the palais. This emphasis on repression and restraint in the acting continually draws attention to the narrative position of the heroines and to their restricted choices in the post-war world.

I have argued that the films of the post-war period in Britain continued the wartime emphasis on women as representatives of national positions and, in their realist emphasis, provide an account that was grimmer and less hopeful than official accounts. If they can be criticized for the limited choices they offered their heroines, the failure is surely not to be ascribed to the limitations of realism but to the difficulties which the post-war settlement had both in reassessing women's roles and in providing the material circumstances which might have made women's lives easier. Thumim (1992) and Mash (1996) both note the way in which the use of women as leading protagonists in British films declines in the 1950s. Given the impasse over women's choices which I have discussed, this decline is not surprising and indicates some deep-seated problems about women's roles in post-war society which, as Wilson has shown, went underground in the 1950s. For, ironically, the good choices made by these post-war heroines turned out to be the 'wrong' ones. As rationing eased and material conditions improved, the association between women and consumption, so long as it was suitably channelled by femininity, became a sign of the modern society much sought after in the 1950s. It is significant, then, that *Dance Hall*, while dealing with issues of the immediate post-war period, also points forward to the rather different role which women will have in 1950s British cinema. In *Dance Hall*, Diana Dors plays Carol, another of the four women whose stories the audience is invited to follow. She is presented in an entirely different fashion from the realist approach adopted for the others. Dors is obviously not an Ealing-type actress and the contrast between her character and Eve runs through the film: her consumerist aspirations are indicated by her streamlined American sweaters and her delight in her diamond engagement ring is clearly material; she has a wisecracking humour, is always ready with a quick remark and a well-placed insult. Sexually upfront, she is determined to get her man. Significantly, her motivations are hidden from the audience and the representation is largely one-dimensional; her dilemmas cannot be representative because they are not shared. Dors's enjoyable but limited appearance is a sign of the rather different portrayal of women in the cinema that is to come in the 1950s.

Notes

1. Street (1997) and Murphy (1992) both offer useful overviews of British cinema during this period, while the work of Cook (1996) and Harper (1994) has led an important reassessment of Gainsborough Studio's melodramas.
2. This doubling is repeated frequently in *It Always Rains on Sunday*. Quite apart from the contrasts between the younger and older Rose, and Vi and Doris, we have Lou and Morrie Hyams as the successful and unsuccessful brothers, whose dubious activities are set against the good works of their sister, Bessie, and the contrast between the gullible Vi and Sadie, Morrie's dark-haired, sardonic wife.

Filmography

Cage of Gold (Basil Dearden, 1950)
Dance Hall (Charles Crichton, 1950)
It Always Rains on Sunday (Robert Hamer, 1947)

Margaret Lockwood in *A Place of One's Own* (1945, UK, Bernard Knowles)
Source: BFI Stills, Posters and Designs
Reproduced courtesy of Carlton International Media Ltd.

CHAPTER TWO

A Place of One's Own? Margaret Lockwood and British Film Stardom in the 1940s

SARAH STREET

Margaret Lockwood's most famous role as bad Barbara Skelton in *The Wicked Lady* (Leslie Arliss, 1945) activated a climate of popular expectation in the post-war years for subsequent appearances as a transgressive heroine. *Picturegoer* frequently reported how her fan mail increased after a performance as a 'wicked' character: Hesther in *The Man in Grey* (Arliss, 1943), Barbara in *The Wicked Lady* and 'Biddy' in *Bedelia* (Lance Comfort, 1946). Lockwood herself recognized that her fans thrilled to her image as a daring adventuress (*Picturegoer*, 8 April 1950: 10–11). It is clear, however, that Lockwood's post-war career was varied and during the years 1945–51, when she appeared in eleven feature films, apart from *The Wicked Lady* only one film, *Bedelia*, gave her a role which required her to perform as a British *femme fatale*. The other post-war films in which she starred are *A Place of One's Own* (Bernard Knowles, 1945), *I'll Be Your Sweetheart* (Val Guest, 1945), *Hungry Hill* (Brian Desmond Hurst, 1947), *Jassy* (Bernard Knowles, 1947), *The White Unicorn* (Bernard Knowles, 1947), *Look Before You Love* (Harold Huth, 1948), *Cardboard Cavalier* (Walter Forde,1949), *Madness of the Heart* (Charles Bennett, 1949) and *Highly Dangerous* (Roy Ward Baker, 1950). Covering a number of genres, including thrillers, contemporary melodramas, costume pictures and a musical comedy, the films offer a range of representations of femininity, some of which can be related to the adjustment of patriarchal norms to peacetime. This chapter will argue that Lockwood's post-war image and star persona are more complicated than a simple continuation of roles which can be identified unproblematically with notions of wartime transgression. As Gledhill (1996: 3) has pointed out, the immediate post-war years were marked by coexisting modernizing and conservative trends which were reflected in a range of cultural products, including films. While the popularity of *The Wicked Lady* can be related to its appeal to women, who had been presented with the opportunity to be more independent during the Second World War, *Brief Encounter* (David Lean, 1945), released in the same year and also dealing with the question of an extra-marital affair, offered a less thrilling, more guilt-ridden perspective. As one of the most popular British film stars of the period, Lockwood's films similarly articulated key issues and discourses which involved negotiating the place of women in the post-war world. She also featured in contemporary discussion about the differentiation between British and Hollywood female stars, which I shall go on to argue can be related to wider questions about national identity.

As other chapters in this book demonstrate, it was common for female roles (for example, the *femme fatale* in French films) to embody a sense of 'national guilt' for collaboration with fascism. In the British context the immediate post-war years were characterized by a different strain of 'national cleansing', as the new Labour government sought to recognize social changes which had been accelerated by the war. However, the resulting legislation was not always as progressive as might at first appear. As Sheila Rowbotham (1997: 247) has commented: 'Despite the gain of family allowances and maternity benefit, the structure of the welfare state was based on the assumption of women's dependence on the man in the family rather than on women's rights as individuals.' Even though women's participation in the peacetime workforce increased after the war, in particular, older married women working part-time, 'full male employment and wifely dependence' remained at the centre of post-war reconstruction (Summerfield, 1996: 49). As far as external relations were concerned, Britain occupied an increasingly minor place in the world economy and in international diplomacy. The country's dependence on America for economic aid to facilitate post-war reconstruction resulted in numerous diplomatic tensions also evident in fraught Anglo-American film relations, culminating in the 'Dalton Duty crisis' of 1947 (Street, 1997: 14–15). Britain's historic dependence on Hollywood films conflicted with the desire to increase national production, and even though British audiences adored the American product, some film fans were also patriotic about British films and stars (*Picturegoer*, 22 January 1944: 9). Thus, debates on the comparison between British and American film stars were caught up in an overall context of ambivalence about America's role as Britain's ally and competitor in both national and filmic terms. It is appropriate, therefore, to make links between the evolution of Lockwood's roles in this period, her representation of various images of femininity and her place within the contexts of contemporary debates about British women and British film stars.

Since Lockwood's most popular films were those in which she appeared as a transgressive heroine, it is interesting to consider why so few of her roles cast her in this guise. Her pre-*Wicked Lady* image was of a wholesome, sensible and talented British actress who took a risk when she appeared as Barbara Skelton, something she acknowledged to *Picturegoer* readers during the filming of *The Wicked Lady*: 'I hope my fans won't mind, even though they seem to prefer me in films like *Love Story*' (*Picturegoer*, 14 April 1945: 7). Lockwood's most famous pre-war films were *Bank Holiday* (Carol Reed, 1937), *The Lady Vanishes* (Alfred Hitchcock, 1938) and *The Stars Look Down* (Carol Reed, 1939) – the first to cast her as a bitter, duplicitous character. By contrast, *Love Story* (Leslie Arliss,1944) was a romantic melodrama in which Lockwood plays a concert pianist stricken with an incurable disease who falls in love with a mining engineer (Stewart Granger) who is going blind. Indeed, she often expressed anxiety about developing her career in a single direction and experimented with a variety of roles in an attempt to avoid becoming 'typed'. This dual concern for, and at times refusal of popular opinion is typical of British stars of the period, who were anxious to differentiate themselves from Hollywood models of stardom and resist being forced by box-office pressures into roles which they did not respect. The opinions of the fans were important, but many stars sought to develop their acting skills on screen, concerned that typing was in conflict with artistic development (*Picturegoer*, 9 December 1944: 11). *Picturegoer* published many articles and readers' letters which debated Lockwood's future career, often disapproving of her choices (*Picturegoer*, 3 August 1946: 9; 6 November 1948: 5). On the other hand, a study by Barbara Kesterton in 1948 showed that adolescent girls held Lockwood as a role model and that her 'wicked' roles were the most popular (Harper, 1994: 139). Within this context it is arguable that her role as a *femme fatale* in *Bedelia*, which reviewers criticized for being a rather diluted version of the American *film noir*, was compromised by a sense of British reserve about imitating American-influenced examples of female transgression (Aspinall and Murphy, 1983: 76–7). Contemporary male commentators sought to distinguish between American 'dames' and British 'ladies', arguing that 'we may lack glamour, and we may be old-fashioned; but our actresses play the parts of ladies – not dames' (*Picturegoer*, 10 May 1945: 11). Within this distinction, being a 'lady' was not associated with overt sexuality, and so it would appear that a major tenet of British female stardom was in conflict with the popular enthusiasm for the American-style *femme fatale*.

In spite of the factors which constrained Lockwood's opportunities (or indeed desire) to exploit her popular success as a 'wicked' lady in the post-war period, her films certainly reference important discourses which were relevant to contemporary women as members of society and as individuals. The rest of this chapter will discuss Lockwood's films in relation to money, profession/employment, class, motherhood and preoccupation with alter egos and split personalities. In a period when women's social positions were being renegotiated in relation to home and the workplace, her films offer a wide range of representations from different perspectives, with a striking emphasis on female characters who are divided in their loyalties, personalities and femininities. I will argue that this latter theme is crucial for an understanding of the post-war years, which were characterized by a revival of spiritualism and concern about the individual's battle to maintain a coherent, stable identity after the strains and fractures wrought by the Second World War. Indeed, after the war the number of National Spiritualist churches increased (from 400 in 1944 to 498 in 1954) and occult movements generally attracted considerable attention (Nelson, 1969: 259). Although the films' narrative closures frequently result in the restoration of coherence and stability, usually via the agency of heterosexual romance, the doubts and fissures which have been suggested nevertheless work to qualify this sense of unambiguous resolution.

Money, profession/employment and class

In most of her films Lockwood plays characters who are concerned about money: even when upper-middle-class and well-placed she desires greater financial security, and there exists a marked association between money, social mobility and sexual excitement. These concerns are notable in *The Man in Grey*, *The Wicked Lady* and *Bedelia*, in which she goes to great lengths to get more money by stealing other people's husbands, masquerading as a highwayman and poisoning. In these films the attainment of greater wealth is a path to greater independence. In *The Wicked Lady* Barbara's adventures 'on the road' with Jerry Jackson (James Mason) provide an ironic example of how downward social mobility grants her greater sexual freedom than her upper-class marriage. Here it is not so much the money that matters but what it represents: the excitement of being able to win it for herself, rather than simply because she is married to a rich, titled man. Barbara's decision to masquerade as Jerry Jackson is prompted by a desire to reclaim her mother's brooch which she has lost at cards. We see her on the road and experience the thrill and excitement of the robbery and dialogue that is full of double-entendre, both of which play on her apparent gender-switch. Once she has won the brooch back and is safe in the house, she clasps it to her and we hear in voice-over that it 'means more to me than the Skelton diamonds'.

In *Bedelia* Lockwood's character has achieved her wealth by marrying and then poisoning her husbands, moving from place to place and changing her identity. In many ways these women are being resourceful, seeking to create a place for themselves outside that dictated by patriarchy. This desperation is also evident in films where the women Lockwood plays are not particularly transgressive. She is often a professional woman or someone who manages to increase her social status. In *A Place of One's Own* she is a companion/secretary who marries an upper-class doctor; in *Jassy* she plays a gypsy who becomes a housekeeper and then marries the owner; in *The White Unicorn* she takes on the role of an upper middle-class woman who becomes the superintendent of a remand home after her divorce; in *Madness of the Heart* she stars as Lydia, a doctor's secretary who marries a rich Frenchman; and in *Highly Dangerous* she plays an entomologist. These films indirectly reference women's uncertainties about their place in the labour market after the war and the extent to which they were able to maintain financial independence from men. This was often extremely difficult, so it is hardly surprising that in many of the films women's financial security could only be achieved through marriage.

Discourses on class are prevalent in many of Lockwood's post-war films. *A Place of One's Own* can be read as a critique of rigid class stratification. In this film Lockwood is employed as companion/secretary to Mrs Smedhurst (Barbara Mullen), whose 'nouveau riche' husband has recently bought a Victorian mansion. The Smedhursts have no truck with snobbery, claiming the right to spaces which were formerly occupied by the titled nobility, and treat Annette (Lockwood) as their daughter. The film can be interpreted as an optimistic statement about post-war society, as a 'new order' threatens traditional class stratification. On the other hand, the film's representation of competing femininities (see below, where I discuss Annette's 'possession' by the spirit of a former occupant of the house, Elizabeth Harkness) can be read as having a class dimension. When Annette is taken over by the spirit of Elizabeth she is upper-class, alluring, mysterious and refined, reciting poetry and playing the piano beautifully, whereas middle-class Annette is gauche and less confident. Upper-class visitors, including her suitor Robert (Dennis Price), respond to her favourably when she is behaving as Elizabeth, perhaps indicating the persistence of class mores and the privileging of refined feminine codes: ladies not dames. In this instance, discussion about what typified British female stars accorded with an aspect of the film's preferred representation of femininity. On the other hand, as I shall go on to argue, its association between Elizabeth, 'hysteria', disturbance and sexuality represented that femininity as potentially dangerous.

Motherhood

A key (and unusual) film which articulates this theme is *The White Unicorn* (adapted from a novel by Flora Sandstrom), although it is also relevant in *Hungry Hill*, where Lockwood plays a mother who spoils her son after the death of her husband. In *The White Unicorn* she plays Lucy, the superintendent of a remand home. The film progresses by means of parallel narratives: Lockwood's marital story is compared via flashbacks with that of Lotty (Joan Greenwood), a working-class woman in her care whom she has befriended. Lotty's child has been taken away from her after she attempted to commit suicide when she was abandoned and left destitute by the father. The two women share their experiences of romance, disappointment and the need to be independent. Both have lost their children. Lucy has been rejected by her daughter after her divorce and Lotty wants to be reunited with her child. Lucy is upper-middle-class and much of the narrative is preoccupied with the story of her difficult marriage to Philip (Ian Hunter), a high-powered lawyer who cares most about his work; her extra-marital affair with Dick (Dennis Price); her divorce from Philip and subsequent marriage to Dick, who is killed while skiing on their honeymoon in Finland; and her eventual inheritance of her aunt's philanthropic enterprise, the remand home. In the end, Lucy helps Lotty to be reunited with her child by taking the case to court with (ironically) her ex-husband as the judge. The details of the case and Lucy's defence of Lotty's right to her child convince him that he must facilitate a reconciliation between Lucy and their daughter.

The film warns women against getting married for the 'wrong reasons', in Lucy's case the pursuit of romance which is not forthcoming in her first marriage and is cut short in her second by the death of her lover on their honeymoon. We are not allowed to see how her relationship with Philip might have developed; possibly it would have become as sour as her first marriage. As soon as Lotty discovers that she is pregnant she is abandoned by her boyfriend, who quickly changes from being a romantic lover to a heartless exploiter of Lotty's body. The film deals with the subsequent pressures on her as a single mother, her poverty and depression, which, together with Lucy's experiences from a different class perspective, combine to produce an extraordinarily agnostic view of the possibility of romantic fulfilment, nearly ending, in Lotty's case, with death.

The film was controversial for its generic mix of 'women's picture'/social realism. An early fight scene between Lotty and another inmate in the remand home was promoted as

> the most violent fight between women ever filmed. This is no ordinary face-scratching, hair-pulling episode. There are kicks and punches and the girls (Joan Greenwood and Joan Rees) fling each other to the ground, and in general battle as vigorously as any British champion defending his title. (Pressbook for *The White Unicorn*)

The *Evening News* was not impressed by this display of feminine brutality:

> They claw each other, sling each other about the floor, punch in the stomach and twist the ankle. It is a revolting exhibition, unnecessary to the proper telling of the story. It is high time the censor took a hand. (16 October, 1947)

The *Mail* criticized its feminism:

> Our feminine colleagues sometimes accuse male critics of using the phrase 'a woman's picture' when they can think of nothing else to say. I apply the label confidently to *The White Unicorn*, as its emotional content is largely

> to do with mothers fighting for their babies; it amiably implies that all men are dirty dogs, stupid dogs, or both; and though its matter is serious, realism is never allowed to intrude on this matter. (17 October 1947)

This last comment is particularly interesting in that it makes explicit reference to the film's critique of male behaviour while at the same time concluding that this is an erroneous representation, 'realism' being identified as a 'correct', masculine position. This confusion about the film's appeal is also reflected in its publicity material. The distributors were unsure exactly how to pitch it, resulting in an uneasy negotiation between star persona and genre. The pressbook recommended that exhibitors should foreground Lockwood as a versatile and hard-working star, suggesting tie-ins with merchandise associated with the film (knitting patterns for *White Unicorn* gloves and jumpers) and detailing her New Look wardrobe:

> *The White Unicorn* has aimed at setting a new standard in the dressing of a British production . . . the accent is on rounded hips, smooth tight waists, and low necklines . . . It is predicted that the dresses, designed by Mattli, of Carlos Place, will be eagerly copied and worn proudly by women of discriminating taste.

This displacement of the 'serious matter' dealt with in the film onto safe, predictable discourses centred on Lockwood's star image (acting abilities, wardrobe, etc.) reveals how the film was at odds with expectations based on her previous four period roles (*The Wicked Lady*, *Bedelia*, *Hungry Hill* and *Jassy*).

Lockwood was not normally associated with realist films, so her appearance in *The White Unicorn* marked something of a departure. What is striking, however, is the extent to which both the period costume and contemporary dramas in which she appeared featured heroines who are torn between different identities. In the case of *The White Unicorn* Lucy identifies strongly with Lotty, even though their problems with men have been experienced from different class perspectives. This is not a difficulty for her and facilitates the narrative's closure, when both women are reunited with their children. In many of her other films, however, split identity means that Lockwood's characters must suffer and repent, returning to a one-dimensional state by their conclusion.

Alter egos and split personalities

In this section I will examine *A Place of One's Own* and *Highly Dangerous*, both of which involve Lockwood in roles where she is 'split' between herself and a threatening, dangerous 'other'. These preoccupations can be related to post-war spiritualism; a fascination with subjectivity (the influence of psychoanalysis) is suggestive of a complex recognition of gender roles. Several films of the period show a woman being possessed by another spirit or inclination which represents the conflict of femininities raging within her. In *Madonna of the Seven Moons* (Arthur Crabtree, 1944), for example, Phyllis Calvert plays Maddalena, a demure, repressed woman who is married to a rich Italian businessman and who periodically 'becomes' wild gypsy Rosanna. Rosanna represents liberated sexuality and recklessness, images which contemporary research suggested were the most compelling for female audiences (Harper, 1995). Similarly, *Black Narcissus* (Michael Powell and Emeric Pressburger, 1946) deals with the striking transformation of a repressed nun (Sister Ruth, played by Kathleen Byron) into a sexual, desiring woman.

In *A Place of One's Own* Lockwood plays Annette, companion/secretary to Mrs Smedhurst. Soon after the Smedhursts have moved into their new home and Annette has been employed, it appears that the house is haunted. Although the film is optimistic about the possibility of class mobility, its treatment of gender relations is more ambiguous. While the male characters are dismissive of the existence of ghosts and the supernatural, Mrs Smedhurst and Annette, representing the feminine 'irrational', realize that Annette is being 'taken over' by the spirit of Elizabeth Harkness, a young woman whose tyrannical father prevented her from marrying the man she loved by confining her as an invalid, a recluse who rarely appeared. A classic case of 'hysteria', Annette is taken over by the spirit of the dead woman and enters into a dangerous world controlled by feminine intuition and (according to the logic of the fiction) disturbing symptoms of the condition which might lead to death, as in the case of Elizabeth Harkness.

There are many references in the film to Annette's possession by another woman: that she is 'not herself' and that too much 'hysteria' is a dangerous, female tendency. In one key scene we watch as Annette is 'taken over' by Elizabeth's spirit while she is playing the piano: beginning the piece rather badly, as she enters her trance she plays Chopin with a delicate and eerie touch. The images of the possessed Annette invest her with a fullsome femininity which is coded as threatening. When she reverts to being 'herself' she is dressed in a far more restrained costume, which includes a white, virginal 'bridal' dress after her engagement has been announced. In a later scene we see Annette looking in a mirror, dressed in a low-cut dress with a flower at her bosom, reciting poetry as Elizabeth rather than Annette. Once the trance is over she realizes what has happened, protesting that she wants to be left alone to marry Robert (Dennis Price), as if Elizabeth is preventing their union. As noted earlier with reference to class, Robert is fascinated when Annette is possessed by Elizabeth, and is attracted by her new class position and her sexuality, although this is also represented as disturbing. The closure of the film, however, seeks to banish both these associations with the supernatural (upward class mobility and assertive female sexuality): the ghost of Elizabeth is successfully exorcized and Annette is free to marry Robert. Those disturbing ideas do exist, especially when the threatening spirit is female. The subtext of the Annette–Elizabeth conflation is, of course, that within accepted conventions of feminine behaviour (Annette) lies the potential for extremity, uncontrolled emotion and sexuality (Elizabeth), rendering 'the feminine' a complex and unstable entity.

In *Highly Dangerous* Lockwood is possessed by a different 'spirit', that of a male radio character, Secret Agent Conway, who inspires her to go on a mission to Eastern Europe in order to gain information about suspected germ warfare. She plays Frances Gray, an entomologist whose most courageous acts are undertaken while she is under the influence of her alter ego. By the end of the film, however, he has been banished from her psyche in favour of normality – a romantic pairing with an American who was largely responsible for the success of the latter stages of her mission. The film can be related to Cold War discourses about being 'taken over' by an alien power, Britain's relationship with the East and dependence on America. Its depiction of 'the feminine' is more straightforward than in the earlier, immediate post-war film. In contrast to *A Place of One's Own* the identificatory symptoms are not complex and do not cause extreme distress, indicating a more routine case of identification with the male domain of activity, a strategy which can be related back to a wartime ideology which recognized that women were performing 'male' roles but at the same time encouraged them to maintain their feminine attributes. In *Highly Dangerous* Frances Gray is trusted, obviously very good at her job and indispensable. It is interesting, however, that she is ultimately persuaded to go on the mission rather than take a planned holiday in Torquay after listening to the radio character. The superior who persuades her to take the job knows of her affinity for Conway and changes her name from Frances Gray to Frances Conway. It is as if there is a complicit recognition that she needs the courage of her male alter ego in order to be brave for Britain; on her return she settles for a more conventional existence.

At the end of *Highly Dangerous*, when her mission is complete, Annette forgets her identification with Agent Conway: she literally turns off his voice on the radio and concentrates on her romance. Yet earlier in the film we get the impression that, as with Barbara's euphoric time with Jerry Jackson in *The Wicked Lady*, Frances enjoys the power and release she feels as Agent Conway. Inspired by his influence, she is far more animated and assertive than in her more cautious, professional demeanour. In one scene, as she listens to the radio programme in her car, she puts her foot down on the accelerator, totally absorbed in and thrilled by the adventures she is hearing. While she has a capacity for adventure and daring, the film's preferred reading seems to suggest that she also desires romance and stability. Less threatening than Elizabeth Harkness, Agent Conway is a suitable role model: male, not complex, disembodied and certainly not sexual. The differences between these two images of female possession and split identity, one from 1945 and the other from 1950, provide a useful indicator of how films of the immediate post-war years generally contained more complex representations of femininity than in the later 1940s and 1950s (Perkins, 1996: 265–80).

Conclusion

Margaret Lockwood's film roles of this period represent the spectrum of competing femininities which characterized it as a transitory decade, bracketed by pre-war pressures for modernity, women's wartime experiences and the conservatism of the 1950s. Onscreen Lockwood could be wicked, duplicitous and sexual but also professional, honest, responsible, a loyal wife and mother. Although fans admired her in her wickedest roles (*The Man in Grey*, *The Wicked Lady* and *Bedelia*), they also tolerated her desire to be appreciated as a versatile actress and to star in a wide variety of roles (*Picturegoer*, 16 May 1942: 9). These roles, together with her offscreen reputation as a patriotic, hard-working and sensible woman, distanced her from the few roles which identified her primarily with transgression. As such, she epitomized British female stardom which linked 'ladylike' feminine qualities to British national identity and differentiated her from Hollywood's *femmes fatales*. However, this position also granted her a 'place' from which to explore social and individual aspects of female experience which were pertinent to the 1945–51 period: work, money, class, motherhood and identity. The films which dealt with these issues thus contributed to the ongoing 'problem' of locating 'the feminine' during a period when a clear, stable representation could only be achieved as a function of narrative closure.

Filmography

Bank Holiday (Carol Reed, 1937)
Bedelia (Lance Comfort, 1946)
Cardboard Cavalier (Walter Forde, 1949)
Highly Dangerous (Roy Ward Baker, 1950)
Hungry Hill (Brian Desmond Hurst, 1947)
I'll Be Your Sweetheart (Val Guest, 1945)
Jassy (Bernard Knowles, 1947)
The Lady Vanishes (Alfred Hitchcock, 1938)
Look before You Love (Harold Huth, 1948)
Love Story (Leslie Arliss, 1944)
Madness of the Heart (Charles Bennett, 1949)
The Man in Grey (Leslie Arliss, 1943)
A Place of One's Own (Bernard Knowles, 1945)
The Stars Look Down (Carol Reed, 1939)
The White Unicorn (Bernard Knowles, 1947)
The Wicked Lady (Leslie Arliss, 1945)

France

CHAPTER THREE

Evil Women in the Post-war French Cinema

NOËL BURCH AND GENEVIÈVE SELLIER

Introduction

The cinema of the post-war years marks the last period of truly popular film in France: audience figures reached an all-time high and everybody without cultural or economic discrimination saw every film. In the face of the Hollywood invasion, cinema became a national cause and political and professional organizations, especially on the left, fought to oblige Parliament to adopt a new law subsidizing French films. They succeeded in 1948.

In this context, it is revealing to look at cinematic representations as vivid expressions of the contradictions in society as a whole, especially at the level of gender relations, central to nearly all French films (Burch and Sellier, 1996). We will try to understand the meanings of these contradictions by examining some significant films of the period in terms of culture and society, rather than by the criteria of cinephilia, predominant among French historians of cinema.

The post-war period in French culture is particularly interesting because of the apparent contradiction that existed between the new political role for women, who won the right to vote in 1944 (a decisive step in emancipation) and the plethora of images of evil women which characterized the cinema and literature, both high and low. The dominant female figure – who appears, according to our research, in 25 per cent of films made between 1945 and 1955 – is a *sale garce* or 'evil bitch', who uses her powers of seduction to exploit, enslave and/or destroy men. Opposite her is a helpless victim – a young man old enough to have been mobilized in 1939, whom life has treated badly and who is unable to defend himself against such a treacherous enemy.

The figure of the malevolent *garce* will appear less frequently but lose none of its virulence right up to the end of the 1950s (the last remarkable instance being Julien Duvivier's 1956 *Voici le temps des assassins/Murder à la Carte*), although 1950 marked the turning point, with the huge success of *Caroline chérie* (Richard Poitier) making Martine Carol *the* female star of the French screen. With the advent of Carol and a host of voluptuous starlets in various states of undress, the evil *garce* of the immediate post-war era was gradually replaced in packed movie houses by the more reassuring image of a sexy woman at the service of a patriarchal figure played, as often as not, by Jean Gabin or Fernandel. The symbolic violence against women expressed in the *garce* figure was no longer necessary once patriarchal authority, badly shaken by defeat and occupation, had (temporarily?) recovered its serenity.

Along with the preponderance of misogynistic representations of women *after* the war, we can also note that it was the female stars accused of actual or imaginary 'horizontal collaboration' *during* the war who were dealt with most severely. As part of the purging of the motion picture industry after Liberation, Arletty and Mireille Balin were both jailed for their affairs with German officers, while Ginette Leclerc, compromised by her French lover, spent almost a year in prison, after which her career never really recovered.

We might perhaps find the missing link between harsh treatment and misogynistic representation in a long-repressed but undeniably widespread ritual which accompanied the liberation of many French towns and villages: women accused of having had sexual relations with the enemy had their heads shaved. According to Alain Brossat (1992), who examines these so-called freak events played down by almost every historian, they were not only an attempt – in keeping with a tradition that goes back at least to the Middle Ages – to exorcize a fear of the female sexuality which men could not control, but also a reminder to women that their bodies did not belong to them and that they could be repossessed symbolically on behalf of the Nation. The fact that a woman had had real or reported sexual relations with the enemy became the very symbol of national humiliation for a patriarchal society whose army, put to rout and then held prisoner for four years, had left women to face enemy soldiers on their own.

Quite apart from this phenomenon of head-shaving, which was limited to a few months in the summer of 1944, women became, at the Liberation, an ideal scapegoat for other forms of anxiety. This was because their *de facto* autonomy during the German occupation sparked the jealousy of those who were absent – prisoners, exiles, Resistance fighters. Cruelly and illogically, once France was free again, women were held responsible for the difficulty returning men had in finding jobs.

Despite the fact that women won the right to vote in 1944 (years later than in most comparable countries and officially presented as a reward for their role in the Resistance), the Liberation was to mark the beginning of a highly conflictual period in male–female relations fuelled by a new and major male anxiety: would women be willing to resume their role as housewives? During the Occupation they had demonstrated, often against their will, that they were as capable of supporting a family as of running a household and dealing with children's education – their more traditional roles (Fishman, 1991). Thus, at the same time as women were being 'granted' – De Gaulle's word in 1944 – the right to vote by their political leaders, the badly shaken male regime felt it imperative to lay down the limits of women's emancipation. Male fears and refusals had been legitimated by the Civil Code, introduced by Napoleon in 1804, which literally codified the subordination of women through legally incapacitating wives and investing all power in father or husband. Even after 1945, in all areas of the *Code civil* women continued to be regarded legally as minors and it was not until the 1960s and 1970s that this monument of patriarchal power began to be seriously eroded.

If one analyses both the stance taken by the main women's organizations which came into being after the war and the terms of the 1946 Constitution, it becomes clear that, at a time when the government was seeking to increase the birth rate, there was a consensus that priority should be given chiefly, if not exclusively, to the defence of women's maternal role – only the Union des Femmes Françaises, which had communist leanings, defended their right to work. Although the political discourse on both left and right was broadly content to re-establish the traditional sexual division of social roles, cultural productions offer ample evidence of the crisis which that consensus was attempting to paper over (Chaperon, 1999a).

The Resistance cycle

The films devoted to the Resistance during this period are invariably misogynistic. This is not surprising when we recall that a film like *Pontcarral, Colonel d'Empire/Pontcarral, Colonel of the Empire* (Jean Delannoy, 1942), the only film made under the Occupation which was perceived by the audience as a call to Resistance, validated the virile integrity of a Napoleonic officer standing up to the Restoration by devoting half the film to his taming of an aristocratic 'shrew'. Most of the post-war films on the subject were produced by film-makers close to the Resistance and thereby had a legitimate claim to authenticity, but they showed only male Resistance activities and skimmed over the vital role of women (as attested by historians of the period) in logistics and liaison work. René Clément's *La Bataille du rail/Battle of the Rails* (1946), the archetype of 'authenticiy', and devoted to the Resistance movement among rail workers, unabashedly established the canon of an exclusively male movement, despite the fact that Colette Audry worked on the screenplay! Only one woman appears, and that briefly in a negative role, as she tries to dissuade her husband from taking risks.

In a more traditional vein, the two most successful films about the Resistance, *Jéricho/Behind These Walls* (Henri Callef, 1946) and *Le Père tranquille/Mr Orchid* (René Clément, 1946), did not feature a *garce* but offered like *La Bataille du rail* a vision of the French struggle against the Occupation which denied the presence and commitment of women. It is a different case with *Un ami viendra ce soir/A Friend Comes Tonight* (Raymond Bernard, 1946), which tells the story of a Resistance group hiding out in a mental home. Simplistically Manichean, often implausible and overacted, the film offers, in Madeleine Sologne's portrayal of a young Jewish woman feigning insanity, the perfect image of a frail and unreliable female: she falls in love with Paul Bernard, who turns out to be the Nazi spy. Realising her love affair has put the Resistance group at risk, she returns to Paul, defuses his time-bomb and kills him. Having saved her comrades, however, she actually does go out of her mind, tortured by her misguided love and the murder she has committed. Thus, when the young heroes come down from the mountains to liberate the village, she has conveniently disappeared from the film.

The most violent version of the misogyny specifically associated with the Resistance came from communist director Louis Daquin. *Patrie/Country* (1946) tells of an episode in the Spanish occupation of The Netherlands at the end of the seventeenth century, which is in fact a reversal of Jacques Feyder's *La Kermesse héroique/Carnival in Flanders* (1935), in which the women save the honour of their village in spite of the cowardice of the men. In the later film, the same screenwriter, Charles Spaak, extols the virtues of Flemish resistance to the Spaniards and inverts the gender roles. Here, it is the Flemish burgher husbands who are heroic, defending their homeland even as they burn at the stake, while one of the women denounces her husband to save her lover. But male bonding saves the day and the lover punishes the treacherous female with his own hands.

This film's grotesque presentation of male heroism and female duplicity is all the more surprising from a militant Communist, once the assistant of the pro-feminist director Jean Grémillon, and who had himself, under the Occupation, directed *Madame et le mort/The Lady and Death* (1943), a detective comedy glorifying the emancipated woman! The explanation for such an astonishing regression (fortunately an isolated incident in this director's career) is doubtless to be found in the acute sense of malaise experienced during the period, especially in Resistance circles, where women's participation (of which, as a Communist, Daquin would have had first-hand knowledge) was experienced as a threat to the restoration of a positive masculine identity.

On the other hand, it is not at all surprising that it should be Yves Allégret, future expert in matters misogynistic, who in 1945 directed *Les Démons de l'aube/Demons of the Dawn*, a third-rate rendering of the exploits of a North African Army commando unit, which extols male fraternity in combat against a background of female treachery. Georges Marshal, a recently liberated POW, is corrupted by a wife who prefers party-going (and her lover) to the Resistance. Having seen the error of his ways, he rallies the Free French forces in Algiers and dies heroically with his men as they destroy a German artillery position on the Mediterranean coast in preparation for the Allied landing.

Mission spéciale/Special Assignment (Maurice de Canonge, 1945), a two-part feature, is the 'secret service' version of the same male heroics, aimed at perpetuating the continuity of a state apparatus 'duty-bound to resist'. The only major female part (played by Jany Holt) is that of a sadistic female Nazi spy. In minor roles, two other women are active in the Resistance, but one dies after being tortured and raped by the Gestapo, while the second is killed after stealing secret documents from a German officer whose mistress she has become to avenge her murdered family. In other words, the only strong woman in the film embodies everything hateful about the enemy, while the women on the side of right are terribly vulnerable. Conversely, the reassuring invulnerability of the group's leader (Jean Davy) is signified by his lack of any female attachment.

Both because of their often mediocre production values and dependence on temporal proximity to the 'events' they narrate, the cycle of Resistance pictures rapidly faded. Their importance, however, is that they proposed (or imposed) an official reading of the previous period in which the triumph of the Resistance, represented as exclusively male, was inseparable from women's return to their 'rightful' subordinate position in society.

Noir realism and misogyny

The trend for *noir* realism in the French cinema has often been perceived either as an emulation of Hollywood *film noir* or else interpreted, like its supposed American counterpart, as a reflection of the ideological disillusionment which grew out of the Cold War. But that analysis fails to take into account the dominant problematic of these French films, quite apart from the specific individual characteristics of scriptwriters such as Jacques Prévert (who was still going strong), but above all Charles Spaak, Jacques Sigurd, Henri Jeanson, Jean Aurenche and Pierre Bost, and directors such as Yves Allégret, Henri-Georges Clouzot, André Cayatte, Claude Autant-Lara, Julien Duvivier, Marcel Carné, René Clément and Henri Decoin. Compared with the pessimism of pre-war 'poetic realism', which those very same scriptwriters and directors had a hand in creating, the new common denominator of post-war films was the articulation between the objectively or subjectively evil nature of women and the victimization of men. Where 'fate' was once personified (and easily recognized) in the guise of a sinister middle-aged man (Michel Simon in *Quai des brumes/Port of Shadows*, Jules Berry in *Le Jour se lève/Daybreak* (Marcel Carné, 1938 and 1939), it now lurked deceptively behind the good looks of a young woman. The social conflicts of the pre-war period had given way to the theme of the battle of the sexes, in which women exerted a destructive power over men.

Viviane Romance's treacherous moll in *Panique/Panic* (Julien Duvivier, 1946), Suzy Delair's over-ambitious music-hall entertainer in *Quai des Orfèvres*, Cécile Aubry's irredeemable whore in *Manon* (Henri-Georges Clouzot, 1947 and 1949), Simone Signoret's gold-digger in *Manèges/The Wanton*, also *The Cheat* (Yves Allégret, 1949), Maria Casarès's portrayal of Death in *Orphée* (Jean Cocteau, 1949), Nicole Stéphane's voraciously incestuous sister in *Les Enfants terribles/The Strange Ones* (Cocteau and Jean-Pierre Melville, 1949) – all these female characters are malevolent in a more lethal way than any of the pre-war *garces*.

Pitted against such women there was no young Gabin, capable of ennobling suffering. The victimized male of the post-war films was very different from the tragic hero of pre-war poetic realism: the spectator was expected to pity him from the start of the film, although he was usually young and often even good-looking. Gérard Philipe's fugitive murderer in *Une si jolie petite plage/Such a Pretty Little Beach* (Jacques Sigurd/Yves Allégret, 1949), Serge Reggiani's street-urchin in love with a movie star in *Les Amants de Vérone/The Lovers of Verona* (André Cayatte, 1948), Daniel Gélin's concert pianist married to a frivolous heiress in *Edouard et Caroline* (Jacques Becker, 1951), Jean Marais' 'psychic war-casualty' in *Les Miracles n'ont lieu qu'une fois/Miracles Only Happen Once* (Yves Allégret, 1951) are typical examples of the phenomenon, but so are the roles played by older and less seductive actors: Pierre Brasseur's circus motorcyclist in thrall to a 'praying mantis' in *Portrait d'un assassin/Portrait of a Killer* (Raymond Bernard, 1949), Michel Simon's long-suffering husband in *La Poison/Poison* (Sacha Guitry, 1950) and Bernard Blier's equally forbearing husband-accompanist in *Quai des Orfèvres*.

At first sight surprising, this emphasis on the weakness of men confronted with female characters of often devastating power can be seen as a paranoid interpretation by men of their own predicament at the Liberation, fearful that they would not be able to recapture their pre-war position of dominance and seeing the emancipation of women as an attempt to destroy male identity.

Among the directors who were to illustrate this unprecedented misogyny, there were as many left-wingers and former Resistance fighters as there were individuals more or less implicated in political compromise with Vichy ideology and Nazi rule. Moreover, the most extreme misogyny to be found in films produced during the Occupation occurs in the tiny handful of explicitly 'resistant' works like Delannoy's *Pontcarral, Colonel d'Empire* or Daquin's *Premier de Cordée/Team Leader* (1944), a situation which casts serious doubt on the hypothesis put forward by historians and 'New Philosophers' that the post-war hostility towards women was a displacement of national guilt experienced by 'forty million collaborationists' (Levy, 1981; Rousso, 1987:201–6). On the contrary, it seems to us that to treat this misogyny as a metaphor for a more serious, 'political' phenomenon, in the exclusive restrictive sense still used by French intellectuals (and the thinkers who propagate this theory are in fact prominent champions of the intellectual machismo still hegemonic in France), is really a way of negating the fact that it was women themselves who were the prime targets of this settling of accounts at the Liberation. Certainly, recent historical research – such as that referred to above – tends to confirm the hypothesis that violence towards women, symbolic or real, was explicitly aimed at them as women, and was no doubt a factor in delaying for some twenty years the struggles for women's freedom and equality that were to develop only in the 1970s. And this in spite of the enormous and unprecedented popularity of de Beauvoir's 1949 feminist polemical study, *Le Deuxième Sexe*, which at least testified to the interest aroused among women by an implacable exposure of patriarchal domination. Today, however, we know that all discussion of this book was deliberately stifled, especially by women's organizations (Chaperon, 1999a, b).

Julien Duvivier, who spent the war years in the United States, was the director who began the new trend with his 1946 film, *Panique*. In it, Michel Simon plays Monsieur Hire victimized in a chillingly topical sense: he is Jewish. His co-star is Viviane Romance, who had been established by the same Duvivier, in his 1936 film *La Belle Équipe*, as the archetypal beautiful bitch of the pre-war years. But the woman she plays in *Panique* has lost all her autonomy: she is in love with a crook (Paul Bernard), for whom she has already gone to prison and for whom she agrees to seduce Michel Simon so as to frame him for a murder committed by her lover.

The cynicism of the post-war cinema is already full-blown in this film's depiction of the hostile crowd that drives Monsieur Hire to his death, a crowd that stands looking up at the rooftops in a sinister echo of the once solidary crowd that watches the doomed Jean Gabin in *Le Jour se lève*. The Viviane Romance character plays a decisive role in the death of Monsieur Hire: he is wary of everyone else but her, while the young policeman (Charles Dorat), efficient, discreet, but ultimately powerless, suspects the real culprit from the very start, but is too late to foil the diabolical couple's plot and save Monsieur Hire.

Duvivier displays a good sense of political opportunism in *Panique*, joining in the exorcism of the Occupation at the expense of the cowardly and profiteering *français moyen* – but mostly at the expense of women. The film manages a veritable *tour de force* by embodying all human evil-doing (aimed at a Jew, in 1946!) in a woman who at the same time is denied any subjectivity (she is a puppet in a man's hands). As a characteristic trope of the film, the moral revulsion she experiences in insistent close-up is systematically annihilated in the narrative by her physical dependency on her lover.

Descending from a long tradition (see Oscar Wilde's *Salomé*, for example), Yves Allégret's 1949 film, *Manèges*, hinges on an evil alliance between mother and daughter (Jane Marken and Simone Signoret). The highly complex organization of the narrative into flashbacks aims to fuse together mother and daughter in an uneven contest between a lone man (Bernard Blier) and two women who are secretly plotting to ruin him. The women in the film are uniformly vicious and their prey, typically for the period, is an ordinary 'average man'. Unlike most Hollywood *films noirs*, where there is generally a girl-from-home representing a possible straight-and-narrow, here every woman on the screen is unequivocally trashed. Significantly, and also in contrast to Hollywood where the hero has generally transgressed and is guilt-ridden, the male figure here is an utterly innocent victim.

One particular scene, in which Blier tries to talk about his hardships in a Stalag to a wife who, rather than listening, is exchanging flirtatious looks with a man at the bar, sheds a harsh light on the misogyny of this film – and all the films that resemble it from the period. It is a prisoner's fantasy: 'This is what our wives were up to while we were rotting in a Stalag (or work brigade or concentration camp or even in the Resistance) . . . But we found them out and they'd better fall in line or get what they deserve.'

Like *Manèges* many films of the period resort to a duality in the figures of the evil women, which derives its phantasmal effectiveness from its ability to combine two logically contradictory ideas: evil and passivity. Although the Signoret character is in fact rather self-aware and calculating, for the most part the young women in these films – those who fascinate men – are passive: their seductiveness operates without their being conscious of it and their bodies act, so to speak, without the intervention of their minds. The mothers, on the other hand, whose beauty has faded with age, play an actively evil role, as though taking revenge for the fact they are no longer attractive. Seduction comes across as a specifically female instrument of power, temporarily camouflaging a much more formidable ambition which takes shape when beauty has faded. This dual figure denies the desired woman any autonomy, while at the same time attributing to her a power which she derives from her submission to maternal omnipotence.

This matriarchal fantasy has its source in a twofold inversion of the period's social reality. On the one hand, the isolation of housewives and their economic dependency placed them more often than not in a position of inferiority within the couple and the family; on the other hand, and above all, the wholesale arrival of (young) women in the rapidly expanding tertiary sector (as opposed to more traditional sectors, such as cottage industry or agriculture) afforded them a new social and psychological autonomy which made the figure of the all-powerful mother appear anachronistic. By reviving it so forcefully, the cinema was working to keep women in their role of eternal minors, condemned to lifelong confinement in the private sphere.

A tale of revenge from 1946, *Un revenant/A Ghost* (Christian-Jaque), carries the derogatory equation of younger and older women to its logical conclusion, as Louis Jouvet, a world-famous choreographer, returns to Lyons (which he had left twenty years earlier in dramatic circumstances) to settle accounts with his enemies and meet again the object of his youthful love, now revealed to us as a docile middle-aged housewife (Gaby Morlay). Written by Henri Jeanson, the film jubilantly runs the gamut of anti-bourgeois satire, but with a place of honour reserved for misogyny, via the Morlay character. Apparently a sympathetic figure, oppressed by a social milieu that obliged her to renounce the man she loved in favour of an arranged marriage, she gradually becomes the object of a sadistic indictment on the part of her former lover (Jouvet), clearly the author's mouthpiece, who ridicules her more and more openly as the film progresses. He feigns undying love and then leaves her stranded on the railway platform after inciting her to leave her husband. As he leaves, he announces he is taking away her son (François Périer) to punish her for having once bowed down to the powers that be. The spectator, led to identify with the role of the demiurgic righter-of-wrongs played by Jouvet, comes to accept the notion that Morlay is entirely to blame for his past sufferings, especially since he is now faced with a middle-aged woman who has lost the fresh beauty and innocence of youth and has sold out to patriarchal and bourgeois power. Gaby Morlay appears as the true face of that misguided passion of long ago, as the ageing process serves to reveal the 'true nature of women' – weak, hypocritical, conformist.

Is not this story of a man's return the re-enactment of the return of the prisoner-of-war, judging the women who, in order to survive under the Occupation, had perhaps been forced to compromise themselves? Thus, the sense of guilt at having left women to fend for themselves in the teeth of the enemy is reversed: women are made to feel guilty for their cushy lives at home while men were risking theirs at war. *Un revenant* also turns class confrontation into male revenge, since Jouvet, claiming to get back at the bourgeois family that tried to murder him, punishes the woman he claims he once loved, going so far as to take away her son, after teaching him, through a cynical manipulation, that any relationship with a women is a con game.

In *Une si jolie petite plage*, the displacement of a social theme (orphans exploited by their foster families) onto the 'sex war' is characteristic of the period: Gérard Philipe returns to the scene of his unhappy teens and finds an alter ego exploited as he once was by the new proprietress (Jane Marken) of the same seaside inn. He broods over his past sufferings, which in his despair he confuses with his seduction and abduction ten years earlier by an older woman, whom he has just murdered for want of the strength to leave her. Jean Servais, playing the role of a sinister character tracking him down like a detective or a jealous lover, turns out to be less threatening to the hero than the tortured memory of the woman from whom there is no escape but to kill himself at the end of the film.

Like an avenging ghost, the murdered woman makes her presence felt through the gramophone record the inn guests listen to – she was a *chanteuse réaliste*, famed for speaking the 'truth of love'. By breaking the record, Philipe gets back at a pre-war myth. From *Paris-Béguin* (Augusto Genina, 1932) and *La Tête d'un homme/Head of a Man* (Julien Duvivier, 1933) to *Pépé le Moko* (Julien Duvivier, 1937) and *L'Entraîneuse/Nightclub Hostess* (Albert Valentin, 1938), Jane Marney, Damia and Fréhel, *chanteuses réalistes*, had the task of authenticating the emotions experienced by the spectator. The young man in *Une si jolie petite plage* violently denounces the fictitious character of that emotion by destroying the last trace: a tune on a gramophone record. *Réalisme poétique* was dead, long live *réalisme noir*!

An unhappy childhood (which had brought together Jean Gabin and Jacqueline Laurent in *Le Jour se lève*) is insufficient to bring together young men sexually exploited by older women: Gérard Philipe fails to gain the confidence of the boy who performs the chores that used to be his and who has himself fallen prey to an older woman staying at the inn, uncannily repeating Philipe's own story. As for the pathetic servant, played by Madeleine Robinson, she is powerless to help the hero: it is as if he were under the spell of some witch who had deprived him forever of the capacity to love. The film is constructed around the absent woman, already dead when the film begins, never to be revived in flashback, but who finally drives the hero to his death: she is tantamount to some malevolent divinity who cannot be abandoned or killed without ensuring one's own death.

The wickedness of women was an eminently consensual theme that enabled ideological differences and discreditable behaviour to be conveniently forgotten. For example, it enabled Clouzot, after undergoing a two-year suspension from film-making activity for his collaboration with Germans, to re-emerge in great style with *Quai des Orfèvres*. The character of Jenny Lamour in this film, a music-hall singer whose unbridled ambition causes her husband almost to commit murder, was probably the finest role of Suzy Delair's career. Bernard Blier is the natural embodiment of the affectionate, kindly and weak husband who has the wool pulled over his eyes. A petit bourgeois whom love has brought down in the world, he plays the piano in the music hall where his wife appears and is forced to look on helplessly as she deploys her seductive charms. Blier and Louis Jouvet, who plays the police inspector, each offer in their own way a fragile and attractive image of masculinity – the young husband who has no defence against his wife's ambition and the ageing policeman who has come back from the colonies with malaria and a half-caste child he dotes on. Between them they constitute two cleverly camouflaged embodiments of the patriarchal law which the post-war cinema relentlessly set out to rehabilitate.

Manon (Henri-Georges Clouzot, 1949), an updating of the Abbé Prévost novel to post-Liberation France, was also a big box-office success. Today it is hard to work up much enthusiasm for this 'modern' adaptation of *Manon Lescaut*. The eighteenth-century heroine, victim of patriarchal oppression as much as of her own desire, becomes a layabout lady saved from the head-shaver's scissors at the Liberation by Resistance fighter Des Grieux who betrays his comrades-in-arms for the blue eyes of the belle. He becomes a small-time black-marketeer, then flees with her to Palestine where the lovers die in the desert. Contrary to the novel, in which the hero survives to tell his *malheureuse histoire*, the victimization of the male character in Clouzot's film gives rise to an endless finale after the death of Manon in which the young man lies slowly dying on the sand, his arms outstretched, a second Christ sacrificed to redeem the sins of Woman . . .

The film is constructed on a flashback principle similar to that of *Le Crime de Monsieur Lange* (Jean Renoir, 1936): a man accused of murder by official justice tries to explain his act to a group who can turn him in or save him. But, as in *Quai des Orfèvres*, the object is to show that only the woman is guilty. The first flashback is a classic of its kind. In the bombed ruins of a newly liberated town, a group of Forces Françaises de l'Intérieur (FFI), the official Resistance fighters, rescue a girl accused of 'horizontal collaboration' from the clutches of a band of hysterical women who are about to shave her head. A group of half-naked women with shaved heads and tattoos go by; FFI member Des Grieux (Michel Auclair) is put in charge of Manon (Cécile Aubry) until she can have a proper trial; she tries to escape; he captures her again; she persuades him to run away with her . . .

It is not a matter of indifference that a director closely involved with the German cultural authorities during the Occupation should, in a 1948 film, make use of the head-shaving of the Liberation. In the first place, he was calling attention to the so-called 'horrors' of the Liberation, in order to deflect from the much more substantial horrors of the Occupation. But Clouzot's vision contains wheels within wheels: he absolves the young FFI men of any responsibility for the head-shaving (contrary to most eye-witness accounts) and heaps the blame on women – head-shaving was a consequence of women settling scores among themselves, not a sexist reprisal. It is only a short step from this image to the notion that, like Cécile Aubry, the *tondues* were merely the young and pretty victims of jealous harpies. Additionally, the scene may also be read, in the light of the rest of the story, as a call for a united front among men (collaborators and resistants alike) against women. Be that as it may, the fact that Clouzot could already afford to be so brazen with such sensitive themes as the purges and the black market indicates that prevailing attitudes had already shifted for him and for public opinion in general (a supposition confirmed by the film's success at the box office).

Clouzot lavished most of his attention on the character played by Cécile Aubry, a systematic reversal of the typical female of the Occupation film who was the subject of the narrative and responsible for the destiny of the community. Here it is the narrator hero who is the subject: the woman is the object of his desire and the source of all his troubles. Our point of view on the heroine is mediated by the desiring male gaze and it is this concentration on a male viewpoint that runs through French post-war cinema like an act of vengeance. As for the female figures, modelled after Hollywood's fetishization of the body, they are represented with a kind of visual eroticism unknown in French films before 1945. The childlike appearance of Cécile Aubry, emphasized by her acting, makes the subtext perfectly explicit: women are fascinating because they are childlike, irresponsible, thoughtless. In other words, they attract men through their capacity to exist as nothing but a body, concerned only with their comfort and their appearance. The scene in which Michel Auclair is shocked to learn that Manon is working in a high-class brothel sums up Clouzot's ideas on man/woman relations: you could murder women (*Bonnes à tuer* is the title of a 1954 Decoin film) but we men always forgive them because they don't know how much they make us suffer.

Over and above Clouzot's own settling of accounts, the fact that the film was a 1948 box-office hit is an indication of the violently conflictual relationships that existed between the sexes at that time. Whether acting consciously or unthinkingly, Manon and each of the female figures like her share an ability to exert a destructive power over the men they will seduce from the moment they elude male control. What these films advocate untiringly, then, is the passive submission of women to men, by using pathetic or, in the case of Auclair in *Manon*, trapped male figures to make women feel guilty. In fact, Auclair is constantly excused for his 'bad behaviour' in the film on the grounds of circumstance or because of the impossibility of resisting Manon's seductiveness, and, as the tragic 'new' ending confirms, he is the victim and not her.

Studies of Weimar cinema or post-Vietnam Hollywood cinema suggest that military defeat gives rise to films that both wallow in and exorcize a crisis in masculine identity. The French defeat of 1940 was one of the most humiliating inflicted on a major power this century, which no doubt helps to explain why few national cinemas have been characterized by the overall swing of gender representations observed in French films, from the idealization of women as social movers or mainstays during the Occupation to the violent misogyny of the post-Liberation years.

To what extent were these 'innocent' men and these 'vicious' women original creations of the post-war years? On the whole, women tended to be relatively innocent objects of conflict and exchange between men, especially in films derived from *théâtre de boulevard* (for example, Guitry, Pagnol . . .), which was so important during the first decade of sound. There were, however, films where woman represented man's sworn enemy. Among these we must cite Renoir's *La Chienne/The Bitch* (1931), as well as films by Duvivier, Genina or even Grémillon, and it was these minority figures, codified for the screen in the 1930s, which became generalized in the post-war era. 'La mère maquerelle' (the pimping mother) in Grémillon and Spaak's *Gueule d'amour/The Look of Love* (1937) –

providing a cynical justification for her 'kept' daughter, Mireille Balin, and participating in the flaunting and taunting that will eventually 'force' Gabin to murder his beautiful tormentress – is a figure that will resurface in *Manèges*, with a similar apologetic veneer of class criticism.

More immediately, the horrible women of the immediate post-war cinema can be regarded as a response to the edifyingly strong women of the cinema of the Occupation. From this perspective villainesses, such as Jany Holt's Nazi torturer in *Mission spéciale*, are 'inverted feminist' types of, for example, Holt's portrayals of sexually independent women in Occupation films like *Les Anges du péché/Angels of the Street* (Robert Bresson, 1943), *Farandole* (André Zwobada, 1944) or *La Fiancée des ténèbres/The Bride of Darkness* (Serge de Poligny, 1944). Similarly, the inept anti-heroines of the Resistance – such as Madeleine Sologne in *Un ami viendra ce soir* stupidly falling in love with a Nazi spy and paying for it with madness – are inversions of the women who took their destiny in hand in wartime films: Sologne herself as the resourceful and athletic adversary of black marketeers in *Départ à zéro/Leave at Zero* (Maurice Cloche, 1941) or, more prestigiously, Madeleine Renaud as pilot heroine in *Le Ciel est à vous/The Sky Is Yours* (Jean Grémillon, 1944).

Minority representations

In opposition to this paranoid mainstream, a small number of remarkable films which tried to look at the 'new deal' of equality between men and women proposed gender roles and relations owing little to pre-war cinema but much to patterns developed under the Occupation. *Antoine et Antoinette* (Jacques Becker, 1947) offers a rare portrait of a young working-class couple (Claire Maffei, Roger Pigaut) in which the woman is clearly the more lucid and level-headed partner. She has no trouble keeping at arm's length the grotesque macho patriarch, black marketeer Noël Roquevert, who resembles a leftover from the cinema of old. Like other auteurs of the period, however, Becker's position oscillates, and in *Le Rendez-vous de juillet/July Meeting* (1949) and *Rue de l'Estrapade* (1951) the revolt of young women against their elders and bourgeois marriage ends pathetically. *Edouard et Caroline* (1951) ridicules the social ambitions of a young wife (Anne Vernon) set against the far more serious artistic ambitions of her pianist husband of working-class background (Daniel Gélin).

On the left, *Les Frères Bouquinquant/The Brothers Bonquinquant* (Louis Daquin, 1947) is somewhat more circumspect: Madeleine Robinson's provincial domestic becomes the victim of a drunken husband, heroically accepts responsibility for his death (in reality accidentally caused by her lover), but then her superstitious nature nearly makes her succumb in prison to the wiles of a malicious priest. And while Lolleh Bellon's worker heroine in Daquin's *Le Point du jour/The Barricade of Point du jour* (1948) is an admirable example of independent womanhood; the film's central theme is the (male) worker-engineer alliance advocated by the Communist Party in those years.

One of the most remarkable of these dissident films was directed by Henri Decoin, a prolific director since the mid-1930s. Throughout his career he stands as an emblem of the versatility of French film-makers, prepared to sail in accordance with the prevailing ideological winds. In the post-war years these came from a very different direction than in the 1930s. *Les Amants du Pont Saint Jean/The Lovers of Pont Saint Jean* (1947) recounts the parallel loves of a couple of ageing down-and-outs (Gaby Morlay, Michel Simon) and a boy and a girl (Roger Blin, Nadine Alari) in their late teens. In the face of men who are not unsympathetic but are prone to cowardice and violence, it is the women who embody courage and integrity throughout. Morlay is accidentally killed by her lifelong companion in a fit of drunkeness and Alari, after a first night of love with her young beau, decides he is not for her . . .

Nearly all directors in France at this time were men. Of the tiny number of women directors, only Jacqueline Audry acquired any recognition. Despised in her day by 'advanced critics' (*Cahiers du cinéma*, *Positif*) as a second-hand exponent of *la tradition de qualité*, she has been systematically neglected by film historians in spite, or perhaps because of, her very acute perspective on gender relations. *Minne, l'ingénue libertine/Minne, the Naive Libertine* (1950) takes advantage of the popularity (since 1940!) of Belle Époque films and of a well-established sex comedy tradition to assert women's right to pleasure in love. *Olivia* (1951) was the first French film to give a broadly positive image of lesbian love and most of her sixteen feature films are marked by a feminist approach to human relations. It is typical of the cultural blindness of the time that the mainstream critics, who often gave her favourable notices, almost never seem to have noticed what actually distinguished her films from those of her male contemporaries.

Finally, among the better-known films, one could mention Max Ophuls's *Madame de . . .* (1953) and *Lola Montès* (1955) and Jean Grémillon's *L'Amour d'une femme/Love of a Woman* (1954) as examples of films which attempt to make visible both the patriarchal oppression of women and their desire to escape from it. They also happen to be profoundly pessimistic and, except for Grémillon's film, highly ambivalent.

Conclusion

The post-war period in France marked the dawn of a collective recognition of the cultural importance of the film industry with its cross-class audience, and of the cultural, social and political battle which led in 1948 to the law on public support for the film industry and to the renegotiation of the Blum-Byrnes agreement expressing the country's determination to resist the invasion of Hollywood films.

In this context, the violently conflictual nature of filmic representations from many genres can be seen as an expression of the attempts to redefine gender roles and identities after the unprecedented disturbances caused by defeat and Occupation. In a profession which was almost entirely male-dominated, the most revanchist male viewpoints could be set forth as self-evident truths, yet the emergence of a feminist current, however small, showed that the need to redefine gender roles was not a one-way affair.

The real balance of power, however, is to be read in the box-office success of the most misogynistic films (*Panique*, *Quai des Orfèvres*, *Manèges*, *Manon*) and in the increasingly spectacular failures of films taking an opposite stand (*Les Amants du Pont Saint Jean* and *Le Point du jour*, 1948), both of which tend to suggest that a consensus was being arrived at in post-war France at the expense of women and with their consent, even as the Cold War was instituting violent political and social divisions. That a Communist director like Louis Daquin should have abandoned the proto-feminist preoccupations of some of his earlier post-war films in favour of a class viewpoint that was more compatible with the predominant misogyny (*Bel Ami*, 1954, and *Les Arrivistes*, 1960) attests to the general repression of a more egalitarian definition of the relations between the sexes.

After 1950, the evil *garce* gradually gives way to sexier, more cooperative figures (Martine Carol, Françoise Arnoul and then Brigitte Bardot), more compatible with a pattern of patriarchal domination. This substitution testifies to the efficiency of the symbolic violence against women through film representations. The Second World War was to establish motion pictures in France as a privileged arena for the expression of social contradictions and to reveal just how genuinely political were representations of 'the private sphere'. While some films suggest a collapse of traditional patriarchal values under the Occupation, others show, just as clearly, the forceful return of those values following the Liberation. They all attest to the extraordinarily persuasive powers of screen representations aimed at stifling the egalitarian aspirations of the women who had grown up in a time of war and resistance.

Filmography

Les Amants du Pont Saint Jean (Henri Decoin, 1947)
Les Amants de Vérone (André Cayatte, 1948)
Un ami viendra ce soir (Raymond Bernard, 1946)
Antoine et Antoinette (Jacques Becker, 1947)
La Bataille du rail (René Clément, 1946)
Caroline chérie (Richard Poitier, 1950)
Les Démons de l'aube (Yves Allégret, 1945)
Edouard et Caroline (Jacques Becker, 1951)
Les Enfants terribles (Jean Cocteau and Jean-Pierre Melville, 1949)
Les Frères Bouquinquant (Louis Daquin, 1947)
Le Jour se lève (Marcel Carné, 1939)
Manèges (Yves Allégret, 1949)
Manon (Henri-Georges Clouzot, 1949)
Minne, l'ingénue libertine (Jacqueline Audry, 1950)
Les Miracles n'ont lieu qu'une fois (Yves Allégret, 1951)
Mission spéciale (Maurice de Canonge, 1945)
Olivia (Jacqueline Audry, 1951)
Orphée (Jean Cocteau, 1949)
Panique (Julien Duvivier, 1946)
Patrie (Louis Daquin, 1946)
Le Point du jour (Louis Daquin, 1948)
La Poison (Sacha Guitry, 1950)
Pontcarral, Colonel d'Empire (Jean Delannoy, 1942)
Portrait d'un assassin (Raymond Bernard, 1949)
Quai des Orfèvres (Henri-Georges Clouzot, 1947)
Le Rendez-vous de juillet (Jacques Becker, 1949)
Un revenant (Christian-Jaque, 1946)
Rue de l'Estrapade (Jacques Becker, 1951)
Une si jolie petite plage (Jacques Sigurd/Yves Allégret, 1949)

Micheline Presle in *Falbalas/Paris Frills* (1944–5, France, Jacques Becker)
Source: BFI Stills, Posters and Designs

CHAPTER FOUR

From Stardom to Eclipse: Micheline Presle and Post-war French Cinema[1]

CARRIE TARR

Micheline Chassagne, born in 1922, took the name Presle from her early role in G. W. Pabst's *Jeunes Filles en détresse/Young Girls in Trouble* (1939) and, according to Roger Régent (1946: 270), was 'one of the only revelations of the last four years [of the German Occupation]'. Presle may have been less well known internationally than her contemporaries Michèle Morgan and Danielle Darrieux, but her Occupation films established her image as a lively, independent young woman and made her France's most popular young female star. In an early 1945 opinion poll in *Écran français* (16 January 1945), 22-year-old Presle figured in fifth place, behind Darrieux, Gaby Morlay, Edwige Feuillère and Viviane Romance, stars who had been well established prior to the outbreak of war. That same year, no fewer than three of Presle's earlier wartime films opened in Paris – *Fausse alerte/False Alarm* (Jacques de Baroncelli, 1940–5), *Félicie Nanteuil/Twilight* (Marc Allégret, 1942–5) and *Falbalas/Paris Frills* (Jacques Becker, 1944–5) – as did her first post-war film, *Boule de suif/Angel and Sinner* (Christian-Jaque, 1945), an instant popular and critical success. Presle then starred in the internationally acclaimed *Le Diable au corps/Devil in the Flesh* (Claude Autant-Lara, 1947) and was propelled into first place in the *Cinémonde* 1948 poll of preferred female stars (Crisp, 1996). After her next film, the less successful *Les Jeux sont faits/The Die Is Cast* (Jean Delannoy, 1947), Presle went on to make two commercially driven Franco-Italian co-productions, *Les Derniers Jours de Pompéi/Last Days of Pompeii* (Marcel L'Herbier, 1948) and *Tous les chemins mènent à Rome/All Roads Lead to Rome* (Jean Boyer, 1949). But by that time she had fallen in love with American actor Bill Marshall (previously married to Michèle Morgan) and, with blithe disregard for her professional interests, decided to follow him to Hollywood in 1948 and allowed him to direct her not particularly distinguished Hollywood career. On her return three years later, after the breakdown of her marriage, she found it extremely difficult to re-establish herself. For example, in *L'Amour d'une femme/A Woman's Love* (Jean Grémillon, 1954) Presle stars as a young doctor who refuses to give up her career for love; but the film's moderately disturbing message about female autonomy meant that it was never given proper distribution. Her subsequent long and varied film and television career (which includes more than ninety film appearances to date) only really took off in the 1960s.

Although the eclipse of Presle's career at the end of the 1940s may be attributable in part to her literal disappearance from France, it may also be due to the nature of her star image and the inability of post-war French cinema to accommodate it. For Françoise Audé (1987: 75):

> She was the most popular actress of the war years, because her vitality, energy and gaiety combined with her sudden pathos and gravity were antidotes to the sadness and weariness of the rest of the world: Micheline Presle represented truth for those who refused to be asphyxiated. She was alive. She was young. She was responsible.

For Françoise Ducout (1978: 120):

> She foreshadowed transformations which were not just those of an adolescent, but rather of a woman who, beneath her carefree exterior, was aware that the times were changing radically and that, to survive in a future which would not always smile on everyone, one had to be alert, and learn new ways of behaving, a new language, a new way of thinking.

Presle's star image would thus seem eminently suited to figure the contemporary French woman facing the challenges of post-war reconstruction. But the dominant tendency of post-war French cinema was to turn away from topics rooted in contemporary reality, for fear of endangering the reconstruction of a fragile national unity after the bitterly divided years of war and Occupation. Presle's three French films of the post-war years 1945–47, all made by established directors in the French 'cinema of quality' tradition, typically fail to address the actuality of women's experiences. They consist of two costume dramas based on literary adaptations and one film set in a fantasy world, based on the very literary screenplay of writer and philosopher Jean-Paul Sartre. All three films are set at times of war or revolution and are therefore readable as displaced reworkings of the Occupation period. Their settings suggest that the sort of woman represented by Presle belongs to the past rather than to the present, and their progressive containment of Presle's star image can be seen as emblematic of the treatment of the figure of the 'new woman' in post-war French cinema.

The articulation of Presle's star image needs to be seen within the wider context of shifts in the representation of gender between the Occupation and the post-war period. As Burch and Sellier (1996) have argued, despite the Vichy government's reactionary legislation pertaining to women, French cinema of the Occupation, marked by a crisis in masculinity, paradoxically gave women more active, dynamic roles than had been available in the pre-war period (see also Tarr, 1995). However, after the Liberation, when women had at last achieved the right to vote (1944) and Brigitte Chevance, writing in *Femmes françaises* (21 September 1944), identified 'the emergence of a new woman whose complex face will not be liked by misogynists', French cinema contributed to the reconstruction of French national identity by reinscribing a patriarchal perspective which required women's roles to be marginalized and contained. Male stars of the 1930s were more popular than female stars (Raimu, Fernandel, Jouvet, Blanchar and Gabin were all ahead of Danielle Darrieux in the *Écran français* 1945 poll), and by the end of the decade, representations of young women in dominant French cinema had been largely reduced either to harmless sex objects (Doniol-Valcroze, 1954) or to dangerous sexual subjects who needed to be punished. They were embodied, too, by a new generation of female stars, typically sex goddess Martine Carol, star of *Caroline chérie* (Richard Pottier, 1951), and the dangerously sexual Simone Signoret, both of whom were still relatively unknown in 1948 when Presle left France for Hollywood. But in any case, Presle's elegance, spontaneity, sincerity and sense of self-worth were not appropriate for the role of either sex object or *femme fatale* (although Joseph Losey was later to make her play both, rather unconvincingly, in *Blind Date* in 1959). The rest of this chapter traces the shifts in the construction of Presle's star image from her first starring role and the progressively autonomous roles of her Occupation films through to the more problematic post-war films in which her role as an independent-minded woman is both foregrounded and progressively constrained and closed over.

Presle's first starring role was in the pre-war film, *Le Paradis perdu/Four Flights to Love* (Abel Gance, 1940), a romantic melodrama in which she plays the dual role of Janine, a humble young woman who marries for love and dies in childbirth during the First World War, and her daughter, Janette, whose own marriage a generation later occasions the death of Pierre (Fernand Gravey), the grieving husband and doting father. The film was screened some months after the outbreak of the war and its pathos was in tune with the mood of the nation. As Janine, Presle's beautiful oval face, long eyelashes, lovely smile and sweet voice inspire Pierre to become a successful dress designer. Her seductive singing voice and her modelling of Pierre's fashion designs are elements which resurface in Presle's subsequent performances. However, the role of devoted wife is not a recurrent theme. For example, in *La Nuit fantastique/The Fantastic Night* (Marcel L'Herbier, 1942), Presle plays the enigmatic Irène, a vision dressed in glorious, diaphanous white robes, who is pursued across Paris in a surreal dreamlike chase by Denis, a student (Fernand Gravey). Though Presle's role is secondary to that of Gravey and owes much to the extravagant costumes she is allowed to model, she is more quirky and independent than the more conventional Janine and Janette of *Paradis perdu*.

If *La Nuit fantastique* still depends on conventional notions of femininity and feminine roles, two of Presle's later Occupation films, *Félicie Nanteuil* and *Falbalas*, begin to question the satisfactoriness of heterosexual romance. *Félicie Nanteuil*, set during the Belle Epoque, gave Presle the role she most identified with (Presle, 1994: 81). As the eponymous heroine, an aspiring young provincial actress, Presle is taken in charge by hammy Parisian actor Aimé Cavalier (Claude Dauphin), becomes a star, falls in love with aristocrat Robert de Ligny (Louis Jourdan), but cannot find happiness in love because she is unable to exorcize the ghost of her former benefactor. Cavalier's unhealthy obsession with her leads to his suicide and Félicie's decision to devote her life solely to her career. *Falbalas*, the last Presle film of the Occupation (shot while Becker and his colleagues were simultaneously working on the clandestine filming of the Liberation struggle), draws on a similar theme and is, arguably, the film which most justifies Presle's image of the modern woman. Based on an original screenplay by Jacques Becker and Maurice Aubergé, *Falbalas* is set in contemporary Paris (albeit free of signs of the German presence) in the world of *haute couture*, echoing *Paradis perdu*. Once again, the Presle character, Micheline (named by Becker after the star), provides the model and inspiration for the work of a dress designer, famous couturier Philippe Clarence (Raymond Rouleau). This time, however, as in *Félicie Nanteuil*, the Presle character comes to reject conventional women's roles and embrace solitude. She refuses marriage with her friend and fiancé, Daniel (Jean Chevrier), a solid, companionable silk manufacturer whom she does not love. And she refuses the love of the seductive but feckless Philippe, who is incapable of treating her as an equal, and whose disarray leads to his death. *Falbalas* works to critique the idealization and exploitation of women, foregrounding images of a community of women at work and independent women in positions of authority. However, the film is actually centred on the drama of its male lead whose suicide frames the narrative, and the ending leaves open the question of the future of 'the new woman'.

In both *Falbalas* and *Félicie Nanteuil*, Presle's role involves a transformation from gaiety to seriousness and from innocence to knowledge, in particular knowledge about the inadequacy or perfidy of men. As a result, a stoical solitude becomes preferable to a conventional role within the couple. In both films, she is initially represented as a source of male inspiration, through her engaging stage performance in *Félicie Nanteuil* and through her beautiful softly lit face in *Falbalas*, set off in each case by the film's stunning costumes. But Presle's role is not that of the sex object, for she is allowed to assume a measure of subjectivity. Nor is she the *femme fatale* of *film noir*, since her motivation is transparent and she does not wilfully set out to seduce and destroy her male counterparts. The films are sympathetic to the choices her characters have to make and much more ambivalent towards her male counterparts, whose weaknesses typify the problematic representation of masculinity in Occupation cinema. The men are unable to summon up the talent or the emotional depth necessary to match the women they claim to love, and their inadequacies lead them of their own volition to death. The solitude of the 'heroine without heroes' at the end, then, is freely chosen rather than being imposed as a punishment for transgression. Nevertheless, despite or because of their implicit justification of female autonomy, these films were not particularly successful at the time of their screening (just after the Liberation) when representations of masculinity in crisis were already less desirable and comprehensible.

After taking second place to Raymond Rouleau in *Falbalas*, Presle herself moved on to head the credits of her first post-war film, *Boule de suif*, in which she stars as a Resistance heroine, albeit disguised through its costume drama adaptation of two short stories by Guy de Maupassant, *Boule de suif* and *Mademoiselle Fifi*. In this film, Presle, the elegant Parisienne, was cast against type (the role was originally destined for Viviane Romance) as the comfortably rounded, sensual figure of Maupassant's prostitute, a role for which she was required to dye her hair blonde and put on weight (not easy in post-war scarcity). Elisabeth Rousset, nicknamed Boule de suif (Dumpling), is a well-known prostitute who is also a serious figure of Resistance, as is made clear in the film's opening sequence in which she puts her life at risk by sheltering an armed partisan in her boudoir. Boule de suif joins a coachload of other citizens – an aristocratic couple, two bourgeois couples, two nuns and Cornudet the democrat – fleeing the Prussian invasion of 1870. Though she is treated with disdain by all the characters except Cornudet, Boule de suif shows her generosity of heart by sharing her copious supply of food with them. However, when their departure from an inn depends on Boule de suif agreeing to sleep with a Prussian officer, her fellow travellers shamelessly put pressure on her to do so. To her chagrin, they then ignore her and refuse to share their food with her on the next stage of the journey. In the second half of the film, Boule de suif is allowed to get her revenge, both on the French citizens who have mocked her and on the Prussians. When the coach is ambushed and the women taken off to a château occupied by the sadistic Prussian officer, nicknamed Fifi (Louis Salou), and his friends, Boule de suif is the only character to defy the Prussians and uphold the dignity of the French. She turns drunken Fifi's grotesque advances into a splendid act of heroism by stabbing him and making her escape. She is then saved from detection by the local priest who hides her in the belfry, thus leading to the final image of the film when she tolls the bells in joy at Fifi's funeral.

To a greater extent even than *Félicie Nanteuil* and *Falbalas*, *Boule de suif* foregrounds a heroine without heroes, for the French men in this film are all grotesquely inadequate, and even the sympathetic Cornudet gets shot in the leg (a sign of his impotence) when he tries to come to Boule de suif's aid. The partisans remain shadowy figures; the priest is unable to save the life of his parishioner; the innkeepers and the other coach passengers are fools, cowards and hypocrites, willing to collaborate with the enemy when their interests are at stake. As 'the first film about the Occupation' (Bazin, 1975:145), *Boule de suif* is significantly also the first and last 1940s Resistance film to feature a female protagonist. Later films like *La Bataille du rail/Battle of the Rails* (René Clément, 1946) and *Jéricho/Behind These Walls* (Henri Calef, 1946) secured the figure of Resistance as a masculine one, marginalizing and trivializing women's roles, while in Henri-Georges Clouzot's *Manon* (1949), women are clearly identified with collaboration and blamed for the ignominy of the period. However, even in *Boule de suif* a number of devices work to undermine the significance of its representation of an active, articulate, resourceful and effective heroine, starting with the choice of the stereotypical, sexualized prostitute with the heart of gold as the figure of feminine Resistance (rather than, for example, the female equivalent of the ordinary middle-aged man played by Noël-Noël in Clément's *Le Père tranquille/Mr Orchid* of 1946). Presle's star performance carries the film in part because she is so clearly playing against type, lending Boule de suif more elegance, honesty and class than she would have had if performed by Romance, for example. But Boule de suif is often absent from long sections of the narrative and, when present, tends to be caught up within a prurient, voyeuristic male gaze or undermined by nods and winks from characters whose narrative knowledge is greater than hers. The film's ambiguous, even hypocritical attitude towards its heroine is exemplified in its end title, which seeks to appropriate and contain her potentially threatening autonomy: 'Shortly afterwards, a patriot fell in love with her for her glorious action, married her and made a lady of her, worth many others.' The spectator can thus be reassured that transgressive femininity is a function of the disorder of wartime, that it only involves prostitutes and that in peacetime, order and domesticity will be restored.

After the success of *Boule de suif*, producer Paul Graetz of Transcontinental Films offered Presle the starring role in an adaptation of Raymond Radiguet's 1923 novel *Le Diable au corps*. Presle, who now had the right to choose her director, screenwriters and co-star, suggested working with Claude Autant-Lara, Jean Aurenche and Pierre Bost, the director and writers of *Douce* (1943), a successful woman-centred Occupation film, and proposed Gérard Philipe as her co-star, a prescient choice which gave Philipe his first major film role and led to a best actor award. The film was a popular and critical success at home and abroad, enjoying a *succès de scandale* because of its provocative topic. Set during the First World War, it is Presle's best-known film of the 1940s and marks the pinnacle of her fame as a young star. She plays Marthe, a young middle-class woman who is engaged to be married to Jacques, a soldier, but who falls for François, the adolescent schoolboy she meets outside the makeshift hospital where she is supposed to be assisting her mother in caring for the wounded.

Marthe's subsequent affair with François is trebly transgressive in that she commits adultery with a schoolboy while her husband is away at the Front, fighting for his country. The film thus depicts a youthful rebellion against family, church and patriotic duty, values which are embodied in particular in the figure of Marthe's censorious mother (Denise Grey).

In *Le Diable au corps*, Presle's role again develops from object to subject of desire, and from a position of innocence and frivolity to one of knowledge and responsibility, a position linked to her recognition of the inadequacies of her young lover. However, like *Falbalas*, the narrative of *Le Diable au corps* is focused as a male-centred story, firmly constructed through a series of flashbacks from François' point of view. Though it is Marthe's death and funeral which constitute the present time of the diegesis, and frame and punctuate the main narrative, that death is perceived through images of François' grief and solitude. As the crowd in the street celebrates the Armistice, the lonely figure of François is seen, first revisiting the flat in which their love affair took place, then witnessing the funeral, visually and spatially isolated from the legitimate mourners, and finally stepping out into the outside world where the church verger cannot wait to hang out the flags of peace. The three long flashbacks which evoke his tragic love affair are signalled by the soundtrack's slowing down of the sound of the church bells, a sign of the disorder of the past represented by Marthe, only returning to normal when the film restores the spectator to the present moment. The principal subject of the film, then (as in the novel), is male rather than female subjectivity.

Within this limiting framework, however, Presle's Marthe bursts out of the screen and assumes a certain limited autonomy as when, at the beginning of the first flashback, she appears in the place of François' self-reflection in the mirror, larger than life, beautiful, gay, smiling and, as events quickly reveal, disturbingly amoral beneath her pert, period bourgeois outfits. Like François, Marthe resents and resists traditional figures of authority and she quickly succumbs to François' schoolboy charm and defiance of convention. Although to a large extent it is François who manipulates their relationship, his youthfulness prevents him from fully assuming his responsibilities. Marthe, therefore, is obliged to take responsibility for her own actions and, after her marriage, lives out her adulterous passion in open defiance of her mother and her loathsome neighbours, regardless of the consequences. She seduces François with a hot toddy, takes him boating in broad daylight, refuses to answer her husband's letters from the Front and dances to the gramophone with the curtains open during a blackout. But she also faces up to the realities of her situation when she realizes that François cannot be relied on. When the childlike François is unable to confront Jacques with the truth about their relationship, she takes steps to ensure that Jacques thinks he is the father of her unborn child. If Marthe's role illustrates an option available to women during the disorder of wartime, namely, the exercise of personal and sexual freedom, it is also clear that the arrival of peace will bring her idyll to an end.

What is significant about *Le Diable au corps* is that it is the woman who pays the price for the young couple's transgression. Marthe's deathbed scene, from which François is of necessity absent, echoes the scene following the couple's first night of love, but shows her now suffering alone, calling out in vain for her lost love as her mother and husband stand helplessly by and the fire in the grate is extinguished. The film firmly, even excessively, links her death with the end of the war. As the verger says outside the church, 'This is the first funeral of the peace. It's time for women to die now. Everyone in their turn.' The dangerous autonomy of the young married woman who takes advantage of wartime to defy conventional morality, provoke uncertainty over paternity and live her own life without feelings of guilt or remorse has no place in peacetime and must be punished. The closure of Presle's role is firmly secured, both by the film's structure, which returns the spectator from her death to the present-day suffering of her unhappy young lover, and by the First World War setting, which relegates her transgressive life to a past world which no longer exists.

After *Le Diable au corps*, Presle was one of French cinema's hottest properties. Her next film, *Les Jeux sont faits/The Die Is Cast*, also promised to be a prestigious cinematic event, with a screenplay by Sartre, direction by Jean Delannoy (whose 1946 film, *La Symphonie pastorale/Pastoral Symphony*, starring Michèle Morgan, had been immensely successful) and Marcello Pagliero (star of *Roma, città aperta/Rome, Open City* (Roberto Rossellini, 1945)) as her co-star. The film was chosen to represent France at the 1947 Cannes Film Festival, but it was neither a commercial nor a critical success. A whimsical parable set in an unidentified country which is suffering from a military dictatorship, it constitutes yet another transparent metaphor for France during the Occupation. Eve Charlier (Presle), the wife of the leader of the security police, and Pierre Dumaine (Pagliero), the leader of the Resistance, are killed and meet in the afterlife, where they discover that they were 'made for each other'. They are allowed to return to earth for twenty-four hours to see if they can make a success of their new-found love. The artifice of the setting and plot, based on an attraction which lacks any clear motivation, is reminiscent of the use of fantasy in French cinema of the Occupation. Delannoy seems to have returned to the aesthetics of Occupation cinema, too, with his use of long, static takes and elaborate, unrealistic sets. The pace and rhythm of the film render it lifeless, the acting is wooden and the soundtrack leaden. Even Presle has difficulty in summoning up the emotional register necessary to make her part convincing. But perhaps this is not surprising in a role which not only denies her the youth and seductiveness of her earlier roles but also begins with her death and dwells on the improbability of her coming back to life.

It is disappointing, if not unexpected, to note how *Les Jeux sont faits* divides up the gender roles according to classic patriarchal assumptions. Pierre is the working-class hero whose life is dedicated to revolutionary struggle, an entirely masculine affair, but who is killed by a collaborator while plotting an insurrection; Eve is a wealthy bourgeois woman, who is intent on preventing her fascist husband from getting his hands on her beloved younger sister, but who is poisoned by her husband in order to secure her sister's dowry. Pierre and Eve are separated not just by wealth, class and the prejudices of others but also by their separate spheres of interest. Eve's life is confined to the private (feminine) realm of domestic intrigue, Pierre's to the public (masculine) domain of political action. Both are altruistic and both attempt to overcome the barriers which separate them, as when they dance together in the park in full view of Eve's contemptible bourgeois friends. For a brief moment in Pierre's modest flat their love affair seems to become a real possibility, and Presle as Eve is allowed to manifest a more carefree side to her nature, softening the lines of her severely elegant dress and hairstyle by placing a rose in her hair. But it is not enough to prevent Pierre from going off at the last moment to try and save his friends from a fascist plot, leaving Eve to try in vain to save her sister from her husband by forcing them to listen to her at gunpoint! The couple's inability to put the past behind them means that they fail the test and must return to the land of the dead, Pierre once again shot by a collaborator, but Eve collapsing when she realizes that her lover will not return to her in time. The film provides a bleak view of both the Resistance and relationships between the sexes and marks a low point in Presle's image as an independent-minded woman. Whereas in *Le Diable au corps* Marthe's death is gratuitously imposed on a narrative of female transgression, in *Les Jeux sont faits* Eve's desire to defy her husband and start life again with a new lover is foiled by her inability either to persuade her sister of her sincerity, or to unmask her husband's deviousness, or to seduce Pierre away from his political commitments. Powerless and defeated, death is her only remaining option.

From an analysis of the last three films Presle made in France before leaving for Hollywood, it is clear that her image as the modern, independent young woman of French Occupation cinema was being progressively displaced and contained in the 'quality cinema' of the period 1945–47. These films demonstrate, if obliquely, the tensions between women's aspirations towards autonomy fuelled by their wartime experiences and the post-war reimposition of conventional patriarchal social structures. If Presle is a 'heroine without heroes' in *Boule de suif*, the film makes use of narrative and audiovisual strategies which distance the female character and attempt to close off her role once the war narrative is over. In *Le Diable au corps*, the Presle character's joyful sexual transgression is contained, both by a punitive narrative which ends in her death and by a point-of-view structure which privileges the subjectivity of her male partner. By the time of *Les Jeux sont faits*, the war narrative has been rewritten to minimize the destabilization of gender roles evident in the earlier two films and to reinstate patriarchal power, however contemptible. The Presle character's revolt against her husband's abuse of power is doomed, therefore, to failure and, consequently, death. None of these films, then, offers a satisfying representation of the contemporary 'new woman'. But the temporary suppression of the Presle character can be read as a tribute to the power of Presle's star image at a time when dominant discourses on femininity required women on screen to be either domesticated, objectified or demonized.

Note

1. Some of the material used in this chapter has already been explored in an article entitled '"Now you don't": women, cinema and (the) Liberation', in H. R. Kedward and N. Wood (eds), *The Liberation of France: Image and Event*. Oxford: Berg (1993), pp. 103–16, and is reproduced with the permission of the publisher.

Filmography

L'Amour d'une femme (Jean Grémillon, 1954)
Blind Date (Joseph Losey, 1959)
Boule de suif (Christian-Jaque, 1945)
Les Derniers Jours de Pompéi (Marcel L'Herbier, 1948)
Le Diable au corps (Claude Autant-Lara, 1947)
Falbalas (Jacques Becker, 1944–5)
Félicie Nanteuil (Marc Allégret, 1942)
Les Jeux sont faits (Jean Delannoy, 1947)
La Nuit fantastique (Marcel L'Herbier, 1942)
Paradis perdu (Abel Gance, 1940)
Tous les chemins mènent à Rome (Jean Boyer, 1949)

Simone Signoret in *Manèges* (1949, France, Yves Allégret)
Source: BFI Stills, Posters and Designs

CHAPTER FIVE

The Tainted Woman: Simone Signoret, Site of Pathology or Agent of Retribution?

SARAH LEAHY AND SUSAN HAYWARD

Simone Signoret's film career began during the Occupation with walk-on parts in some eleven films, but it was only after the Liberation that she was given larger roles. With *Dédée d'Anvers* (Yves Allégret, 1947) she became widely known to the French public. During the Occupation, her half-Jewish identity prevented her from obtaining an actor's card (issued by the German-controlled *Comité d'Organisation de l'Industrie Cinématographique*, COIC). After the Liberation she emerged as a fresh face at a time when many directors were busy avoiding the painful subject of the war and when established female stars (Arletty, Mireille Balin, Ginette Leclerc) were being punished for consorting with the Germans. A regular at the Café Flore (from 1941), Signoret became known, from the mid-1950s onwards at least, for her left-wing convictions. And it is with her role in *Dédée d'Anvers* that she gained the reputation of being an 'intellectual' actress, a reputation which lent weight to the 'truthfulness' of her performances. 'Intelligent', 'natural', 'authentic' are words found again and again in connection with her film roles of this period.

Although by 1947 Signoret was not yet a star, she had an aura that marked her out as distinct from other existing or emerging stars of that time. One of the most distinguishing features of her performances remains that, despite often playing the role of either victim or (as she put it) *garce* (bitch), she is always the subject not the object of her own desire. In this respect, she goes against the prevailing norms of the times as far as prescriptions for femininity were concerned and, as an agent of desire, her performance style aligns her with the image of independent womanhood more readily associated with the 1970s. Her strength and independence come through in at least three ways. First, through her very corporeality: when she walks, she strides purposely forward, she smokes and stamps out cigarettes with her shoe with a wonderfully insouciant vulgarity, and to show her determination she firmly but sensuously plants her hands on her hips. Second, her gestures are at a bare minimum and yet express volumes: a glance, a lifting of the eyebrow, a moue from her very full lips, a shrug of the shoulders, dismissive hands. Finally, she embodies a strong sense of the everyday, of being part of the 'real world'. The rough, seemingly untrained edge to her voice reinforces this, inviting audiences to identify with her apparent ordinariness. In virtually all her films there is an expression of concern with contemporary society. For example, in *Dédée* and *Manèges/The Cheat* (Yves Allégret, 1949) she embodies two responses (prostitution and bounty hunting) to the problem of women caught in the poverty trap, a very real concern for women in the immediate post-war years and, indeed, well into the 1960s.

Let us now briefly consider this period in France's history when Signoret was an emerging star. Post-Liberation France was a time of paradox. On the one hand, the country was attempting to rebuild its sense of national identity after the humiliating Occupation by the Germans. On the other, it was busily looking for scapegoats for the national shame and guilt over the acts of collusion and collaboration during the Occupation. Reconstruction of the image of France came in the form of a heroization of France's Resistance. Retribution took the form of a Purification Committee, which dispensed sentences (including death) to the few who served as embodiments of France's shame. Retribution also took the wider form of a nationwide punishing of women who were accused of 'horizontal collaboration' with the enemy – they came to embody the ugly whoring France that had given itself over so passively to the enemy.

The hypocrisy latent in the strategies of rebuilding and retribution would not be openly addressed until well into the 1970s with the lifting of censorship, and indeed, where women are concerned, an investigation of this history of culpabilization has only just begun. Similarly, the role of cinema during this period of rehabilitation (1944–50) has also come increasingly under scrutiny, particularly in relation to the representation of women. Here too the construction of femininity has served as an embodiment of contained and displaced guilt. The representation of women became the site upon which the repressed guilt of a nation humiliated by defeat got played out.

It should also be remembered that if the Occupation years presented female stars with greater opportunities and scope on screen (albeit in a superficial way and, of course, still firmly rooted within patriarchy), then, after the Liberation, the roles attributed to women were often quite contradictory. Although a certain number of films provided women with heroic roles, mostly placed in some historic past, a great many more represented women as whores and as *femmes fatales*. The punishment and vengeance wrought on women in films during the post-war period were clear indicators of a masculinity and a nation in crisis.

One thing which did change radically at the Liberation, however, was the return of American movies to French screens. These included not only new productions but also the back catalogue of movies which had been banned during the war, notably a large number of *films noirs*. Jill Forbes (1997: 35) points out the importance of *film noir* in the French post-war context and, in particular, how 'in its perception of the ambiguities of reality and the uncertainties of appearances, it also challenges the perception of realism in film.' The extent of collaboration and denunciation, and the large numbers of eleventh-hour resisters, gave rise to uncertainties about the roles people had played during the war. The emphasis on investigation and psychological processes in *film noir* revealed the cinema as a place in which the pathologies left over from the years of Occupation could be expressed (*ibid*.: 35–8).

It is within these contexts that we must consider the two Signoret/Allégret films. Both *Dédée* and *Manèges*, unsurprisingly given their blackness, gained the epithet of *réalisme noir* (by analogy with the *film noir*). What is striking in our case study of these films is the shift in representation of the post-war pathologies over a two-year period. In *Dédée*, Signoret is the victim of betrayal and exploitation. By the time she stars in *Manèges* she is the embodiment of these same evils. In *Dédée* she is the site of the tragedy of France as an occupied country. In *Manèges* she is the evil woman incarnate, the site of the duplicity and corruption motivated by greed, who cares nothing for an honourable France.

Dédée d'Anvers: agencing desire and retribution

It is worth remembering that when *Dédée d'Anvers* was released in 1947, the Purification Committee was entering its third year of purging France of its past; that the Fourth Republic was in its second year of government with some thirty-five women *députés* – one of whom was the Minister of Health; and that, thanks to the 1946 *Loi Marthe Richard* (which in turn had been helped by the effect of *les tondues* – the women who had their heads publicly shaved for 'horizontal collaboration'), brothels had been officially closed. In other words, the men and women of post-war France were cleaning up their nation and setting their sights on a healthy, well-fed new generation of French citizens. But France was also feeling the first effects of the Cold War. Three years into peace the threat of another war loomed. As if that were not enough, men and women who had survived the Occupation were still being told that some of them were guilty by association and that the intellectual had had no right to err. The mood of the times was one of profound disappointment and depression. The bleakness of Allégret's film, *Dédée d'Anvers* seemed to match the social climate perfectly.

In the film, Dédée (Signoret) is the so-called 'top-quality' prostitute and favourite of the proprietor, Monsieur René (Bernard Blier) of the Blue Moon bar where she works. Thanks to her distinguished and distinctive manner, men have ennobled her with the honorary title of D'Anvers (it should be noted that Anvers is the French name for the Belgian town, Antwerp, where the film takes place). In the opening sequence she sets eyes on a sailor and, through an exchange of glances, the mutuality of their desire is established. Her subsequent love affair with the sailor, an Italian called Francesco (Marcello Pagliero), sets in motion a tale of sordid jealousy and revenge enacted by her pimp Marco (Marcel Dalio). The two lovers plot their escape by sea, but on the night of their assignation Marco finds out about the plan when René blurts out the truth to humiliate him. In a fit of drunken rage, Marco goes to the assignation and shoots Francesco in the back, killing him. Dédée turns up at the appointed time and discovers her lover dead. With the help of René, she finds Marco and instructs René to kill him by running him over with his car.

This excessive closure differs from the original novel by Ashelbé (1949)[1] in which it is René who strangles Marco to death. The film adaptation, in its ultimately less misogynistic ending, makes for a far more complex set of readings around both masculinity and femininity. Until the very end of the film, Dédée (while clearly an agent of her desire for Francesco, as the opening exchange of gazes indicated) is not a woman in her own right – she is the property of others (as Marco never ceases to remind her, often 'branding' her by burning her flesh with his cigarette). But at the end of the film it is she who decides how Marco should die and orders René to carry it out. Dédée occupies a position of authority for the first time. Her decision about the way Marco will die is thought-through – a taking of the moral high ground and an intellectual counterpart to the baseness of Marco's burning her with his cigarette and of his callous and cowardly murder of Francesco.

Part of the way in which we can read Signoret's construction of Dédée is to see her as a foil to the weak masculinity so much in evidence in this film. Her eyes flash with contempt when she looks at Marco. When it really matters, it is she who pushes René on to track down Marco after he has murdered Francesco. Physically, Signoret occupies more space in the frame than her pimp, and for the most part swamps him. The one major exception is the scene in bed when he tortures her by burning her breast with a lighted cigarette.

Throughout the film, men behave in ways associated more readily with female characterizations in *film noir*, a reversal that is surely significant. Men are responsible for denunciation (René) and murder (Marco) – that is, of careless talk (that costs lives) and treachery. Heroic masculinity is far removed in this film of *réalisme noir*. Indeed, not only is masculinity in crisis but it is also clearly fragmented. There is a sense throughout the film of a deep unease and a lack of clarity: Marco is constantly ridiculed, René's sexuality is ambiguous, and Francesco, the only 'masculine' man, is involved in dubious business activities. This representation of masculinity as ambiguous and cruel when under threat echoes the unease and lack of clarity associated with both the Occupation and post-Liberation periods.

For all that Marco seeks to humiliate Dédée, in the end it is he who is deeply humiliated, including his ignominious death. For all that Dédée lacks a full and proper place in society, she does briefly occupy a decision-making space both as agent of desire (her love for Francesco) and as agent of retribution (cleansing?) in removing Marco from the world. Close attention to the camera work shows that whenever Dédée is in a two-shot and there is a cut to a single shot within the same scene, the point of view is almost without exception hers. The most exemplary sequence of Dédée's overriding subjectivity, positioning her as agent of desire, is the moment when she visits Francesco on his boat. We see Francesco in full view and Dédée, in medium shot with the camera behind her, reflected in one of the portholes. As she reaches out towards Francesco and we see only her hands and arms, Francesco becomes the viewed object, desired and eroticized by Dédée. This process of eroticization of the male body occurs elsewhere. On two occasions, Dédée refers to his smell and says how much she likes it. We see her touching his lips, running her hands over his face and neck. Apart from the specific use of close-ups which make her the central subject of desire, the way in which she is lit for these moments of agencing desire is quite remarkable. The full light makes her eyes glow with passion and renders her lips voluptuous.

Having said this, it is also important to note that just as the men are ambiguously positioned (in terms of a shady past or a questionable masculinity), so too is Dédée. This point is best exemplified when, at one point in the film (a crucial one incidentally, since it brings her to Francesco's door and their first meeting), she visibly enjoys watching men beat each other senseless in a street brawl. The scene, a vicious conflict between workers, where some men are handcuffed by others to railings, summarily punched and kicked until they bleed, is watched with ever-increasing glee by the gorgeous Dédée. It is a shocking moment in the film, more so than the *mise-en-scène* of Francesco's murder, because it is so unexpected and apparently uncharacteristic of Dédée. Furthermore, because of its realistic depiction (as opposed to the very staged shooting of Francesco by Marco) and more significantly because of the point-of-view shot which is Dédée's – we watch it as she watches it and become sutured into her point of view – there is a shock effect as we shift from a position of victim (which is the position she has occupied until now) to that of semi-sadistic voyeur. And her words to Francesco, who is surprised by her enjoyment, only partially assuage our discomfiture. 'I like seeing men fight. They never hurt each other enough really,' she declares to Francesco, who then enquires, 'Don't you like men?' 'No,' she replies, 'or rather I like them too much which is the same thing.' Signoret's acting makes us uneasy with what has just happened. In the crude way in which she plays the role, exposing a tough side that we did not expect, we become uncertain whether she is the innocent we have constructed her as. As Dédée enters the realm of the ambiguous we are made aware that the issues at stake are not simple ones, any more than the answers.

With its ambiguities, what this scene does make possible is the denouement. For it is Dédée who stages the whole killing scene from beginning to end. It is a chilling performance – Dédée remains icily determined until Marco is dead – and yet it is incredibly moving as this woman of so few words contains her pain to make sure that what must be done is done. It is she who cleans up the scene. She orders Francesco's body to be taken back on to the boat and throws Marco's gun into the water. It is she who insists on the search for Marco, who when found is dragged back to the scene of his crime. Finally, it is she who chooses the car rather than the gun as the instrument of Marco's death (it would be too kind to shoot him, she declares, and this way it would look like an accident – thus disguising the truth of this act of retribution) and instructs René to drive over Marco's body slowly. A powerful ending for a woman who had no power, whose identity (as one of her women friends points out) was totally dependent on men. Even her dress code marks her as changed, as masculinized. Gone is the frilly dress, the half-length fur coat and the extraordinarily impractical stiletto heels, replaced now by a black shiny trench coat and a beret – a mixture of Michèle Morgan in *Le Quai des brumes* (Marcel Carné, 1938) and any number of police inspectors in thrillers of the time. The meting out of justice is done in a silent, unostentatious way. Only Marco is weak and pathetic as he protests his innocence. There are no tears until it is all over, and again they are silent, gently falling down her cheek. In the process, Signoret's performance has shifted Dédée from being an agent of desire to embodying an agent of retribution.

It is tempting to read this ending as a metaphor for the way in which punishment was meted out to traitors in the Resistance and to collaborators after the war. And certainly Marco's cowardly methods of vengeance and retribution can also be read as symptomatic of Occupation actions, particularly by the fascist police, the Milice. But these are readings we only have with hindsight and by way of films made much later about this period in France's history (an early example is *L'Armée des ombres/Army in the Shadows* (Jean-Pierre Melville, 1969) starring Signoret). At the time there were no images to represent the realities of retribution. The Resistance was presented as heroic and unified (*La Bataille du rail/Battle of the Rails*, 1946, by René Clément, for example) and, as far as the general public was concerned, very little was revealed about what happened to collaborators. *Dédée d'Anvers* was one of the few films of this time which attempted to depict a less glorious reality, but even if the film does pay tribute to a woman who finds inner strength despite all odds, the bleakness of the ending holds out little hope for a better life. We assume Dédée will return to the Blue Moon. She is avenged but socially no further advanced. She has not made the world a cleaner place, even though she has rid it of a treacherous and exploitative man. In redressing the betrayal she has merely taken the law into her own hands. If we view the film within its historical context, then the ending, if anything, points to the confusion of a nation which during the Occupation had behaved in unseemly ways and after the war continued to act in ways which at best could be described as schizophrenic (personalized revenge, denial of and inability to deal with the larger scale of recent events). As we shall now see, this bleak post-war mood of treachery, betrayal and uncertainty becomes even darker by the time Signoret stars in *Manèges*.

Manèges: the malevolence of desire

Manèges appeared in January 1950 to a somewhat mixed reception from critics. The film was overwhelmingly praised for the quality of the direction and acting, but fell foul of many reviewers for its bleak vision of humanity. Despite critics' reservations about the subject matter of the film, Signoret was unanimously praised: they agreed that *Manèges* confirmed her great talent and underlined the authenticity of her performance, which they linked to her minimalist style of acting: 'Simone Signoret possesses all the talent required for cinema: she expresses her thoughts without a word, by removing her make-up, or simply by looking at her nails' (Lauwick, 1950).

The film opens in a hospital. Dora (Simone Signoret) has been seriously injured in a car accident and her much older husband, Robert (Bernard Blier), waits anxiously for news of whether or not she will live. The events leading up to her accident and the story of how Dora and her mother (Jane Marken) together systematically bled Robert dry are revealed to the spectator through a series of flashbacks shown first from Robert's point of view (initially at least encouraging spectator identification with him) and then from the two women's viewpoints.

There are three sections to the film and each is composed substantially of a flashback which represents the thought processes of the three major protagonists (Robert, Dora, her mother). The first section of the film starts with Robert's arrival at the hospital and includes the flashback sequence, narrated from his point of view, which presents a rosy picture of his marriage to Dora and of their successful business, a riding school. By showing his version of events first, the film underlines how oblivious Robert is to what is really going on. Thus, when the women reveal how they cruelly duped him, through subsequent flashbacks shown from their points of view, Robert's gullibility is exposed as well as the women's perfidy.

The end of Robert's reminiscences is signalled by a change in viewpoint – a long-shot pan around the hospital room at the moment that Dora wakes up and realizes that her husband is in the room. Her vision is slightly blurred and it is only with difficulty that she manages to focus on her sleeping husband. She is drenched in perspiration from the pain and, after the camera zooms in on Robert, dozing in the corner, it cuts to Dora's expression of disgust. She tries to speak, but is obviously suffering and gives in to her own memories in the form of a flashback devoted to her relationship with her lover, François (Frank Villard). These flashbacks present Dora as a woman with a sexual appetite who equates love with sex. The poignancy of these images is that they contrast with the present reality of Dora completely stripped of her sexuality – the sexually aggressive woman is now paralysed.

The third part of the film is heralded by the arrival of her mother at the hospital, sobbing and violently blaming Robert for what has happened. Dora asks her to tell him: 'Mother, tell him everything. I want to hear.' The mother takes a kind of aggressive pleasure in announcing to Robert that he has been deceived since the beginning, and Robert backs away, closing his eyes in disbelief. Many of the scenes that follow repeat those of the first part of the film, but this time they are narrated sadistically by the mother and shown from an angle that reveals the nods and winks exchanged between mother and daughter. The women's cruelty is heightened even further by the intensification of the points of view: the story, although now narrated by Dora's mother, is revisualized by all three protagonists.

The representation of women generally in this film is deeply misogynistic. All women are constructed as wayward: Dora and her mother, the snobbish female clients at the stables, the woman in the restaurant who laughs at Dora and, finally, the nurse who insults Robert as he leaves the hospital at the film's end. His comment as he walks out ('They're all bitches, all in it together') is justified in the context of the film.

It is not difficult to read this demonization of women and especially of female sexuality in the context of post-Liberation retribution. And it is surely significant that Dora has her back broken – paralysed, she is no longer a threat. The mother in *Manèges*, who because of her lack of name and her role as narrator acquires a kind of archetypal status, is emblematic of this demonization. Embodying past crimes against patriarchy, she is the Mother-Nation who colludes with the enemy and betrays the patriarchal state (and where, one might ask, is the father?) Furthermore, she is ensuring that her daughter follows in her footsteps. As Burch and Sellier (1996: 280) point out, she has lost her looks and therefore her weapons, and so she uses her beautiful daughter to entrap and exploit 'ordinary men, ugly men incapable of resisting the charms of a beautiful woman.'

One must ask whether or not this seemingly irredeemably misogynistic text can be subverted, allowing the female spectator to find some expression of her desire. Is it the case that the structure in flashbacks only privileges the male viewpoint, as has been argued by Burch and Sellier in their analysis of the film (*ibid.*: 279–83)? How can this be if two of the flashbacks are those of the daughter and mother? Could it not be argued rather that this structure also permits the agencing of female (Dora's) desire and spectator identification with that desire through Signoret's perfomance?

It is possible to offer a counter reading. Richard Dyer (1986), in his work on stars, explains how film texts can be 'subverted' by the spectator through identification processes. In the light of his work, *Manèges* can be read, if not as an expression of female desire, then at least as articulating desire from a female viewpoint through the women's flashbacks and, more importantly, through Signoret's performance, a crucial factor in spectator identification with this female agency.

Several elements of her performance combine to present an image of independence and sexual agency: her striding, self-confident walk, the frank vulgarity she exhibits when flirting with the workmen and crucially her voice and her eyes. She uses her voice to denote either firmness of purpose or vulnerability. She conveys her desire for François, and later her disappointment when he takes her home to his hotel room, through the look in her eyes.

Signoret's ability to express so much with just a look or a gesture makes the moments in the film when Dora takes control of the gaze even more loaded with significance. During her flashback scenes, the spectator (without necessarily approving of her actions) can easily identify with Dora's desire for François, eroticized as he is through her gaze. The story she tells him about her older husband who cannot 'fulfil her needs' is corroborated by the flashback's depiction of Robert. And this does allow us to understand her disgust with her husband. Thus, when she looks at Robert coldly or laughs behind his back, he might well solicit our sympathy as a victim of her exploitative and manipulative ways, but he certainly does not elicit our empathy: he is now too ridiculous for the spectator to identify with him.

Signoret's physical presence adds to her dominance onscreen: as tall as the men, she is often shown in movement, rushing around or away from the stables, riding (in comparison to Robert, usually seen sitting at his desk doing his accounts). Her voluptuousness marks her out as 'all-woman' rather than a girl who 'needs' to be seduced. Signoret is firmly in charge of her sexuality. Dora is a desirable woman but, rather than being presented as an object of male desire, her attractiveness becomes a weapon which she manipulates in order to ensure her own survival, as when she makes sure that she is 'noticed' by rich male clients at the stables and laughs at the ease with which she conquers them. This adds to the contrast between the desiring/desirable woman we see in the flashback sequences and the broken body in the hospital bed. Now she is deformed by bandages and sweat, her varnished nails are visible on the hand stretched out on a splint at an unnatural angle. The severity of her punishment is indicative of the extreme means required to contain her within patriarchy and even then she is unrepentant. When she asks her mother to tell Robert the truth, she does so not to repent but out of a sadistic desire to witness his pain.

In his analysis of *Gilda* (King Vidor, 1946), Dyer (1980: 91–9) suggests that by positioning the male character as in some way deviant from 'normal' masculinity, the female character gains validity. Although job and social status position Robert in *Manèges* as ultra-normal, *moyen*, his extreme passivity is far from 'normal' masculine behaviour, since passivity is more readily associated with femininity. In *Manèges*, however, it is the women who actively *reveal* their secrets to Robert; it is they who open up Pandora's box, driving the narrative to its close. And undynamic Robert, lacking any 'masculine' investigative impulse, shuts his eyes and tries not to hear. Robert's downfall is in large part due to his own stubborn refusal to heed repeated warnings when there was still time to save his business.

It is only at the end of the film, after a quick succession of images which represent the scales finally falling from Robert's eyes, that he begins to act decisively, displaying a violence not even hinted at in the rest of the film. He brutally informs the mother that Dora will live but remain paralysed.

In representing Dora as always in control of her malevolent desire, her punishment at the end is all the more severe. What gets restored, however, is a truly violent form of patriarchal order. Robert discovers and recovers his 'masculinity' only through cruel (if seemingly justified) aggression towards the mother and his final insult (which includes the 'innocent' nurse). Despite his newfound assertiveness, Dora's punishment does not change the fact that he has lost his business. This film could be read as a warning of the consequences of upsetting patriarchal order, of undermining masculinity and of the danger and abnormality of female desire. A more symptomatic historical reading, made possible by Signoret's powerful performance, would suggest that it is also a drama of the troubled relationships between the sexes in the post-war period, the anxieties produced by economic and sexual insecurities and the confused and uncertain need for retribution.

Conclusion

It is instructive to see how Signoret's projected image compared to the real situation of French women at this time. As Burch and Sellier note in Chapter 3, during the Occupation women found themselves playing a greater part in public life than ever before, and had been given the vote immediately after the Liberation (1944). Women had become the breadwinners and many men returned to find their wives coping without them. Not only were women dominating the public sphere, traditionally a male preserve, they were also beginning to encroach on the most public male terrain of all, namely the world of politics (not only by voting but also by being elected to parliament). The image of femininity was, then, in considerable flux and the 1950s marked a period when great efforts were made to return woman to the home – to re-feminize her, as it were.

Viewed in this context, Signoret's body becomes a site upon which this contradiction is played out. On the one hand, she was the woman in her own sexual right (and not the infantilo-sexual object of her contemporaries Martine Carol and Brigitte Bardot). She was a strong and independent woman who threatened the patriarchal order. But, conversely, in the roles she played during these post-war years, she was also either the victim of men's treachery (*Dédée*) or was portrayed as so evil that she got the punishment she deserved (*Manèges*). In other words, narrative closure brought punishment to the strong independent woman – an attempt by the narrative, one could argue, to put her back in her place.

What is interesting about many of her films, however, is that although retribution or punishment are meted out, Signoret does not succumb and return to her supposedly rightful place. Far from it. Unlike her American celluloid sisters of the time, she is not co-opted back into the patriarchal order of things. In many of her roles she refuses to give in to the expectation that she submit, and what excites in her performances is that Signoret represents herself as subject of desire, refusing to be the site of structures of exchange and looking. She achieves the empowering position of agency and does so in ways that are unequivocally authentic. She defies becoming the province or the property of either sex, that is challenging dominant representations of woman either by being 'more' than the role (because she is agent of desire) or 'less' than it (because of her understated performance). It is arguably because of these performance qualities and because she was so obviously of the period that she appealed to men and women alike. In her understated performances, her strength, independence and bodily self-assurance, she offered women an alternative image of themselves to gaze upon and an exciting image of womanhood for men to dream about.

Signoret's roles conflicted with the images of femininity that were being privileged elsewhere in the media: those of marriage, motherhood and sacrifice. Her onscreen presence was marked by a mixture of sensuality, vulnerability (the lisp) and vulgarity, but above all by the intelligence and realism which she brought to her often excessive roles and which she managed to counter through her minimalist performance. A close reading of her post-war French films allows us, then, to go further than Burch and Sellier's (1996: 224) reading of Signoret as a displaced embodiment of the misogyny of the times where women were represented as malevolent and men as victims. The inference of their reading is that women were represented as dangerous and needing to be contained, and that Signoret was a *femme fatale*, in the American *film noir* sense of the term, the one difference being that the men she brings down are victims and presumably, therefore, innocent.

While we do not disagree about the intentionality of the films' narratives and their attempts to represent Signoret as needing to be contained (because of her apparent ability to destroy men), we challenge the premise that the men who are destroyed are innocent. As we have argued, none of them is free from a shady past, even Robert (in *Manèges*), whose fragile masculinity leads to his humiliation. Rather, we have argued that Signoret, through her performance, draws attention to the space vacated by the men (through their loss of masculinity, doubtless) which leaves room for women to have agency. Our argument, then, is that Signoret occupies a position more readily associated with the male and that hers is the privileged viewpoint, the driving force of the narrative. She is the prostitute or manipulator who sees herself as worth more, who attempts to take control of her life (and sexuality), even if in doing so she brings about her lover's death. It is made explicit in her films of this period (even *Manèges*, where the lack of economic independence partly motivates her greed) that it is male insecurity which prevents her from successfully fulfilling her own destiny.

Signoret, then, in her cinematic roles during this period of France's rehabilitation, becomes something of a double-edged sign. On the one hand, the narrative attempts to produce her as a particular construction of femininity: the embodiment of a victimized France, tarnished by her past and embodying the repressed guilt of a nation humiliated. On the other hand, Signoret's performance resists this essentializing of woman as victim or object of opprobrium, suggesting instead that there is such a thing as female subjectivity and that women are quite capable of assuming responsibility for their actions. Finally, it should be noted that neither Dédée nor Dora are the perpetrators of male defeat or emasculation. In the first instance, Dédée exposes male insecurity and weakness. In the second, Dora both exposes and exploits them. And she does so, and admits doing so, in full consciousness. Wicked she may be, but she owns up to the truth!

Note

1. Although the novel was clearly written before the film, the only copy to which we have had access is the 1949 version (Ashelbé, *Dédée d'Anvers*. Monaco: Éditions des Rochers). This includes a preface by Ashelbé giving his views on the film.

Filmography

Dédée d'Anvers (Yves Allégret, 1947)
Manèges (Yves Allégret, 1949)

Germany

Hildegard Knef and Wilhelm Borchert in *Die Mörder sind unter uns/ The Murderers Are among Us* (1946, Germany, Wolfgang Staudte)
Source: BFI Stills, Posters and Designs
Production Company: DEFA/Progress

CHAPTER SIX

Sweeping up the Past: Gender and History in the Post-war German 'Rubble Film'

ERICA CARTER

It is spring 1945. The war is over, Nazi Germany defeated. A train pulls in to a Berlin station. Dishevelled travellers cram the carriages: refugees, war veterans, returning prisoners. Out of the crowd steps a woman in white (white light on her face, white coat, light scarf). This is Susanne Wallner, a concentration camp internee returning home. The camera keeps a respectful distance as she passes through streets piled high with rubble, her luminous figure a haven of light against the dark silhouettes of ruined buildings.

So begins the film that heralds the post-1945 rebirth of German cinema: Wolfgang Staudte's *Die Mörder sind unter uns/The Murderers Are among Us* (1946). As the narrative of this first post-war production unfolds, it becomes an emblematic tale of the guilt of a murderous nation, a people responsible for the Nazi crimes of genocide in the death camps and bloody massacres in war. Susanne returns to the bomb-damaged flat that was once hers. She encounters the volatile Hans Mertens (Wilhelm Borchert), an ex-army doctor who has moved in uninvited. Susanne is mystified by Mertens's moods, his anger, his drunkenness. But she falls in love nonetheless, and nurtures Mertens through his confrontation with the traumatic memory that plagues him, the memory of a massacre on the Eastern Front, an atrocity he witnessed, but could not stop.

Mertens's despair persists. This is a man who faints at the sight of blood, a doctor who has lost the power of healing. Then he encounters ex-Hauptmann Brückner (Arno Paulsen), the commanding officer who ordered the massacre. Brückner has set up a new business manufacturing cooking pots from old steel helmets. This murderer-turned-entrepreneur, unlike Mertens, is flourishing.

Mertens resolves to execute Brückner. He leaves the house, revolver in hand. Just in time, Susanne stops him and the film draws to its didactic close. 'We have no right to pass sentence,' says Susanne. 'But', replies Mertens, 'it is our duty to accuse.'

Directed by one of the major auteurs of the post-war period, Wolfgang Staudte, *Die Mörder* has rightly gained a status as a pivotal text in German film history. There are two senses in which Staudte's film sets the tone for the cluster of films made between 1945 and 1949 that are known – set as they are among the ruins of devastated towns and cities – as Germany's 'rubble films' (*Trümmerfilme*). First, though neither a genre (they were too stylistically diverse) nor strictly speaking a movement (film personnel were too dispersed, their project never defined by manifestos or through coherent collective organization), the 'rubble films' nonetheless shared a common preoccupation with issues of individual and collective guilt, and with the historical responsibilities of the German nation. In *Die Mörder,* Mertens's pursuit of Brückner is lent historical weight when, at the film's close, he demands a national settling of accounts with Nazi criminals: 'It is our duty to accuse.' That same clarion call echoes through countless literary works, philosophical tracts and press commentaries of the period. Karl Jaspers's (1946) *Die Schuldfrage/The Guilt Question* represented perhaps the most significant philosophical exposition and critique of the concept of collective guilt that framed Allied policy after 1945. But there were numerous literary works, too (Hans Werner Richter's *Die Geschlagenen/The Defeated*, 1946, is an important example), as well as a crop of cultural journals (*Der Ruf, Die Wandlung, Der Aufbau*), all preoccupied with similar questions of German responsibility for fascist crimes.[1]

And then there were the films. After *Die Mörder* came Kurt Maetzig's *Ehe im Schatten/Marriage in the Shadows* (1947), a Holocaust narrative based on the life story of the actor Joachim Gottschalk, who committed suicide with his Jewish wife and child when they faced deportation to the death camps in 1941. There followed Helmut Käutner's *In jenen Tagen/In Those Days* (1947), a montage film depicting disconnected episodes from the life of a twelve-year-old car. The vehicle first sees the light of day at the dawning of National Socialism (January 1933), but its owners' lives tell a more private and less barbaric tale of the Third Reich, a story of the moral incorruptibility of some Germans, even under Nazi rule: so there is the Gentile husband who dies in a death tryst with his Jewish wife, or the deserter who rescues a refugee and her child from destitution. Another 'memory-text' (Kuhn, 1995) is *Zwischen Gestern und Morgen/Between Yesterday and Tomorrow* (Harald Braun, 1947), the story of an artist returning to a hotel he once visited before the war and unearthing memories of fascism and its crimes. He remembers the Gestapo's pursuit of a Jewish woman to her death by suicide, or his own forced flight into protracted exile from Nazi Germany. Then there is the first film made under British licence, *Film ohne Titel/Film without a Title* (Rudolf Jugert, 1947), a comedy with serious intent that thematizes the corruption of the German cinematic tradition after National Socialism, and opens with an only partly playful debate between a screenwriter, an actor and a director on the pitfalls (practical and moral) of making comedies for mass consumption in post-war Germany.

All these titles and more, then, display a preoccupation with the Nazi legacy, and explore the possibilities of what the German language knows as *Vergangenheitsbewältigung* ('overcoming the past'). But there is a second sense in which *Die Mörder* may be seen as representative of the broader spectrum of 'rubble films', and that is in its quality as what might be called a transitional artefact, an object in between historical moments and cultural locations. By the end of the war, the industrial infrastructure of German cinema had been shattered. Theatres and cinemas were closed between March and July 1945; after the Allied victory in May, all German film-making was banned, the Ufa studios seized and remaining copies of pre-1945 German titles impounded (Fehrenbach, 1995). Film production was slow to restart, especially in the western zones where, in the early post-war months at least, denazification procedures for German film-makers were protracted and production licences hard to come by. Staudte's experience with *Die Mörder* exemplifies the difficulties. Already active as a screenwriter, actor and director in the Third Reich, he wrote a treatment for *Die Mörder* in the last months of war. The film was rejected by film officials in the western zones and finally passed the Soviet authorities only on condition that he change the ending (it was originally envisaged that Mertens would shoot and kill the war criminal Brückner) (Gregor, 1966: 21).

The complexities of negotiation with the licensing authorities represent only one of the many elements that gave film-making in post-war Germany its provisional quality. Following the break-up of the Ufa concern after 1945, the conditions of industrial production, in the film industry as elsewhere, were unpropitious in the extreme. Facilities were in short supply and film-making personnel dispersed or unavailable. The Ufa star system had collapsed; many of Ufa's favourite actors and directors were refused licences to work in film during this period. The sheer physical difficulty of film-making in the immediate aftermath of war was immense: cast and crew were often undernourished, film studios bombed out, film stock scarce. Then there was the issue of competition: on the one hand from Hollywood (as is well known, Hollywood was quick to launch onto the German market its recycled product from the wartime years), and on the other, the so-called 'overflow films' (*Überlaufer*), German entertainment films that had either been withheld during the Ufa era, or were relaunched after gaining clearance from Allied authorities (Fehrenbach, 1995; Kreimeier, 1989).

But this was not only a transitional cinema in terms of its conditions of production but also at the level of textual form. Again, *Die Mörder* is a typical instance. Eschewing the mannered realism of the Ufa style, Staudte returned for this film to a pre-Nazi model, that of Weimar expressionism: witness the chiaroscuro lighting and grotesque *mise-en-scène* that are the film's hallmarks (see page 90). The films that followed *Die Mörder* shared its apparent scepticism about Ufa models, though they were sometimes more radical still in questioning the adequacy of any extant model, expressionist or other, for post-war German film. Thus, for instance, *Film ohne Titel* opens with a debate between scriptwriter, director and actor (the latter played by Willy Fritsch, a major screen idol of both late Weimar and Third Reich cinema) about the impossibility of finding a story that will make a film 'appropriate to our times'. In fact, of course, the film does tell a story – that of the lovers Martin (Hans Söhnker) and Christiane (Hildegard Knef) – but their narrative is punctuated by scenes that play out alternative modes of cinematic narration. The film perpetually cross-cuts from the space of what is signalled (initially at least) as the fictional narrative of Christiane and Martin to a space beyond narrative (a tree in an open field, with no props to signal historical time or geographical location), where the dialogue shifts from character interaction to metacommentaries on issues of film style and narrative plausibility. Moreover, Fritsch's apparent dissatisfaction with the style of the fictional passages leads him at one point to re-enact, in a parody of the Ufa style that made him famous, a love scene previously played in naturalist mode by Knef and Söhnker.

The unease around film style displayed by *Film ohne Titel* is reproduced in different but related ways in numerous films of the period. It is evident, for instance, in the frequent recourse of the rubble films to cinematic modernism: Expressionism in Staudte's case, while Helmut Käutner chose a Surrealist mode for his parody of the Adam and Eve legend, *Der Apfel ist ab/The Apple Has Fallen* (1948). A desire for a radical break with 1930s and 1940s style was also registered in the genre-mixing that characterized such films as *Straßenbekanntschaft/Street Acquaintance (*1947–8). The film was received by contemporary critics as an *Aufklärungsfilm* (an established category used in German cinema to refer to sexually explicit narrative films ostensibly devoted to the propagation of sexual health), but the director Peter Pewas rejected that designation ('Ohne Tendenz und Sensation. Peter Pewas über seinen Film *Straßenbekanntschaft*', *Berliner Zeitung*, 8 April 1948). *Film ohne Titel* locates itself as comedy, at the same time directly thematizing the inadequacy of classical genre models to the social conditions of the post-war moment, while Helmut Käutner's *Der Apfel* offers what is for this director a characteristically whimsical mix of popular comedy with high modernist experimentation.

Finally, the rubble films' impulse towards stylistic rupture is evident in their eschewing of classical narrative form. We will consider below the disruption of coherent narrative time that is a special feature of the rubble films; and their handling of narrative point of view is a further instance of a preference for open over closed form, ambiguity and contradiction over univocality and closure. Many of the films (*In jenen Tagen*, *Straßenbekanntschaft*) have multiple narrative voices, none of which is especially privileged. In some (including *Zwischen Gestern und Morgen* and *Straßenbekanntschaft*), a female narrative voice replaces the classical masculine perspective, and in one (*In jenen Tagen*), the post-war crisis of human narrative authority itself is referenced. The latter film opens with two mechanics dismantling a car for scrap, and debating, as they work, the past and future of a defeated Germany. When they despair over the capacity of humanity now to find redemption, the voice of the car intervenes and takes up a role as narrator. The suggestion here is that the human voice has lost its narrative legitimacy, an inference reinforced by one of the mechanics when he complains that 'all humanity is gone'.

The rubble film and gender

The rubble films belong, then, to a cinema of ruptures, breaks and unfinished transitions. This is true, not only in terms of their tendency to formal experimentation but also in their status as a bridge to future efforts at cinematic *Vergangenheitsbewältigung*. Bruce Murray (1991: 261), for instance, referring to the concern with the fascist past that would resurface in New German Cinema, describes Staudte's *Die Mörder* as establishing 'guidelines for the further development of a post-war cinema that would continue the enquiry into the past and link it to questions about social development in the present and future'.

Largely overlooked, however, by Murray as well as other critics, is the status of the films as texts from a cultural interregnum, not only in terms of their relation to history but also in their representation of gender. If one focus of post-war public discourse in Germany was the question of history and its 'overcoming', then a second was what was widely perceived as a crisis in gender. Families were split by war, gender roles transformed: women worked in transport and heavy industry; they had been independently sexually active in their husbands' absence; the war had forged female communities on the home front into which returning male soldiers had no point of entry. Some films of the period directly thematized this turmoil in gender roles and identities. *Straßenbekanntschaft* offers perhaps the best example, not least because it explicitly constructs its subject matter (venereal disease) as a women's issue. The film addresses changing gender roles through its depiction both of strong female friendships and women's working lives, and – in its treatment of figures such as the house-husband Herbert (Harry Hindemith) – of the breakdown in masculinity inaugurated by men's defeat in war, as well as by their difficulty in accepting changes in the women they left behind. Thus when Herbert accuses his tram-driver wife, Marion (Ursula Voss), of infidelity, she places their confrontation in the context of what is, she suggests, a wider breakdown in male–female communication:

> There's not a single one of you who really knows how we've been living here at home. Off to the factory every morning, home late in the evening; the hunger, the cold, the sirens, then the fear and the helplessness. Is it so strange that we wanted to forget everything, just for a moment?

Marion touches on an issue that is central to the handling of gender crisis in the films under discussion here: the different relation of women and men to memory and recent history. We will return below to what is figured here as a female wish to 'forget everything, just for a moment'; but what, first, of masculinity and its relation to history in the rubble film?

Masculinity and memory

Dr Mertens in *Die Mörder sind unter uns* is a broken man. The war has left him an alcoholic, an erratic figure plagued by guilt and moral indecision. The ethical ambiguity that surrounds him is figured visually in the film by dramatic side- and under-lighting that distorts his features and casts menacing shadows around him. Mertens prowls Susanne's flat like a caged animal, stalks the streets with no clear destination. His acting style combines intense physical agitation with a guttural, growling vocal delivery that signals his distrust of language and of its power to name historical reality (indeed, it is at first only in nightmares that he can speak of his war experiences). Gone are the clipped tones and barking delivery of such male stars of Nazi cinema as Willy Birgel or Carl Raddatz. Gone too is the assertive militarism of fascist soldier males in such films as Veit Harlan's *Kolberg*, Goebbels's 1945 swansong, for which he recalled 180,000 men from the front to fight a last stand on the silver screen in a reconstruction of the glorious defeat of the fortress of Kolberg during the Napoleonic wars. Gone (though he will resurface in the war films of the early 1950s) is the German male as guardian of moral rectitude and national stability: Gneisenau and Nettelbeck, the defenders of Kolberg, for instance, or Christian Faber, the defender of Aryan honour in Veit Harlan's 1940 anti-Semitic propaganda piece *Jud Süß*.

The men of the rubble films, by contrast, grapple with a masculinity in crisis. Some, like Mertens, are morally tainted by their involvement in the war crimes of National Socialism. Men in other rubble films may not be so actively associated with fascist crimes, but they are at least culturally and socially displaced by the experience of defeat, exile or imprisonment. Herbert, the returning soldier in *Straßenbekanntschaft*, can find no work, and is forced into the role of house-husband to a working wife. Michael, in *Zwischen Gestern und Morgen*, had a promising artistic career before the war. He returns from political exile expecting to be welcomed, but finds himself branded instead as an outsider and petty criminal. And in the parodic scene from *Film ohne Titel* in which Willy Fritsch lampoons his own former star persona and acting style, we see the problem of gender identity re-enacted as a crisis in cinematic representation. There is now, this scene suggests, no film language adequate to the representation of a post-war generation of defeated German men.

That the dislocation of masculine identity evident in the rubble films is a result of men's now fractured relation to the Nazi past is clearly evident, and not only at the manifest level of the protagonists' recurrent preoccupation with remembrance of times past. That disruption of past-present relations is inscribed in the very narrative structure of the rubble films. In the classical narrative paradigm that had dominated German cinema since the early 1930s, narrative coherence – as in classical Hollywood – was established through temporal structures that emphasized linearity and teleological progression. Flashbacks, for example, were never a prominent feature of the Ufa style: moments of necessary narrative disruption – the numbers in musicals, for instance – were always narratively motivated, as were such formal devices as montage, which, though perhaps required for reasons of economy or scene-setting, involved a reordering of, or ellipsis within, the story's time line.

The rubble films, by contrast, regularly used fragmented narrative structure to raise the same questions about the relations between past, present and future that were so central to public debate in the period. There is never a straightforward storyline in these films. *In jenen Tagen*, for instance, is structured as a montage of fragmentary episodes from the lives of the owners of the car which is the film's narrator. The past/present/future continuum is to an extent sustained in this film, in that the episodes are organized chronologically owner by owner. Other films, however, more radically disrupt the temporal continuum. Not only is there extensive use of flashbacks but they are also signalled as compulsive, involuntary bearers of affect-laden memories inaccessible to the rationality that structures linear narrative. The use of flashbacks in *Die Mörder* clearly exemplifies the disruptive quality of memory within the film narrative. That Mertens's memories will resurface, despite his efforts to suppress them, is signalled early on: during a drunken chess game, for instance, when he orders his pieces to be sent 'straight to the mass grave'; or later in the hospital, when he collapses at the sight of suffering patients, and screams deliriously, 'the women! the children!' For the spectator, who knows nothing yet of Mertens's war experiences, these are unsettling interludes, moments of narrative disruption and enigma. The expectation is established at these points of a flashback that will begin to unravel Mertens's mystery; but importantly, the first flashback does nothing to restore narrative coherence. Mertens is prompted by his first encounter with Brückner to remember their time together at the Front: he hears battle noises, sirens, marching songs, the refrain from 'Lili Marleen', distant screams. For the film audience, there are no images: only Mertens's face in close-up, accompanied by a flashback that is no more than a disjunctive montage of offscreen sound.

That the past is a source of narrative incoherence is similarly signalled in other films of the period. The flashforward is a rare device in narrative cinema, disrupting as it so easily does the realist illusion of an equivalence between narrative and historical time. *Film ohne Titel*, however, is structured around an extended flashforward. We are presented with a romantic melodrama that might in future be made by the three protagonists, yet the ontological status of the images onscreen remains unclear. Are we watching a film that has already been made? Or does the extensive cross-cutting to the film-makers' metacommentaries constitute the fiction entirely as a fantasy, a director's/screenwriter's/actor's projection of a cinematic future that the corruption of the film-making tradition in Nazi Germany has placed beyond reach?

One final instance of the rubble films' characteristic disruption of temporal coherence is their use of recapitulation and repetition. Although always compulsive, repetition in these films may be traumatic, as in the case of Dr Mertens's involuntarily resurfacing nightmare memories; or it may be part of a quasi-therapeutic process of working through inchoate memories. This is certainly its function in *Zwischen Gestern und Morgen*. Here, the fact that the protagonist Michael Rott (Viktor de Kowa) has, like Mertens, a compulsion to remember is signalled by a series of sound flashbacks in opening passages of the film. Shots from Michael's point of view of random objects in the *mise-en-scène* – the corridor of the ruined Hotel Regina, the rubble that was once the hotel bar – are the cue for non-diegetic music that evokes pathos, though its meaning is unclear. Memories of pre-war experiences (Michael last visited the hotel in March 1938) resurface initially, then, as pure affect: memory, as yet, is pre-linguistic and beyond narrative, signified only in musical form.

Later, Michael dines alone in the upper gallery of the makeshift hotel restaurant. This time, a point-of-view shot of a deserted space below him triggers a memory that is now capable of surfacing in narrative form: there is a dissolve to the same space in its pre-war guise as a hotel swimming pool. The story of Michael's last visit unfolds: the narrative of a romance, of his love for the equally smitten Annette (Winnie Markus), of the tragic interruption of their affair when he learns of his imminent arrest for 'subversion' and flees.

Back in present time, Michael re-encounters Annette, and is devastated to find her married to the hotelier Rolf Ebeling (Viktor Staal). There ensues a second flashback, this time figured (by a dissolve from a close-up of his face) as Ebeling's, not Michael's, memory. Michael's story is now recapitulated, but in sequences in which the composition and framing of shots have been altered to imply a new perspective (Ebeling's).

Before leaving, Michael had been entrusted with a task. On his way to Annette's room on his last evening, he was stopped by a Jewish guest, Nelly Dreyfuss (Sibylle Schmitz). Nelly has risked her life to spend one last night in a hotel from which race laws now disbar her. Unaware of her identity, Michael agrees to take from her a necklace and deliver it the next day to her actor ex-husband Alexander (Willy Birgel). But by the next morning, Michael has escaped across the border, and Ebeling recalls that the necklace too had disappeared without trace. In Ebeling's flashback, then, Michael figures as a romantic adventurer and petty thief. Until this moment, Michael has dominated the film, both as main protagonist and as narrator. At this point, however, the truth of his autobiographical narrative (and by extension, his legitimacy as narrator) are called into question by Ebeling. As in *Die Mörder*, then, flashback functions in *Zwischen Gestern* to destabilize the narrative perspective of the film's central protagonist, Michael.

There are several issues here that are of larger significance for questions of masculinity, memory and history in the rubble film. First, the disruption of temporal order in these narratives – their use of flashback, flashforward and repetition, most often of scenes viewed from a male perspective – suggests an instability in men's position as narrative agents. In classical narrative, the male subject is the agent of narrative progression, the figure who, in Laura Mulvey's (1989: 20) seminal formulation, is 'the active one in forwarding the story, making things happen'. The men of the rubble films, by contrast, are thwarted in their efforts to move their story on: for, at crucial moments of potential narrative development, a memory of times past interrupts the temporal flow and blocks narrative progression. In *Die Mörder*, when Mertens first visits a hospital – when he stands, then, on the threshold of a new life in his former profession – he experiences an involuntary flashback to wartime trauma, and falls unconscious. Similarly, in *Zwischen Gestern*, Michael's reunion with Annette – the moment when he, as romantic hero, might regain her love – is marred by Ebeling's flashback to a vision of Michael as common thief. And finally, in *Film ohne Titel*, the fictional film director's memories of Nazi cinema render the making of new films quite impossible; again, memory intervenes, not just to block narrative progression, but the very construction of film narrative itself.

A second effect of the flashback in the rubble film is to deprive the male protagonists of the moral authority they need to function as historical agents in the post-war present. Like Mertens's flashbacks to war, Michael's memories of pre-war days in the hotel reveal him as a character of possibly dubious virtue: Mertens is perhaps a war criminal, Michael a potential thief. That Mertens has not fully renounced his violent past is evident in the final scene of *Die Mörder* when, in a misplaced effort at blood-for-blood justice, he attempts to gun down ex-Hauptmann Brückner. The cloud of suspicion that descends on Michael during flashbacks to the necklace incident similarly bars his access to a new life with the lover (Annette) whom this returned exile had hoped to make his wife.

But it is not only men's legitimacy as historical agents that is undermined in these films by memories of the recent past. It is their very access to historical time that is threatened. Julia Kristeva (1981), among others, has observed that memory lies outside 'time as project, teleology, linear and prospective unfolding; time as departure, progression and arrival – in other words, the time of history'. Memory-time is cyclical, repetitive, 'hysterical' in the Freudian sense, if we understand the hysteric as someone who 'suffers from reminiscences [and] eruptions of involuntary memory' (Modleski, 1987: 330). Thus, memory in *Die Mörder* and *Zwischen Gestern* returns both Mertens and Michael to a cyclical re-enactment of scenes from times past: in Mertens's recurrent nightmares, for instance, or the obsessive flashbacks to Michael's hotel sojourn before the war. Similarly, in his re-enactment of a pivotal love scene in *Film ohne Titel*, Willy Fritsch is revealed as trapped in repetitions of the now meaningless gestures he remembers from his heyday as an Ufa star.

This relegation of men to 'hysterical time' highlights the close links in the rubble films between the crisis in historical narrative that they address and a crisis in masculine identity. Modleski suggests that, in classical cinema, hysterical time is inhabited primarily by women: thus, for instance, she links the importance of melodrama as a women's genre to the melodramatic concern with 'what Julia Kristeva calls the "anterior temporal modalities", these modalities being stereotypically linked with female subjectivity in general (with the "cycles, gestation, the eternal recurrence of a biological rhythm which conforms to that of nature")' (Kristeva, 1981, cited in Modleski, 1987: 330). As Modleski (*ibid.*: 332) further notes, however, some films – and this is certainly true of many of the titles under discussion here – situate men too in cyclical time, and thus tend 'to feminise the man, to complicate and destabilise his identity'.

Women, memory and history

Modleski's work usefully highlights the connections between the rupturing of historical narrative – in particular, the destabilizing of narrative time that characterizes the rubble films – and a concomitant destabilizing of masculine identity. But her analysis of time, memory and gender in the women's films also sheds light on a second feature of the rubble film, namely its treatment of women, history and memory. The observations cited above derive from Modleski's discussion of Max Ophüls's *Letter from an Unknown Woman* (1948). Like Mertens, Michael and other post-war German film protagonists, Ophüls's romantic hero Stefan is caught, argues Modleski, in the 'hysteria' of involuntary repetition and cyclical time. The 'unknown woman', Lisa, whose letter triggers flashbacks to the romantic narrative that makes up the main body of the film, is a former lover whom Stefan, a philanderer and womanizer, has apparently forgotten. 'Unable to remember the women who alone gave his life significance,' Modleski continues, 'Stefan is doomed to a life of meaningless repetition, especially in relation to women, who become virtually indistinguishable to him' (*ibid.*: 331).

Importantly, however, Stefan has, by the end of the film, moved beyond what Modleski identifies as the 'feminine' position of one who compulsively repeats old histories. In retelling the story of a life Stefan has repressed or forgotten – the story of his early love for Lisa, of the child she bore him, but whom he never knew – her letter performs a quasi-therapeutic function of 'work[ing] through the pain of loss and nonfulfilment' that Stefan experiences (*ibid.*: 332).

For many male protagonists in the rubble films, there is a woman who will perform a function which, though analogous to the 'talking cure' enacted in *Letter from an Unknown Woman* by Lisa's letter, is more contradictory. Thus, while for Lisa the memories that she uncovers in her letter are, in part at least, her own, it seems a prerequisite of remembrance in the rubble films that women will subject their own memories to a process of erasure. Again, it is *Die Mörder* that sets the tone for many later titles. Despite passing references early in the film to the female protagonist Susanne's concentration camp experiences, her memories are metaphorically and literally 'swept under the carpet' when, on returning home, she dons scarf and apron and cleans her flat with a gusto that borders on the obsessional. To Mertens's growled protests at her attempted restoration of 'bourgeois order' in the home, her (non-verbal) response is an ever more determined onslaught on wartime grime; for, as she says to a neighbour when she first comes home, 'I want to work, to live, at last to live.'

That the work that Susanne performs is in part the physical labour of rubble clearance – sweeping up debris in her home – is, of course, an authentic reference to women's historical experience in the immediate aftermath of war. As is well known, the so-called 'rubble women' (*Trümmerfrauen*) were set to work in their thousands after 1945 to clear the rubble from German cities and to take on other forms of heavy manual labour – construction work, lorry driving, factory work and so on – in preparation for the physical and economic regeneration of the two post-war German states.[2] Unsurprisingly, given this context, Susanne is not the only woman in post-1945 film to work so enthusiastically to clear the debris of the wartime past. The young female protagonist in *Zwischen Gestern* survives (as did many women attempting to carry families through this desperate period) by scavenging among the ruins. In *Straßenbekanntschaft*, tribute is very explicitly paid to women's reconstruction work: thus, women are represented and positively valued in this film in myriad capacities, as tram drivers, street traders, laundry women and so on.

Women are seen as central, then, to the physical labour that erases the traces of war and paves the way to reconstruction in the socio-economic and political domain. That this erasure of the material traces of a traumatic past also involves the obliteration of female memory is clear in *Die Mörder*, for instance, in Susanne's amnesiac relation to her concentration camp past. But this is not to say that women in these films have no involvement in the work of memory. On the contrary, their suppression of their own past seems to facilitate that very process of male remembering that has led the rubble films to be critically acclaimed as important works of *Vergangenheitsbewältigung*.

Mourning and gender

In their much-discussed book, *Die Unfähigkeit zu Trauern*[*The Inability to Mourn*], Alexander and Margarete Mitscherlich (1967: 9) famously argue that public life in post-war Germany was characterized by an 'inability to mourn' the 'national catastrophe' of German fascism. What the Mitscherlichs describe as a collective process of 'stubborn and sustained defence against memory' rendered the post-war nation, they argue (in relation specifically to West Germany), incapable of the 'working through' of traumatic past events that is central to the mourning process.

The Mitscherlichs' essay is indebted to Freud's 'Mourning and Melancholia', in which he characterizes mourning as a process in which the lost object (and this may take many forms, from a cherished intimate friend to an abstract ideal) is recalled to memory, in order that its loss may be recognized and the object gradually relinquished. Mourning, in other words, is a 'psychological process in which the individual, by repeated and painful remembering, slowly learns to bear and to work through a loss' (Mitscherlich-Nielsen, 1989: 405).[3]

One central loss that the rubble films register, as we have seen, is that of a viable male identity. Looking back at their past selves, the men in these films confront an ideal ego – Michael the anti-fascist artist, Willy Fritsch the Third Reich heart-throb, Mertens the good soldier – whose integrity has been undermined by the events of war and the experience of German fascism. Significantly, however – and contra Mitscherlich – a mourning process *does* occur in these films. Our discussion of flashbacks above reveals how many of the rubble films are structured around a process of retrieving memory, revisiting and reviewing the lost object (the male protagonists' former selves), then finally relinquishing it in favour of new identities more adequate to the post-war present.

Crucially, though, it is often not the men themselves who are the active agents of this work of memory, but rather the women with whom they are fortunate enough to have achieved romantic liaison. In *Die Mörder*, it is Susanne who pieces together the fragments of Mertens's memories of times past. Discovering a letter from Brückner that Mertens has never delivered to the wife for whom it was intended, she forces him to visit Brückner, to confront this ghost from his past, actively to remember. When Susanne reads Mertens's diary in the closing sequences of the film, the working through of his past is complete, and he can seek a new self more adequate to present time. Even now, though, it is Susanne who must force an acknowledgement of the need to change from Mertens when she stops him shooting Brückner, and he concurs with her that 'we have no right to pass sentence'.

In *Zwischen Gestern*, it is again Hildegard Knef, this time as Kat the former hotel barmaid, who subjects Michael's memories to the reworking that will lay them finally to rest. As in Ebeling's flashback (discussed above), it is the necklace incident that is important here. Michael has claimed throughout that he delivered Nelly Dreyfuss's necklace to her ex-husband, Alexander, that he did not steal it, as many now believe. At the film's denouement, his story is finally corroborated, this time by a flashback from Kat's perspective to a scene in which she witnessed Alexander hiding the necklace behind the hotel bar. It is Kat, in other words, who – like Susanne in *Die Mörder* – completes the memory-work that will redeem Michael and restore his masculine integrity (his masculinity being proven in the film's closing moments when he takes Kat/Knef in his arms).

Here, then (as, in Modleski's view, also in the contemporaneous *Letter from an Unknown Woman*), we see women 'enact[ing] a process of mourning for the man', working through their memories in an effort to lay the ghost of a problematic past to rest (Modleski, 1987: 334–5). Sadly, however, the completion of this vicarious memory-work does not make women fit for participation in the (masculine) histories whose progression they have helped secure. Instead, the women of the rubble films are ultimately repositioned in the ahistorical temporality that Modleski suggests is typical of classical cinematic representations of femininity. In the first instance, this occurs through the restoration of female figures – characters who might surely, given women's very active socio-economic and political roles in post-war regeneration, have figured more centrally as narrative agents – to a position as ahistorical objects of visual pleasure. It has for many years been a central tenet of feminist film criticism that women occupy a position in classical narrative cinema predominantly as spectacle (Mulvey, 1989). Late 1940s German cinema might have been expected to question this, given its commitment – in its use of modernist visual style, or its fracturing of the point-of-view and temporal structures of narrative cinema – to challenging classical narrative convention. Yet the challenge dissipates in the rubble films' approach to post-war femininity. Ulrike Sieglohr's article on Hildegard Knef in this volume traces Knef's development after 1945 as a popular star; and many of the visual strategies employed in that process – for example, the extensive use of close-up, back- and top-lighting that extract Knef from a darker backdrop, and so on – locate her as an object of spectacle whose 'visual presence tends to work against the development of a story line, to freeze the flow of action in moments of erotic contemplation' (Mulvey, 1989: 19).

But this reassertion of classical codes of feminine representation is not the only strategy employed in the rubble films to place their female protagonists outside narrative and beyond history. In a recent survey of images of women in post-war German visual representation, Mariatte C. Denman (1997: 199) has noted the predominance of the Madonna as a key figure in 'gendered visualizations of Germanness' after 1945. Focusing on visual culture of the period – newspapers, women's magazines, election posters, fine art (she cites here especially the work of the sculptress and graphic artist Käthe Kollwitz) – Denman concludes that the Madonna image was regularly mobilized to represent the universal experience of pain and loss caused by war (*ibid.*: 195).

References to the Madonna surface repeatedly, too, in films of the period. The opening sequence of *Die Mörder* shows Susanne walking the streets on her first return to her former home. During that sequence, the camera lingers on a statue of the Madonna and Child before returning to Knef via a dissolve that suggests a symbolic equivalence between the two female images. Later, Susanne is pictured working on a charcoal sketch for a poster captioned *Rettet die Kinder!* (Save the Children!). The sketch is unmistakably a pastiche of Käthe Kollwitz, and it clearly echoes that artist's preoccupation with the maternal gestures of 'mourning, sacrifice and pleading' that the Madonna evokes (*ibid.*). The Madonna is found, too, in *In jenen Tagen*: the car's last owner is named Maria, and is first seen in a barn (or stable?) sequence nestling with her child in the arms of Josef (*sic*) the deserting soldier. In *Film ohne Titel*, finally, the ubiquitous Madonna image is gently satirized when Willy Fritsch, in the parodic scene discussed above, calls Knef his 'little Madonna' and his only love.

As a universal symbol removed from linear narrative, the Madonna possesses neither memory nor history. Similarly, many women in the rubble film, though they remember vicariously for their men, suffer a curious amnesia in relation to their own part in previous histories. Susanne in *Die Mörder* is apparently never compelled to remember her life in the camp; it is referenced only once, and then fleetingly. The reference to her status as ex-inmate is, however, important, in that it situates Susanne as a universal victim, a figure who suffers so that others (in her case, Mertens) may achieve redemption.

This figuring of the amnesiac woman/mother/Madonna as the primary victim of German history is, ultimately, of course deceptive. Forgetting, as psychoanalysis has clearly shown, is more than merely a passive process, a loss of the past externally imposed on history's victims. Crucially, to forget is also to become involved in the repression of past affects and memories. More than this, repression is not only an active (if sometimes involuntary) psychic process, it is also one that must be constantly repeated, since the repressed (if we follow Freud) will inevitably return, despite the most strenuous efforts to contain it (Freud, 1915: 143).

In this light, let us take one last look at the women of the post-war rubble film. In the film texts from this period, there are indications that the women are as haunted as are their menfolk by repressed memories of a former self: a self that was not merely the victim of historical circumstance (of war, hunger, political oppression) but also the perpetrator, or at least the facilitator, of past crimes.

Among feminist historians of Nazi Germany, the issue of women's status as either victims or perpetrators in the Third Reich has in recent years been hotly contested. While early feminist work focused on such issues as women's war work, their legal status and their position in eugenics programmes (especially in programmes of forced sterilization) to highlight the hardships many women endured under National Socialism, more recent discussions have centred on women's roles in Nazi organizations, as well as their activities as nurses, teachers, social workers and indeed mothers whose role was to support and implement Nazi racial policy and eugenics programmes. The argument advanced here is that women played such a key role in social and racial policy in particular that we must perforce 'speak of guilt, or least of complicity' by women, for example in the persecution of so-called social undesirables, or in the genocide against the gypsies and Jews (Grossmann, 1991; von Saldern, 1994).

In the films of the immediate post-war period, memories of this repressed female complicity repeatedly surface. A number of films feature flashback or dream sequences in which women's participation in the crimes of the past is explored (if sometimes obliquely). *Zwischen Gestern und Morgen* and *Straßenbekanntschaft* offer particularly illuminating instances – in the first case of a flashback, in the second, of dream and nightmare sequences – in which 'the repressed' (the female protagonist as perpetrator, not victim) is brought to mind by the 'return' of figures of ethnic or sexual difference – Jews, blacks, homosexuals – in whose oppression she may have been complicit.

In *Zwischen Gestern*, Kat (Knef) wins the love of Michael by returning to him the necklace which he is suspected of having stolen. Throughout the film, the necklace has evoked for many protagonists memories of a Jewish fate, that of Nelly Dreyfuss, who entrusted her jewellery to Michael before his departure from Germany. An early flashback in the film shows Nelly being harassed by Gestapo officers. To avoid arrest and deportation to the camps, Dreyfuss commits suicide – as do, incidentally, all the Jewish figures in the post-war rubble films. As if this were not enough to underline the failure of these films to confront German complicity in genocide against the Jews – the Jew must die by her own hand, not by that of any ethnic German – *Zwischen Gestern* goes on to perpetrate a yet more extraordinary form of historical repression. When Nelly Dreyfuss's necklace resurfaces after the war, its narrative function is not to remind the audience of the tragedy of her death, nor indeed more broadly, of the crime of Nazi genocide against the Jews. Instead, the recovery of the necklace serves to remove a cloud of suspicion that has hovered over Michael since the start of the film, when he was accused of stealing it. Importantly, it is the female protagonist, Kat, who is the agent here of historical repression: it is she who transforms the necklace from an object that recalls the complicity of the German gentiles in this film (men and women both) in a Jewish death into one that, perversely, proves Michael's innocence and seals their romantic union.

This suppression of the ethnic other as a means of guaranteeing the moral integrity of both hero and heroine is repeated in a rather different way by the heroine of *Straßenbekanntschaft*, Erika. Early in the film, Erika's moral decline (she falls into vagrancy and prostitution) is signalled by a party sequence whose status as a representation of the heroine's fantasy is indicated – in contrast to the social realism of the rest of the film – by expressionist *mise-en-scène* and subjective camera.

What Erika sees here is a mass of anonymous bodies gyrating to American jazz, a scene whose climax is an exhibitionist display of lesbian kissing. This stereotypical association of moral degeneracy with the ethnic other (through jazz) and with sexual deviance (the lesbian kiss) lies in a direct line of descent from Nazi cinema, with its portrayal of jazz culture as degenerate, ethnically hybrid and sexually perverse. *Straßenbekanntschaft* mobilizes the same iconography, not to celebrate the value of jazz culture, but to represent the repressed other which the heroine must overcome if she is to find moral redemption. The seedy milieux through which Erika moves in her descent into prostitution and venereal infection are figured regularly in the film through the imagery of jazz, physical degeneracy and sexual deviance. Finally, in a closing sequence figured, again, as Erika's fantasy, she flees like a woman possessed from the darkened streets and sleazy bars that have been the scene of her decline. The inference is that it is not only her street life as a prostitute that she must abandon but also her affiliation to apparently dubious ethnic and sexual identities. Here as elsewhere in the rubble film, the heroine's moral redemption is made dependent on her disavowal of figures of ethnic and sexual difference: Nelly Dreyfuss in *Zwischen Gestern*, the jazz pianist or the homosexual lovers in *Straßenbekanntschaft*.

From rubble film to New German Cinema

I quoted above Bruce Murray's assertion (and it is a common one in critical writings on this period) that the rubble films of 1945–49 established 'guidelines' for a post-war German cinema that has been regularly preoccupied with the fascist past and its 'overcoming'. Absent from Murray's analysis, however, as from that of other critics, is any comment on the gendered nature of the 'guidelines' that these films lay down. The recognition of the guilt and moral responsibility of German *men* that occurs in such titles as *The Murderers* (when Mertens remembers his part in a wartime massacre) or *Film without a Title* (when Willy Fritsch recalls and repudiates his former star persona) is weakened by an assertion – in the ubiquitous Madonna image, for instance – of German women's moral purity, their non-participation in fascist history. The engagement with the past in these films is thus fundamentally gendered: while men struggle to remember, their women, 'forgetting' their own histories, help them.

What presents itself, in other words, as an engagement with the past by men who act on behalf of the collectivity of the German nation is in fact a selective rewriting of a masculine history: the story of male war crimes (Mertens), men as exiles (Michael), men in the public culture of National Socialism (Fritsch). The broader feminist arguments against this figuring of men as the sole bearers of national histories are surely too familiar to need rehearsing in any detail here.[4] Close attention does need to be paid, however, to the implications of this repression of women's narratives in the specific context of the Third Reich and its post-war representation. Many of the rubble films, as we have seen, position their female figures symbolically beyond history, and obscure these women's memories of their own past in favour of a vicarious remembering for their men. In so doing, they also erase from view what the feminist historians I cited earlier have identified as the history of German (male and female) complicity in Nazi racial crimes; and they do so by mobilizing certain conventions of representation that, as my discussion above should indicate, structure the presentation of femininity across a range of rubble films.

It appears that three symbolic positions are reserved for 'woman' in the rubble film; and in each of these, the image of woman produced has the function of screening out that history of social and racial oppression between 1933 and 1945 in which women were at least as actively involved as the men whose guilt these films more obviously trace. The figuring of women, first, as transhistorical symbols (the Madonna) or sexual spectacle (Hildegard Knef in her function as emergent star) situates femininity in the rubble film within a mode of representation that is iconic rather than narrative-based. Importantly, this favouring of the iconic in female representation renders impossible the recovery of historical narratives in which women might have figured (as they do in some recent feminist histories) as the agents of political or social oppression. Women survive in these films, then, as unsullied images whose personal stories, with their attendant moral ambiguities and ambivalent narrative positions, are lost.

The second feminine position I identified above was that of bystander or observer to masculine histories. For many female figures, the passivity of this onlooker function is underscored by their simultaneous representation as the victims of the histories they watch. Whether in Marion's passionate plea for an understanding of women's suffering in war in *Straßenbekanntschaft,* in Kat the barmaid's bravado-in-adversity as she scavenges among the ruins and bomb-damaged streets of *Zwischen Gestern*, or – most tellingly, perhaps – in Susanne's reference in *Die Mörder* to her concentration camp past, there is an implication that the Third Reich's primary surviving victims are not, say, the Jews or gypsies (as the films seem at pains to demonstrate, those groups have been ruthlessly liquidated), but rather a generation of suffering German women.

It was the Mitscherlichs who most famously observed the widespread tendency of post-war Germans to identify themselves as the primary victims of war. That identification, they further claim, functioned as a defence mechanism against the work of mourning which, in the Mitscherlichs' view, remained unachieved by successive post-war generations:

> Identification with the victim is very frequently substituted for mourning; this is above all a logical defence against guilt. . . . To the conscious mind the past then appears as follows: We made many sacrifices, suffered the war, and were discriminated against for a long time afterward; yet we were innocent, since everything that is now held against us, we did under orders. (Mitscherlich and Mitscherlich, 1967; see also Santner, 1990: 6ff.)

Though there is, in the rubble films' attention to issues of male guilt, an effort at some kind of work of mourning, their sustaining of an image of German women as innocent victims maintains at least partially intact what the Mitscherlichs identify as a defence against collective guilt. The image of woman functions here as a screen which, in reflecting back to the German audience a representation of its (female) self as victim, blanks out memories of those figures who suffered more directly from fascist crimes.

To illustrate this point more clearly, let us look at a third and final convention of feminine representation in the post-war rubble film. In his important work on whiteness, Richard Dyer (1988) uses a discussion of the relationship between Bette Davis's character, Julie, and Theresa Harris's Zette in *Jezebel* (William Wyler, 1938) to show how the symbolic purity of the white woman in Hollywood film may be attained through her definition against an exotic (often black) double or other. The exotic double both acts out tabooed emotions and experiential states for the white woman and functions as a figure of otherness in relation to whom the white woman defines the values she embodies, indeed her very identity.

In the rubble film, too, there is repeating evidence not only of the binary ethnic differentiation that Dyer references but of a more variegated splitting of the social totality into hierarchies of the pure and impure – a splitting that was of course particularly characteristic of the racialized social policies of National Socialism. Thus in the rubble film, the symbolic split that Dyer identifies as dividing figures of the feminine in Hollywood film occurs most regularly between the white German woman who is the main female protagonist (Kat, Erika, Susanne) and a range of others whose ethnic and social legitimacy is conventionally more questionable, from the Jewess Nelly Dreyfuss in *Zwischen*

Gestern, to the lesbian lovers of *Straßenbekanntschaft*. Like Dyer's Hollywood heroine, the rubble woman both sympathizes, indeed identifies, with her exotic double(s) – and in so doing is able to borrow from them a capacity to evoke emotion and melodramatic pathos – but at the same time gains her dominant status as heroine precisely through her difference from the more marginal figures with whom she associates. For instance, *Straßenbekanntschaft*, as we have seen, strives to secure spectactor identification with its heroine Erika through a dual process in which, first, she is identified with the social marginals Nazism despised (the homeless and destitute, prostitutes, jazz musicians, homosexuals). Second, however, her moral integrity is secured through her distancing from these figures of alien ethnicity and social or sexual deviance. Similarly, in *Die Mörder*, the figure of Susanne derives much of its pathos from her implied identity with concentration camp victims. Unlike *Straßenbekanntschaft*, however – whose social realist 'urban underworld' sequences give at least a glimpse of everyday reality among the social outsiders with whom Erika associates – *Die Mörder* denies to the camp victims even the most fleeting participation in cinematic representation. The camp inmates are never figured: instead, we share only in an emotional experience of their fate, filtered through our encounter with the figure whom my opening comments in this essay identified as an icon of whiteness *par excellence*, Susanne.

If, then, the rubble films establish guidelines for a post-war tradition of filmic *Vergangenheitsbewältigung*, they do so, it seems, by mobilizing conventions of gender representation that obscure as much as they reveal of the multiple histories of guilt and innocence under German fascism. More precisely, they establish a tradition in which representations of an ethically unsullied German femininity can function to displace more ambivalent histories of racial and social oppression and female complicity. Many of the films of the New German Cinema that have been criticized for their repression of the Holocaust and its related histories (Edgar Reitz's *Heimat*, 1984, is one example) have at their epicentre an icon of suffering and/or morally irreproachable womanhood: Maria in *Heimat*, the mother Lene in Helma Sanders-Brahms's *Deutschland, bleiche Mutter/Germany, Pale Mother* (1980) or, more recently, the rape victims of Helke Sanders's documentary on the mass rape of German women by occupying troops after the Second World War, *Befreier und Befreite/Liberators Take Liberties* (1992).[5] The reappraisal of the rubble films that I have attempted here perhaps allows us to situate these later titles in a longer film history, and to position them within what is surely a more complex history than has yet been written of the gender and race politics of post-war German cinematic representation.

Acknowledgements

An earlier version of this chapter appeared in *Debatte,* Vol. 4, No. 1 (1996), 109–22. Thanks also go to Ulrike Sieglohr and Jim Cook for their valuable comments.

Notes

1. For surveys of cultural debate in the immediate post-war period, see Bullivant and Rice (1995), Murray (1991) and Carter (1997a), pp. 432–53.
2. On women's work in the post-war period, see for example Kuhn (1984), Kolinsky (1989), pp. 7–40, and Carter (1997b), pp. 45–76.
3. I should here acknowledge my indebtedness to Monica Pearl for her discussion of Mitscherlich-Nielsen in her PhD thesis 'Alien tears: mourning, melancholia and identity in AIDS literature', University of Warwick, 1999.
4. The text that launched debates on women as 'hidden from history' is Rowbotham (1977). For a critique of the binary paradigm of suppression/revelation established by the early second-wave feminist histories, see Scott (1988).
5. For examples of these debates on the historiographical limitations of *Heimat* and *Liberators*, see Hansen (1985) and Grossmann (1995).

Filmography 1946–9

This filmography relates only to titles discussed in this chapter; it is not a full list of German titles released during this period.

Der Apfel ist ab (Helmut Käutner, 1948, Camera-Film, Hamburg)
Ehe im Schatten (Kurt Maetzig, 1947, DEFA, Berlin)
Film ohne Titel (Rudolf Jugert, 1947–8, Camera-Film, Hamburg)
In jenen Tagen: Geschichte eines Autos (Helmut Käutner, 1949, Camera-Film, Hamburg)
Die Mörder sind unter uns (Wolfgang Staudte, 1946, DEFA, Berlin)
Straßenbekanntschaft (Peter Pewas, 1947–8, DEFA, Berlin)
Zwischen Gestern und Morgen (Harald Braun, 1947, Neue Deutsche Filmgesellschaft, Munich)

Hildegard Knef and Wolfgang Staudte, production still of *Die Mörder sind unter uns/The Murderers Are among Us* (1946, Germany, Wolfgang Staudte) *Source:* Deutsches Institut für Filmkunde, Frankfurt/Main.

CHAPTER SEVEN

Hildegard Knef: From Rubble Woman to Fallen Woman

ULRIKE SIEGLOHR

Introduction

> Knef is a child of the German collapse. . . .
>
> Historically tragic epochs always benefit the newcomer: they alone have the stamina of have-nots to start from zero; the public tired of its old friends demands newness, new faces, strange sounds. (Améry, 1955: 316)

Although Hildegard Knef became one of the most popular German stars only in the later post-war period, effectively after she had left Germany, the career of 'Germany's favourite rubble girl' (Heinzelmeier, 1980: 114) was forged in the immediate aftermath of the Second World War. Between 1945 and 1947 when she was only *becoming* a star, she appeared in three key films – *Die Mörder sind unter uns/The Murderers Are among Us* (Wolfgang Staudte, 1946), *Zwischen Gestern und Morgen/Between Yesterday and Tomorrow* (Harald Braun, 1947) and *Film ohne Titel/Film without a Title* (Rudolf Jugert, 1947–8) – always playing contemporary women, in relation to whom the ascription 'rubble girl' does not connote glamour but instead invokes the hard labour of the ubiquitous *Trümmerfrauen* ('rubble women') who cleared the debris from the ruins of bombed-out towns and cities. It is this early unglamorous emblematic[1] dimension of an otherwise glamorous and charismatic star which is of significance here. In these three films, and perhaps above all in her fourth film, *Die Sünderin/The Sinner* (Willi Forst, 1951), Knef's roles negotiate the gender conflicts and contradictions of the real post-war situation in Germany, namely that of women emancipated by the war nurturing tortured males broken by it, only then to be reintegrated into a newly reforming and repressive patriarchal society.

To complement Erica Carter's essay, which discusses more broadly what was at stake in 'memory-work', women's historical agency and the manifestations of these issues in the 'rubble films', I would like to examine the emergence of Hildegard Knef's star persona between 1945 and 1951. In trying to understand how her personal life and the roles she played develop into a signifying star persona we need to consider, as well as the films themselves, three dominant overlapping discursive trends: first, the 'rags to riches' teleological account of Knef's life and career progress (the most common and popular discourse); second, a retrospective feminist appropriation of the star persona; and third, a 'new history' approach which engages with her status as national icon. Crucially, we need also to consider these trends in context and to recognize that for all their strengths the ahistorical tendency of cultural theory approaches to the representation of women must be countered by a 'new historical' attention to specific moments. Thus, with regard to the construction of Knef's star persona, it is important both to note that each discursive perspective foregrounds different concerns relating to the implicit or explicit agenda of the writer, critic or indeed Knef herself, *and* historically to ground these varying ideological concerns by taking into account when a contribution to the construction of the persona is made.

Biography of an emerging star

Born in December 1925 in the provincial town of Ulm, Knef grew up in Berlin, and, at seventeen, trained as a graphic designer at Ufa's special effects department while also taking acting lessons at the government-run Babelsberg Film School. Although this was not public knowledge until the 1970s, during this period Knef had an affair with a high-ranking Nazi film official. In the mayhem of spring 1945, fearing rape, she disguised herself as a soldier fighting the invading Soviet army, was captured but subsequently escaped, and returned to Berlin close to death from starvation, exhaustion and disease (Knef, 1970: Chapters 8 and 9). Immediately after the war she experienced recurring problems with the Allied military police for her Nazi connection and she was briefly barred from accepting a couple of theatre roles (*ibid.*: 141). For a while she had occasionally to dupe the authorities by giving a false identity when moving between sectors of the divided city.

Knef's first brief appearance in the 1944 film *Träumerei/Dreaming* (Harald Braun) got cut on the editing table, but in 1945 she appeared fleetingly in three more films, including *Unter den Brücken/Under the Bridges* (Helmut Käutner). Immediately after the end of the war she was involved with a small theatre group, Tribüne, and took part in a cabaret programme of contemporary comment which was speedily premiered on 1 June 1945 (*Neue Illustrierte*, No. 50, 1960). Subsequently, the critical acclaim she received for the play *Zum goldenen Anker/To the Golden Anchor* led to the starring role in the first German post-war film, *Die Mörder*, a Soviet-licensed DEFA production. So, while during the day she was shooting the film in the Soviet-controlled sector, in the evening she was performing on stage in the American sector. Working conditions were marked by extreme deprivation and, as she recalled (Knef, 1970: Chapter 10), people were always hungry.

At this time Knef got involved with an American film officer, Kurt Hirsch, a Jew of Czech origin, and became a protégée of Erich Pommer, the powerful former Ufa producer who had returned in 1946 from US exile (*ibid*.: 163). Other markers of rising stardom included a photo-series of her in the American journal *Life* (May, 1947), which romanticized the deprivations of living among the ruins, and her appearance on the cover of the first issue of the weekly magazine *Der Stern* (1 August 1948). Knef continued alternating between theatre and film and her next major film role was in the American-licensed *Zwischen Gestern und Morgen*. As a result of all the positive criticism she was declared most promising new actress by the talent scout, Elly Silman, another former Ufa employee and German émigrée working under Pommer, and through Silman's promotion but against Pommer's advice (Knef, 1970: 177) in 1948 she landed a Hollywood contract with David O. Selznick. Her next film, the much-acclaimed British-licensed *Film ohne Titel*, was premiered on the eve of her departure for Hollywood. Ironically, she left Germany just as she was finding success, only to discover that her German identity was a problem in Hollywood. On arrival, and newly married to Hirsch, Selznick imposed compulsory English lessons, but the various screen tests that followed never resulted in her being offered a role.

Knef returned to Germany in 1950 when director Willi Forst offered her the starring role in *Die Sünderin*. While still shooting the film, which became the biggest West German post-war film scandal (see below), Twentieth Century Fox signed up Knef for a major role in Anatole Litvak's *Decision before Dawn* (1951). Throughout the 1950s she acquired an international reputation, starring in films not only by major Hollywood directors but also in French, British and a few German films, and she had a great Broadway success as Ninotchka in Cole Porter's musical *Silk Stockings* (1954). When in the 1960s her career was declining she made a successful comeback as a Marlene Dietrich-style cabaret *chanteuse*, and in 1970 renewed public interest by publishing her best-selling autobiography, *Der geschenkte Gaul [The Gift Horse]*, which was subsequently widely translated. She featured in Helma Sanders-Brahm's film *Flügel und Fesseln/The Future of Emily* (1984–85), and in the 1990s she has maintained her celebrity/star persona by making regular appearances on TV chat shows.

Knef's films and their historical reception

> [Knef] simply is . . . a nearly hundred percent product of our time. She represents the closest approximation of the contemporary type, what we designate as today's woman. (Pommer, cited in *Der Spiegel*, No.19, 7 May 1952: 28)

If we return to an earlier phase of Knef's career, it is apparent that she had no film experience to speak of and only some theatre work to her name when in 1946 Staudte offered her the leading role, Susanne Wallner, in *Die Mörder*. By many accounts she had an impressive appearance: although very young, the deprivations of the war had already left their traces and her angular figure was that of a survivor. In the film she plays a young woman returning from a concentration camp only to find that a stranger is now living in her flat. They decide to share the flat and Susanne takes care of the stranger, a war-damaged and guilt-ridden surgeon Dr Hans Mertens (Ernst Wilhelm Bochert). When Mertens discovers that his wartime superior officer and Nazi war criminal, Brückner (Arno Paulsen), is still alive and already re-established as a manufacturer, he plans to kill him to avenge the atrocities, even though he had complied with Brückner's orders after resistance to them had failed. Discovering Mertens's intention, Susanne intervenes claiming that they have no right to kill but only to accuse the war criminals. Crucially, it is Mertens's past that the flashbacks investigate and not Susanne's story or her past as a concentration camp survivor. (See also Chapter 6.)

Knef was barely twenty years old, blonde, tall and still gangly with strikingly expressive features – austere rather than conventionally beautiful – a nose slightly too prominent for the face's oval shape, wide eyes and sensual mouth. As Susanne she conveys an impression of decisiveness, accentuated by the clipped enunciation of a Berlin accent (albeit muted) and mellowed by a low pitch. Characteristically her expression is often serious and defiant but then lapses into an engaging smile which softens her face; her movements are forceful, exuding vitality; and in most of the scenes her youthfulness, rather than connoting naive optimism, comes across as a practical determination to have a future: 'I want to work, to live, finally live.' It should be pointed out that while Knef's physical appearance, her blondness, still signifies Aryanness, her plain dress style and unfussy behaviour break with the tradition of the Ufa glamorous star image.[2]

The *mise-en-scène* throughout is expressionistic, with dark shadows, oblique angles and spiky ruined buildings. While Mertens's unkempt figure is constantly engulfed by darkness, Knef, although occasionally touched by his encroaching shadow, remains a figure of light. Additionally, whereas Bochert's acting recalls the stylization of Expressionism, Knef acts with restraint, thus appearing 'natural'. The following scene is typical and establishes Susanne as a practical and forward-looking character in marked contrast to Mertens's tortured inwardness. Having decided that they can share the flat, the next morning finds Susanne filling a bucket full of debris. Wearing an apron over her trousers, hair tied back with a headscarf and jumper sleeves rolled up, she is ready to make the flat habitable again. When a little later Mertens tells her that he is a surgeon who now cannot bear the sight of blood, she counters his tortured outburst with stillness. The play between agitation and calm is captured by the *mise-en-scène*, which frames Mertens's face on the right in a diagonal marked by strong shadows, while Susanne, in profile on the left, has her eyes wide open and her lips slightly parted. When he storms out she slowly lowers her head, closing her eyes in resignation.

Inevitably, reviews of the film were mostly concerned with the political issues, discussing the particulars of the *Vergangenheitsbewältigung* ('confronting the past') and an exploration of who was guilty. The immediacy of the narrated events seems also to have been the most striking aspect of the film for Knef and for her approach to the role. In interviews she linked her role to recent history: 'In some of the scenes I believe that I'm reliving again my own experiences. It feels as if the clock has been turned back twelve months' (*Nachtexpress*, Berlin, 27 June 1946). And in another she stated: 'It is a role that enthused me because I can fashion a contemporary destiny' (*Telegraph*, Berlin: 24 May 1946).

In this context it is interesting to note that, unlike Knef herself, the reviews of this first role, lacking any point of comparison, recognized little that was emblematic in her image and commented more in traditional terms on her performance: 'Hildegard Knef's austere-reticent appearance was perhaps the best choice Staudte could have made for this role. Her acting was a beautiful mixture of energetic, unsentimental practicality and comforting love' (Walter Lenning, *Berliner Zeitung*, 17 October 1946); and even in one of the rare dismissals of the film she was positively singled out: 'Staudte's direction is weak. ... Bochert's [Mertens's] mask makes no impact on camera; but the young Hildegard Knef's face was too good for such rubbish' (Wolfdietrich Schnurre, *Deutsche Film-Rundschau*, No. 8, 5 November 1946).

In *Zwischen Gestern und Morgen* Knef plays Kat, a young woman scavenging among the ruins of a once luxurious hotel. She befriends a returning guest, Michael Rott (Victor de Kowa), who had escaped to Switzerland during the war. Through a series of flashbacks it transpires that a necklace which Kat has recovered from the rubble is the same one that had disappeared on the night of Rott's flight, when a Jewess hiding out in the hotel had committed suicide. Assuming the owner to be dead, Kat had intended to sell the necklace on the black market, but when Rott, who she has fallen in love with, is accused of the theft she returns it as evidence of his innocence. Her public rehabilitation of him leads Rott to realize that he in his turn loves her, and the dead Jewess is totally forgotten. (See also Chapter 6.)

Early in the film, when Rott arrives at the ruined hotel, he hears a voice shouting directions to a crane operator clearing the rubble, and then sees Kat sitting among the debris. When he asks whether the hotel accepts guests, she asks him if he has got anything to barter. He offers her a cigarette, which she puts behind her ear with a casual gesture while barely concealing a triumphant smile. Here we see Knef playing a much more carefree young woman than in her previous film. Usually dressed in a black turtleneck jumper and practical slacks, her body language and gestures are boyish as she jumps effortlessly onto the running boards of cars and trams or struts along with hands in her trouser pockets. Clearly, she is no defeatist: despite being a displaced person and caring for her little brother in the post-war chaos, she manages to survive by making black-market deals. As she says at one point: 'One has to continue, there is no other way.' As the title suggests, the film is concerned to enable the future by rehabilitating the honour of men still compromised by the past. By being able to clear him of the theft Kat is crucial to both Rott's present and future. As one reviewer, deploying now the unfolding terms of the star image, pointed out: 'It is the good girl Kat, the dear *rubble girl*, who holds the key all the time' (W.I.G., *Berliner Zeitung*, 21 March 1948 [my emphasis]).

Critical responses were generally fairly dismissive, noting stylistic continuity with discredited Ufa glamour, most obvious in flashbacks depicting the luxurious setting of the hotel and the rich guests. However, Knef's acting is again praised: 'Knef is impressive as the young girl who undoubtedly and seriously confronts contemporary problems' (Luiselotte Enderle, *Neue Zeitung*, Munich, 15 December 1947). 'Although she plays . . . the most difficult part, she proves again her natural talent' (Axelmann[3]). Another critic comments that although all the parts are well played, 'Knef's natural manner of communication' heightens the effectiveness of the film (*Roland von Berlin*, 28 March 1948).

Overall, however, *Zwischen Gestern und Morgen* did not contribute a great deal to Knef's growing reputation, unlike her much praised next film, *Film ohne Titel*. Here Knef plays Christine, a housekeeper, who during the war has a brief affair with Martin Delius (Hans Söhnker), an art dealer, although class differences prevent their marriage. After the war the tables are turned: Martin, as a displaced person, finds a temporary home at Christine's parents' farm, although now he is no longer good enough to be considered as a son-in-law for a farmer. To prove himself a man capable of the practical and useful skills necessary for survival, Martin becomes a furniture maker.

The film starts in the countryside with a discussion between a director, scriptwriter and actor who are looking for an idea for a new film – neither rubble film nor anti-Nazi film, but socially relevant. While they are still searching for a suitable topic a couple, Christine and Martin, pass by and the scriptwriter, a friend of the couple, tells the team their story. Along with 'imagined' different endings and stylistic variations, this account then becomes the central focus of the film. The self-reflexivity of the framing narrative, an explicit quest for a new beginning formally and generically, was what made the film so interesting at the time, but within this limited formal modernism Knef as Christine is presented in a very conventional manner. Essentially, she is constructed as an icon, visually and narratively, both by the film and by Martin, the 'connoisseur', who repeatedly compares her to a medieval madonna. (See also Chapter 6.) Looking prim and proper in an apron with her hair in a bun or sometimes plaited in peasant fashion, Knef characteristically tidies and cleans. At one point, while she is washing up, Martin comes over to her, turning her head to take a closer look as if she were indeed just an inanimate madonna figure to be appraised by a dealer. She takes offence at this treatment and as 'punishment' he dries up the dishes, at which point, watching his madonna at work, Martin also becomes aware of her erotic appeal.

Interestingly, in each of these films the male protagonists become progressively less guilty, and Martin, an adult in the 1930s unlike the much younger Christine, is only compromised by his age since an injury prevented him from being drafted until the very end of the war. Knef's role, however, is consistent in that she looks after her man and it is her love which redeems Martin by turning him from a non-productive dilettante into a practical man. An interesting departure from, or perhaps extension of her previous roles occurs in the post-war scenes set in an idyllic countryside which becomes a pretext for eroticizing Knef as conventional object of desire: typically leaning against a haystack, she takes off her headscarf, her hair tumbling down as she leans back, and we move to a close-up of her slowly closing her eyes. Thus, while *Film ohne Titel* allows Knef to be more versatile, in that she moves from demure urban housekeeper to self-confident farmer's daughter, she is also increasingly objectified for the male gaze – a key stage in the transformation from actress to star image.

Film ohne Titel was premiered in 1947 on the eve of Knef's departure for Hollywood. Apart from commenting on the film's experimental dimension, the reviews were united in regretting her departure to America and in praising her performance 'as inhabiting the character': 'The departure of this young actress from Germany is a most painful loss for us' (*Neue Zeit*, Berlin, 25 January 1948). 'Hildegard Knef as Christine beautifully fulfils the promise of her great talent, she now really belongs to the "first rank" and we thus have to regret even more ... her departure. For everyone else one would think this an awkward role, but with her one doesn't even consider it a "role"' (Edith Hamann, *Kritik*, 7 February 1948). Following this praise, Knef was awarded the Best Actress prize at the 1948 International Film Festival in Locarno.

After her return from Hollywood, Knef's role in *Die Sünderin* as Marina the prostitute seems a radical departure from her previous typecasting, although there are, in fact, strong continuities in terms of sexual politics. Marina has survived the hardships of the war and the years after by becoming a prostitute, but when she falls in love with a painter, Alexander (Gustav Fröhlich), she takes care of him, nurturing him through his fear of impending blindness. Her love for him is so strong that she returns to selling her body to pay for his cure and when he finally loses his sight she first gives him the poison he has asked for and then commits suicide.

The film starts with Marina's outburst 'Oh my God, I've killed you!', and it is through a confessional voice-over, in which Knef's mellow, slightly husky monologue accompanies the images on the screen, that the film traces through a series of flashbacks her fall into prostitution and her subsequent redemption through love. Such a structure clearly draws on Hollywood *film noir* but with interesting variations: typically the film investigates female sexuality and the woman dies in the end; untypically, it is a woman's voice-over confession which initiates the flashback 'explaining' the killing; typically a 'Hollywood' *femme fatale* destroys the hero; untypically Marina only administers the fatal poison to fulfil her lover's request before sacrificing herself. More generally, unlike her earlier films, here Knef is visually eroticized in typical Hollywood fashion – the film starts and ends with a close-up of Marina's nude portrait. However, while her narrative *position* as prostitute and model justifies Knef's rendering as spectacle throughout the film, the voice-over and flashback narrative *structure*, privileging her point of view, works somewhat to counter this visual objectification.

Although *Die Sünderin* can be seen as mainly a star vehicle, it did offer scope for the actress as well, since she first has to play a gangly teenage girl who lets herself be seduced out of curiosity and then for material gain. She then portrays a sensual and glamorous prostitute, and finally a caring and practical mistress. Knef is convincing in all these personas: as a girl she makes her body look awkward, as a prostitute her movements are provocatively sexy in the way she sits and walks, and as mistress she is both sensual and domesticated.

In completing the move from actress to star, the beginning of the star persona is precisely located at the premiere of *Die Sünderin* (18 January 1951) which caused a scandal. Ostensibly this was because of Knef's discreetly brief nude scene, but implicitly it was the depiction of female sexuality asserted in exchange for material gain which upset the new pillars of society. After the unpoliced sexual mores of the war and the immediate post-war years the moral climate of the 1950s saw a reappearance of a puritanism that required a return to traditional gender values whereby women settled down again into marriage and motherhood. At a point when the ideological tide was turning, *Die Sünderin* was still negotiating the independent female and weak male character configuration associated with the war and after: 'Indeed, in its treatment of masculine and feminine roles, *Die Sünderin* can be read as an allegory of post-war gender relations' (Fehrenbach, 1995: 108). Prior to its release, the self-censorship board of the film industry had feared 'that the film skirts the borders of the acceptable' and wanted cuts, which Forst refused. On the film's release the churches (whose Catholic and Protestant representatives held official positions on the censorship board) spearheaded conservative institutional reaction by attacking it from their pulpits, inciting public protests and debate. (For an extensive discussion, see Fehrenbach, 1995, Chapters 3 and 4.)

A Protestant film commissioner, Werner Hess, lambasting the film for undermining the moral fabric of a still unsettled society, pleaded: 'Who will help prevent such spiritual murder of our young people and [our] women, tested by suffering, and our broken-bodied men?' (quoted in Fehrenbach, 1995: 93); while Cardinal Frings preached: 'I expect that [all Catholics] . . . in justified outrage will boycott the cinemas which misuse the name of art to corrupt the moral fibre of Christian folk' (cited by Prinzler, 1993: 537). Inevitably, thanks to this publicity, *Die Sünderin* became the most seen film of 1951 in West Germany.

Ever since the scandal Knef's name has been associated with the film. She claimed in her memoirs that the conservative majority of the public held her personally responsible for the 'immoral' meaning of the film:

> I had understood nothing. In my absence [in Hollywood] the years of moral rectitude had started to impose order and morality alongside the first glimmering signs of the economic miracle . . . I did not understand that currency reform, regular food, heated bedrooms and a return to twee chasteness meant ignoring, repressing and writing off the incomprehensibility of the past. The reaction to a nude girl, a brief screen moment, made me think that the majority of the outraged public had had a lobotomy to liberate them from the memory of the diabolical past. (Knef, 1970: 301)

It is significant that her potential star ability to play a role as if she embodied the character – her much praised naturalism – was now turned against her. Henceforth Knef evoked and even epitomized the sinner. At the time, Pommer declared that 'Never before had an actress been so identified with her role as in the case of [*Die Sünderin*] . . . In the end it was more a campaign against Knef than against the film' (quoted in *Der Spiegel*, No. 19, 7 May 1952).

Interestingly, despite all the public sensation and outrage generated by *Die Sünderin*, far beyond normal film circles, many film critics simply reviewed the film as an artefact and usually dismissed it as aesthetically heavy-handed. Knef is merely adjudged as an actress: 'possibly a fraction too austere and ponderous – more lover than sinner' (H. H. Kirst, *Der Neue Film*, Wiesbaden, 29 January 1951); 'remaining more a mask and only becomes humanized in the sentimental ending' (egw, *Stuttgarter Zeitung*, 24 February 1951); her type and her artistic ability 'breathes some life into the celluloid figure' (Margret Reich, *Frankfurter Allgemeine Zeitung*, 24 January 1951). Following the *succès de scandale* of *Die Sünderin*, however, the Knef star image had now extended far beyond accounts in film reviews and she was poised to become an international German star.[4] From this point her star biography became sensational, often serialized in the tabloids and weeklies with titles such as: 'Hildegard Knef: I'm Not a Sinner – How an Unknown Berlin Girl Became a World Star' (*Der Stern*, 1952); 'Hildegard Knef: The Path to World Stardom' (*Die Tage*, 1951?); 'Little Miss Nothing' (*Wochenende*, September 1952); 'The Natural Hunger for Life' (*Der Spiegel*, No. 19, 7 May 1952). Photos on- and offscreen document her 'rags to riches' development from German actress starting out in the rubble to the glamour of Hollywood, her return to Germany and to scandal, and finally making it as a Hollywood star: from German Knef to international Neff.

Die Sünderin marked the end of Knef's post-war roles of strong woman as redeemer of weak and dependent men, and she became an international star just when in Germany social roles for women were changing. Men now no longer felt contaminated by the past and were again taking control of building *the* future, while women, having worked towards rebuilding *a* future, were now required to make men (and family) again their sole purpose. In this context, changes and developments in Knef's roles and persona become significant. Whereas her star *image* had been as the 'rubble girl' until her return from Hollywood, the 'sinner' now became her counter star *persona*. Elaborating on the original image, the new persona was consolidated by her often wilful and outspoken star behaviour both abroad and on her return visits to Germany, and by her radical non-conformity in the face of the 1950s German 'nice' woman stereotype, refusing (in roles as much as in her private life) to submit to the demands of the dominant petit bourgeois sexual morality. Sex appeal was now the vital ingredient stabilizing her new international star persona: 'Through the films and their accompanying discourses emerges a second image of Knef, that is still in place today: the lascivious sinner as German embodiment of the "femme fatale"' (von Moltke and Wulf, 1997: 310).

Appropriations

> Hildegard Knef, whether she liked it or not, was always also 'Germany'; like all nations, Germany was caught in a strange yearning to see itself represented as a woman; but Hildegard Knef could not become what elsewhere Marilyn Monroe, Brigitte Bardot or Gina Lollobrigida were. Something was not quite right between Germany and this woman who from time to time had the courage to contradict. (Seeßlen, 1991: 18)

Knef's versatility ensured that she remained a star in the public eye, and in the 1980s German cultural critics started to re-evaluate her career from a feminist and film-historical perspective. Ursula Bessen (1989: 205) examines Knef's roles in these post-war films, arguing that although Susanne, Kat and Christine do not offer a 'physically realistic resemblance to the rubble woman's appearance, she nevertheless embodies their characteristics and qualities'. She claims that Knef's playing of these sexually assertive and practical female protagonists made her a very different star from either the stylized glamorous Nazi divas (*ibid.*: 204) or the 1950s German female star typecasting of 'young lady, companionable fiancée, or motherly wife' (*ibid.*: 225). What is implicit in this appropriation of Knef's star image is a wider recognition by feminists that even though the rubble women were coerced back into traditional feminine roles, their feminist daughters could still reclaim both their strength and their independence from the war experience which had irrevocably morally tainted the men, their fathers. (See also Chapter 6.) Although Knef's immediate post-war roles are discussed, to refigure her as a feminist prototype also required a grafting of her 1950s star persona onto that of the rubble woman. She thus becomes an embodiment of the resilient feisty survivor who had not been contained by the resurgent patriarchal ideology.

The feminist film-maker Helma Sanders-Brahms, in a short homage to Knef,[5] also finds it necessary to refer to her rebellious 1950s star persona in order retrospectively to glamorize the practical determination of the rubble women with the sex appeal of the 'sinner': 'She was so beautiful, so provoking, so German. . . . She was very different from all the provincial cherubs who the audiences of the Adenauer era approved of' (Sanders-Brahms, 1985: 228). Similar sentiments inform Georg Seeßlen's (1991: 16) critical portait: 'The first star of German post-war films is also a rudimentary utopian image of a new woman . . .'. In short, the image of the redeemer of tainted masculinity in itself was not sufficient as a feminist role model.

Even more pervasive than a feminist inflection is Knef's discursive reconstruction as national (West German) icon: 'Like a phoenix she emerges from the ashes of the German film industry' (Christa Bandmann, 1979, cited by von Moltke and Wulf, 1997: 314). Although oversimplified, this metaphor of Knef's career being forged out of the ruins of Germany implies the recurring trope in discourses about her stardom. In most of the appraisals and biographies the origin of the making of Knef's reputation is constructed as being synchronous with the establishment of post-war Germany. The hour zero of the nation, 8–9 May 1945, required a new face and a new talent, an untainted figure to signify the future:

> Knef was then a product of that time, with her arrived the war and post-war landscape onto the screen: night-bombings, ruined towns, hunger, coldness, blackmarket. She appeared as a symbol of a betrayed youth, who nevertheless did not give in. (Heinzelmeier, 1980: 113)

Asked in an interview 'whether she believes that she embodied the post-war woman' (Bessen, 1989: 232), Knef replied:

> Well, I would say more the post-war girl. I was not yet twenty . . . And I had experienced an incredible lot . . . and perhaps because of this I had a different face and was a different type – neither the careless youngster, nor the so-called typical young lover. We no longer had an image of them, they were lost to us amongst the bombs and guns.

Marked by these war experiences she seemed to be eminently suitable as an embodiment of the nation's desire to clear up the mess of the past: unfussy and energetic, in these films of the immediate post-war years she represented the new type who takes control of the situation. (See also Chapter 6.)

Although Knef's emblematic star function seems just too neat and convenient to be taken at face value, empirical research does reveal, as noted above, that these meanings were already latent in some of the contemporary reviews (especially those for *Film ohne Titel*), which regularly commented on how she 'inhabited' rather than played a role. However, although during the immediate post-war period her natural performance style, conjoined with the contemporary relevant roles she played, did seem to authenticate the experience of women at the time, the explicit national-symbolic conception of her is a more recent construction from the vantage point of the 1980s onwards.

Von Moltke and Wulf (1997: 308) recognize this fact and the tensions it gives rise to. They perceive Knef's redemption of war-damaged masculinity as crucial to the construction of her as national icon, but they also acknowledge that the construction will always be a difficult one and subject to contestation: 'Her image carries from the very beginning the burden of national symbolization: in a continual balance between high representational power and distanciation Knef is identified with historically different versions of Germanness.' In the construction of a national icon as opposed to a feminist one, different strategies of retrospective appropriation begin to emerge. While for feminists it was necessary to read back the rebellion of the 'sinner' in the sacrifice of the 'rubble girl', for constructors of a national icon it is Knef as rubble woman who unproblematically represents German history. For them the 'sinner' retrospectively invokes a repressed aspect of the war, that many women survived through fraternization with soldiers and prostitution.

Historicizing Knef

Both feminist and national cultural appropriations of the star are, perhaps inevitably, shaped by preoccupations of the 1980s and 1990s. Valuable as these are, by ignoring the different stages in the growth of the star image and persona they tend to ignore what meanings were available when. At this point, establishing the star persona chronologically becomes important particularly since, as Carter argues via Modleski, 'ahistorical temporality . . . is typical of classical cinematic representations of femininity' (see p. 100). Contemporary with the films' original exhibition was a concentration on the acceptable dimension of women's (i.e. Knef's) experiences surviving among the ruins – as depicted by Susanne, Christine and Kat – which was then challenged in the 1950s by the figure of Marina. Out of these two images grew the complex

German/international, resilient/sexy star persona of the later 1950s and 1960s. It was not until 1970 that the revelation in her autobiography of more compromised aspects of her past prompted a return to her wartime origins.

The book's publication was coterminous with a more general *Vergangenheitsbewältigung* of the Germans. Like so many others of her generation Knef had kept some of her wartime experiences secret, but in the autobiography she is remarkably frank about her love affair with a Nazi film official close to Goebbels, Ewald von Demandowsky (head of Tobis Production), alongside whom she fought when he was drafted (Knef, 1970: Chapters 8 and 9).

> I thought the time was right, twenty-five years after the war, to write what it was like to live as a child [*sic*] in Nazi Germany during and after the war. *How do you live with the collective guilt that you have totally accepted but that you also resent because you do not feel guilty*. (Interview with Catherine Stott, *Guardian*, 29 September 1971 [my emphasis]).

In the national 1970s context of West Germans finally confronting their past – accepting collective guilt but not really individual guilt – her experiences carried powerful social resonances for her contemporaries, and the fit that made her their star was very close. For them her youth was clearly a redeeming factor when assigning guilt. A counter reading, of course, is also available. Like her generation, Knef was inevitably shaped by the Nazi ideology and even though she intended her memoirs to demolish prejudices and intolerance, she effectively plays down the horrors of National Socialism while blatantly promoting anti-communist sentiments – a facet of her persona largely ignored, particularly in the feminist reappropriations.

Finally, whatever reading one makes of the life, what is crucial to note is that, as with any star, it is not just the roles but also the actions and events of Knef's life during this period that are available for reconstruction. Thus, a symbolic post-war (West) German history needs to consider not just the star image in the films, nor just the sensations of the life, it must also connect the persona with the context. As a first step in this direction it could be profitable to think through the tensions she might be seen to incarnate: how working across the different Allied sectors could be seen as paralleling the division of Germany, or what purchase on understanding a troubled national symbolic is offered when an American Jew replaces a Nazi lover, when National Socialist ideology gives way to American capitalism. Knef had an affair with a Nazi during the last months of the war and married an American Jew in 1947. To return to our starting point in cinema, even the unproductive contract with Hollywood might symbolically imply the national contract between the German film industry and Hollywood, whereby power is wholly on the side of Hollywood, while Germany waits and hopes for success once the rules are understood.

Conclusion

Through a consideration of her biography, contemporary reviews of the films she made between 1945 and 1951 and subsequent appropriations of her star image and persona I have tried to show how the star persona of Hildegard Knef – textually and extra-textually – reveals the intertwining of roles and 'real' person, of public and private history. This interface characterizes the social function and the historical relevance of many other stars, but Knef is probably exceptional in the way her persona so readily offers itself up for emblematic status. Decisive moments and encounters in her roles and life can be seen retrospectively to reflect, mesh with and comment on public history, 'As if she was a piece of the Republic' (Gerhard Rohde, *Frankfurter Allgemeine Zeitung*, 28 December 1985).

Acknowledgements

Thanks to Renate Bleistein, librarian at the Deutsches Filmmuseum (Frankfurt am Main) and to Hanni Forman for sending me a wonderful selection of books. Thanks as well to Erica Carter and Martin Shingler for their helpful comments. Finally, thanks to Jim Cook for invaluable help. His editorial comments contributed significantly to clarifying my ideas and to shaping this essay.

Notes

1. I use the term 'emblematic' in the sense of expressing or suggesting something socio-historically concrete, and as such distinct from the more abstract quality of symbolic representation.
2. A revealing anecdote refers to the casting of Christine in *Film ohne Titel*. A British film officer initially had suggested Kristina Söderbaum – the former Nazi Ufa diva and wife of the much-compromised director, Veit Harlan – for this role (Jary, 1993: 43).
3. Horst Axelmann, newspaper name and date missing. See microfiche archive at the Frankfurt Film Museum.
4. While still shooting *Die Sünderin* Fox signed Knef for a major role in Anatole Litvak's *Decision before Dawn* (1951). Interestingly, the filming of *Decision before Dawn*, which took place in Germany, coincided with the scandal of *Die Sünderin*. Thus, Hollywood reclaimed Knef just prior to the public outrage, and it is her performance in *Decision before Dawn* which led to other Hollywood films and launched her career as an international film star.

5. Knef featured in her film *Flügel und Fesseln/The Future of Emily* (1984–5). In some sense this is an emblematic film about generational conflict between the mother (Knef) and the daughter (Brigitte Fossey). The mother is frustrated at having missed out on life because of the war, and she turns against her sexually liberated daughter accusing her of having stolen her life.

Filmography

Film ohne Titel (Rudolf Jugert, 1947–8, Camera-Film, Hamburg)
Die Mörder sind unter uns (Wolfgang Staudte, 1946, DEFA, Berlin)
Die Sünderin (Willi Forst, 1951, Deutsche Styria Film)
Zwischen Gestern und Morgen (Harald Braun, 1947, Neue Deutsche Film Gesellschaft, Munich)

Italy

CHAPTER EIGHT

What about Women? Italian Films and Their Concerns

LESLEY CALDWELL

Introduction

Massive political and social upheaval followed the collapse of fascism in 1943 and exacerbated the severe internal chaos produced by the continuing war being fought on Italian territory. An armistice with the Allies had been signed, but a war of liberation which stressed national unity continued after the liberation of the north in April 1945. These events all contributed to shaping post-war Italy, where the first general elections took place in 1948. Despite the claims for the republic as a new Italian nation, offering a new place for women, there were many continuities between the old regime and the liberal democracy, not least in ideas and policies about women and the family.

The films associated with neo-realism were also associated with the new nation and its aspirations, and there seemed to be a distinctively different ethos from that of the preceding era. But there were also significant links with the film industry under the fascists. A questioning of the dominant themes and propaganda of the fascist period had already made an apppearance in some films which predated the end of the war: *Quattro passi fra le nuvole/A Walk among the Clouds* (Alessandro Blasetti, 1942), *I bambini ci guardano/The Children Are Watching Us* (Vittorio De Sica, 1942) and *Ossessione/Obsession* (Luchino Visconti, 1942) all disrupted the unquestioned conflation of women with motherhood and family that was to be found in the policies and statements of fascism.

When it comes to the representation of women in the films of 1945–51, any methodological approaches prioritizing a coherent set of ideological concerns should be treated cautiously. For the most part, the films extended, to a certain extent, the range of women represented, but, in doing so, they drew uncritically upon familiar stereotypes. Moreover, the sheer variety of films with women characters, the roles those characters assume in the narratives and the concerns of the film-makers all militate against claims for any homogeneity of approach.

However, an apparently different range of images where women embodied various feminine possibilities not available previously can be discerned in some films, and since the system of film production itself contributes to the circulation and dissemination of definitions and ideas about women, these were important. On the whole they tended to be associated with particular stars, as in the case of Anna Magnani (see Chapter 9), or they sought to 'Italianize' a kind of heroine familiar through socialist-realist iconography. The extent to which such roles could be understoood as assisting in the project of nation-building and national unity characteristic of the immmediate post-war period is uncertain, but the presentation of a range of popular female figures undoubtedly participated in and contributed to a more general leftist cultural climate.

Shifts and developments are apparent in the films discussed here, not only between the immediate pre-war precedents and neo-realist films but also, more significantly, among the post-war examples. These developments probably owe less to any explicit interest in national preoccupations about the roles between the sexes and rather more to the personal and film-making concerns of their directors. Such concerns registered a continual development throughout the period and were instrumental in establishing a very different terrain of investigation for films of this kind into the 1950s and beyond.

The number of films referred to precludes any really detailed study, but in outlining three films from the last years of fascism, and four post-war examples where women feature in different ways, it is possible to identify a more active, autonomous role for women in the films that were made after 1945. In addressing themes directly at odds with the dominant emphases of the fascist regime and of Catholic accounts – problems of adultery, illegitimacy, heterosexual dilemmas and homosexual desire – the three earlier films questioned the values and aspirations of both fascism and Catholicism. But, with the exception of the woman's desire in *Ossessione*, their accounts of femininity remained conventional and limited. The films of Blasetti and De Sica, *Quattro passi* and *I bambini ci guardano*, explored issues with social and familial, sexual and personal implications, but they were only indirectly concerned with women.

The most noted films of the years 1945 to 1951 are those associated with neo-realism and the films discussed here form part of that committed film-making. Neo-realism occupies a place of undisputed centrality in the history of cinema, but, since only about 5 per cent of the output of Italian production was constituted by films described as neo-realist in the years from 1945 to 1954, they were neither widely circulated in Italy nor, usually, great box-office successes. Seen in terms of the overall output of the time, their contribution to a cultural concern with explicit accounts of femininity (were there to have been one) would anyway have been very limited. Nonetheless, their cinematic significance was, and is, widely recognized.

Through its commitment to the depiction, often in a documentarist and collectivist mode, of the social reality of 'the people', neo-realism apparently marginalized any overtly individual focus. However, the societal thematic of neo-realism was one which emphasized Italian family life as the refuge through which 'the people' sought to gain support in the face of a largely uncaring and uncomprehending society. By taking for granted some of the strongest cultural assumptions about Italian life and its familial base, the films of neo-realism re-emphasized those very values. An account of women was indirectly implicated in this, since the uneasy fit between women's family roles and their problematic social status was confirmed and endorsed in these representations. The writer Fortini justly described the overt concern with 'the people' that dominated discourse – political, cultural and artistic – of the time as residing in that term's easy alignment with ideas of nation, and its avoidance of the more specific associations of 'class' (quoted in Ferrero, 1978: 242). Since 'the people' is a non-gendered category, it also acted to efface the differences between men and women, presenting them as united in the general project of nation-building. Despite the moves to produce a society based on more equality between the sexes, the Italy of 1945–51, its films, its film-makers and its politicians, were deeply rooted in conventional assumptions about the differences between men and women.

The legislative position of women in the new nation was one that sought to endorse their rights as citizens, while insisting that motherhood was still their major contribution to the building of the new collectivity, a nation united. A generalized rhetorical appeal to all women was the norm; its basis, supported by the cultural traditions that reinforced the links between the biological and the social, was still the capacity to reproduce. At the level of the image, it is less clear how a general project aimed at harnessing particular images of femininity to ideas of the republic and a new identity for Italians could be argued for in the films of the time. The signification of woman particularly relates to sexual difference and desire. In romance and fantasy, the basis of most narrative cinema, motherhood and the family usually represent the attempted resolution of the disruption occasioned by desire. All the post-war films referred to here feature childless women, most of them seeking love, so that a major discursive arena aimed at incorporating women into an explicitly national agenda was absent. If an appeal to national identity registered significantly in the depictions of femininity available in these years, it was one whose force lay in its association with ideas of 'the people' and the denial of difference embodied in that term's attempted universalism.

Four films dating from 1946 to 1950 are discussed to illustrate these points. The first two, most clearly neo-realist, *Paisà* (Roberto Rossellini, 1946) and *Riso amaro/Bitter Rice* (Giuseppe De Santis, 1947), may draw upon cinematic female stereotypes, but they also assign a qualitatively different place to their women characters. Despite their association with the sentiments in *Paisà*, and their centrality as eroticized objects in *Riso amaro*, women in these films are protagonists who work, who desire and who act. By 1949, Rossellini had further extended his cinematic concerns. In *Stromboli* (1949) he was engaged in a kind of film-making whose techniques, themes and approaches are distinctively modern. What was dismissed as a shift towards the individual and an abandonment of the more collective social issues of *Paisà* was also a continuation of some of the structural and technical issues that had shaped the earlier films.

In both *Stromboli* and in Michelangelo Antonioni's first full-length film, *Cronaca di un amore/Story of a Love Affair* (1950), the modern theme of the couple in difficulties is approached with a psychological awareness absent from the great films of the immediate post-Liberation period, and through a concentration on the woman character. In these films the female characters have a certain autonomy of interest in their own right.

For Rossellini, a combination of personal and cinematic interests, for Antonioni, his interest in formal, technical problems and in the mental states of his characters – both as they appear in the *mise-en-scène* and through the relations between them – were instrumental in producing this more complexly articulated image. The shift is one that occurs through the attention to interiority and its representation via what happens between and within the characters, in the elaboration of the space within the shot, and through the relations of the one with the other. Through these essentially cinematic concerns, women come to signify in a different way, one which emphasized an examination of the problems of more egalitarian roles between women and men. These films abandon any gesture towards collective, societal emphases or any account of national reconstruction. Rather they concentrate upon issues whose relevance to the future existence of Italy depended less upon the familiar rhetorics of 'family as nation' that fascism had also sought to further and more upon a different, more modern problem, that of desire and its fate in a world beginning to be organized upon less traditional assumptions. In this investigation, the very form of film itself prioritized and embodied the differences.

The early 1940s

In their attention to a social reality which exposes, as unequal to the tasks rhetorically demanded of them, the families of those classes traditionally seen as most strongly supportive of fascism, *Quattro passi* and *I bambini* propose a tentative investigation of the problems of marriage and familial difficulty. The family provided a basis for the films' narratives, but no sustained account of it was really developed. *Ossessione*, Visconti's first great film, an overt and generalized challenge to Catholicism and to fascism, was withdrawn. A tale of destructive adulterous passion and murder adapted from James Cain's novel, *The Postman Always Rings Twice*, in this case it is a woman, Gina (Clara Calamai), whose explicit interest in Gino (Massimo Girotti), a casual passer-by who stays on at the roadside café run by her and her husband, that, unusually, initiates the narrative. All three films make for a tentative questioning of a cultural climate, potentially illuminating a shifting terrain around the place of women and of familial identifications in a society devastated by war, and emerging from a twenty-year regime whose policies were of the most restrictive kind.

In *Quattro passi* two pillars of fascist rhetoric and policy, the family and the countryside, are exposed as inadequate to bear the cultural weight they were called upon to sustain. *Quattro passi* is the story of a country girl led astray by a man from the city. On the bus home to confess her pregnant state to her peasant family, she meets a travelling salesman in chocolates, whose own strained home life has been recorded in the film's opening shots. She persuades him to come home as her husband for the day. At first incredulous, he then agrees; when, inevitably, he is exposed as an impostor by her brother and father, he acknowledges it with dignity, and then makes an argument for their correct treatment of the girl. The film includes a good-humoured fantasy pastiche of country life and its pleasurable effects upon a man from the city. The family's responses to the daughter's situation and the city man's place in effecting a resolution present a study in the position of fathers, of men from the city, and of the future of the Italian family and its female members.

I bambini ci guardano exposes the place of the child in a society supposedly organized round children. Prico first witnesses his mother's affair, then, when she leaves, he is passed from one unwelcoming family situation to another. A visit to his tyrannical grandmother makes him ill and his mother returns, but during a holiday when the lover reapppears the child runs away to his father, who first consigns Prico to boarding school, then kills himself. The child refuses to see his mother. Like his later *Ladri di biciclette/Bicycle Thieves* (1948), De Sica's film ascribes considerable importance to the point of view of the child.

In Visconti's *Ossessione*, an unemployed wanderer and the wife of a roadside cafe proprietor become passionately involved and plan the murder of her husband. The adulterous plot is further complicated by the homosexual subtext and a privileging of the male (gay) character as the exemplar of real feelings in the film. *Ossessione* was exceptional in its approach to film-making, in its imagery and in its choice of themes, which offended both in their eroticism and in the account of the deprived lives of ordinary Italians. Gina, having begun the train of events through her desire for Gino, is quickly reduced to a less interesting character, as passion is subsumed into petit bourgeois aspiration, carping domesticity and an avarice whose roots in poverty and deprivation provide both the rationalization for her failure and a condemnation of fascism. The husband's murder is followed by the death of the wife as the lovers flee from the scene of the crime.

It is clear from these brief synopses that these films engage a range of issues beyond the boundaries of the ideal family, and of women as, first and foremost, wives and mothers. Whether originating in comedy or melodrama, they represent aspects of Italian society at odds with official accounts. They expose the crisis in the family, but their major challenge is to paternal authority. *I bambini* has been accused of vilifying the mother (Cannella, 1966), but, although her negative presence is telling, the film is not really a study of the place of the mother.

While these films address the personal, familial and emotional thematically, their treatment of them primarily refers to a socially weighted area where women are comparatively insignificant. For De Sica, the focus is really on the child; for Blasetti, the genre itself counters any in-depth appraisal; and *Ossessione* remains a powerful examination of passion and its devastating effects for both women and men, notwithstanding the limits of the woman character and the way her wishes seem to lead to general destruction.

These films are cultural records of the social difficulties of the last years of fascism and provide a background to the first years of the republic. Their versions of femininity are restricted, not only in the accounts of the women themselves but also, in their placing of the emphasis elsewhere, they effectively failed to recognize some of the contributing factors in the issues they do address.

Neo-realism

Politically and ideologically neo-realism is linked with the liberation movements, with post-war reconstruction, with anti-fascism and with the establishment of a democratic Italy. Cinematically it is a development from the cinema industry under the fascists. From the 1930s there had been debate, not only among government propagandists but more especially among committed film-makers, about how the cinema could deliver a specifically Italian vision. It was from this context that these films, and neo-realism itself, arose. With its foundations in accounts of ordinary Italians, its commitment to naturalism as realism, its vivid use of location and landscape, its investment in the capacity of the cinema to deliver a form of truth, one which it is argued emerges through the representation either of an ethico-morality or a socio-political one, neo-realism marks a high point in the history of world cinema. Discourses about neo-realism have also formed part of a cultural consolidation of ideas about the Resistance and Liberation, ideas whose emotional claims upon the understanding of modern Italy have been extremely significant.

To raise the issues of naturalism and realism in the Italy of that time, to mention the use of the landscape and the influence of other film-making traditions, to point to the apparent dismissal of other genres, especially melodramas, in the concern with realism and the fidelity of the documentary lens was not only to describe the features of what became known as neo-realism but also underlined the links between cultural and aesthetic debates, and their political affiliation. After the war these emphases became predominantly identified with the workers' movement, but they originated earlier. In a presentation forming part of the retrospective, *Before Neo-Realism: Italian Cinema 1929–1944*, at the Museum of Modern Art in New York, Aprà and Pistagnesi (1978: 3) argued:

> practically everyone involved in the neo-realist movement was formed within the fascist orbit, the film industry, apart from damages from the war, remained, (built up by Freddi and the general cinema direction since 1934), and neo-realism owes a large debt to the professionalism that developed in these industrial structures . . . some of the themes around which the poetics of neo-realism developed had precedents in the thirties. The taken-from-life aesthetic, documentarism, the realism of everyday life, the demand coming from several quarters for a 'committed', anti-escapist cinema, tied to political themes of the moment – fascist themes naturally. This way of understanding the political cinema, as opposed to the genre cinema, as a cinema of present-day events, was supported also by the so-called left-wing fascists, who were more interested in real social problems than in a sterile glorification of the regime. One can see in this left-wing fascism the origins of the group of radicals gathered round the journal *Cinema* (De Santis, Puccini, Pietrangeli, Visconti, Lizzani, Mida, etc.).

Neo-realism's concern was 'reality', variously interpreted, but generally presenting a concentration on and depiction of ordinary Italians, and incorporating a populist reading of class. Rossellini, De Sica and Visconti attempted to record the reality of the people in the aftermath of war and fascism. They chose themes that reflected a social urgency, where the family and its centrality was assumed and where the concentration on real people in real situations, on ordinary Italians, men or women, and their dilemmas, largely evaded intra-familial drama.

Though the presence of the child, and what is elicited in the representation of children, remained De Sica's focus, the relation between father and son developed in an ostensibly more social environment in *Ladri di biciclette*. The loss of the father's bicycle and their shared search for it through the streets of Rome is organized around the strength of the relationship between father and son, and the father's renewed awareness of it. This, rather than any real social critique, forms the basis, an emotional basis, of the film. In opting for a focus on the relation between father and son, De Sica bypasses the personal relations of husband and wife. Criticism may be externalized vaguely onto a society where family subsistence is dependent upon the bike, and where social reality is wanting and brutal, but the personal relation of father and son is presented as the basis of endurance and continuity. As with many of the films of the period, a private and personal resolution of social issues was preferred. Commentators have argued that the use of the child in neo-realism further substantiates its tendency to record injustice and its inability to move beyond it, thus confirming a quality of passivity and helplessness (Kolker, 1983; Deleuze, 1989). The majority of children in these films are children without parents, who, lacking the ordinary indicators of childhood, reveal an Italy without its usual points of reference. But it is also the child who, through the capacity to evoke an excess of emotionality, is deployed as the register of national hopes and a possible future.

Paisà (1946) and _Stromboli_ (1949)

Rossellini cast women as central protagonists in three of the six episodes of *Paisà*, a film whose humanitarian depiction of the reality of Italy, of war and its results makes it a serious anti-war film. It is all the more impressive for its distanced view of its characters and their difficulties, framed through Rossellini's account of the difficulties of Italy itself.

The six episodes begin in Sicily and move upwards to the valley of the Po, a journey from one end of the peninsula to another which has been repeated or travelled in reverse through many later Italian film journeys. In the first episode, Carmela, a young uneducated Sicilian, agrees to guide some American soldiers; she leaves the village with them, already an indication of some independence in those years. When she is then left alone with Joe from New Jersey, the film records their attempts to find ways of communicating without a common language. When Joe shows her a photograph of his sister, she seems dismayed; lighting a match to reveal the likeness to himself, he is spotted by the Germans and shot. Carmela avenges him by shooting a German, thereby drawing attention to herself. When the Americans return they assume she has killed Joe. But the camera takes in the cliffs, revealing to the spectator the dead body of Carmela at their base. This sequence is one where Rossellini movingly juxtaposes the massive images of cliffs and sea with the frailty of the devastated body of the young Sicilian, and of human beings in general. Although, in the film's terms, her death might be anticipated as the inevitable consequence of her action, Carmela's fierce response to the Germans would seem to confirm the real human contact that had been forged between her and the American, and to display a hatred of his killers, who, in turn, have insulted and threatened her.

Bondanella (1993: 67) reports that Rossellini found this young woman on the road near Naples, and her presence carries both a primitiveness and an eroticism often linked to the south. In his book on Rossellini, Brunette draws attention to this quality of the corporeal that Carmela's body promotes; he repeats the response of another American male critic, Robert Warshow, to her body: 'to an American eye almost repellent in its lack of physical charms and at the same time disturbing in its persistent suggestion that charm is irrelevant'(quoted in Brunette, 1987: 73). Brunette adds:

> When the male spectator is confronted with what seems to be a real woman, an unglamorous non-professional, a subliminal sense of risk is at some level reestablished. The very presence of the girl – slovenly and directly sensual in a way no real actress would ever chance – gives an edge to her encounter with Joe that makes the film seem bracingly out of control. (*ibid.*)

Brunette quotes the feminist critic, Dalle Vacche as, like him, seeing Carmela as the symbolic representative of Italy, crushed by invaders of every kind, 'her body serves as a site of reconciliation between region and nation'(*ibid.*).

Dalle Vacche herself dismisses as trite Rossellini's equation of women, or the woman's body, with the land (*ibid.*: 199). But the traditions that Rossellini exploits in constructing this equivalence between women, the land and the nation have different, extensive iconographic and cultural histories. Not only is there the resonant traditional association of the landscape with mother and child in Italian painting but also the more persistent connotations of fertility, nature and origins with the Mediterranean, and with women and women's bodies, all associations that have a firm place in the European imagination. Speaking of Rossellini, Adriano Aprà (1978: 296) says: 'Woman heralds the future through her physical, earthy presence; something that comes from her identification with the origin of all, with mother earth and the motherland.' Fascism, and Blasetti in particular, in his earlier movies, *Sole/Sun* (1929) and *Terra madre/Mother Earth* (1931), had emphasized the land as a signifier of traditional Italian values, the container of its civilization. This, therefore, is a theme that partakes of a complex and continuing history, one enmeshed in ideas of Italy that preceded fascism but were revitalized by it.

Rossellini's use of the three women, Carmela, Francesca (the woman at the centre of the Roman episode) and Harriet (the protagonist of the fourth episode set in Florence) is interesting. His choice of these very different women as the protagonists of half of the episodes implies that the results of war and of national reconstruction are the shared concern of women and men, despite the hackneyed recourse to the prostitute employed in the Roman sequence. Francesca, after earlier meeting and falling in love with an American, has been forced into prostitution. When her former lover later pays for her services, but fails to recognize her, she gives him her address. In the morning, he throws it away, dismissing it as the address of a whore. Harriet, an American woman, pursues her search for her partisan lover across the front lines of the streets of Florence, only to discover the news of his death from another partisan, as he himself dies in her arms. Brunette (1987: 66) devotes some time to these rather different women, describing them all as 'passive creatures, those upon whom history acts and those therefore who history makes to suffer'. He links what he describes as their acting impulsively and without political opinions – 'acting solely from what their nature tells them' – to his reading of Rossellini's association of women with passion: 'Rossellini clearly admires these gestures which he sees as manifestations of a direct intuitive naturalness' (*ibid.*: 66). But Brunette's own associations of some essential femininity with impulsive action and intuition are countered by the narrative centrality and the cinematic importance ascribed to these women. Nor are melodramatic events confined to the episodes with women. Aprà (1978: 296) suggests, more carefully, that while it may be women who feel in Rossellini, their feeling and suffering is limited to their announcing and signalling a future that will be carried forward by men. These assessments draw upon a sort of 'women who feel/men who act' dichotomy, which is also attributed to Rossellini, but, in this instance, the passionate account of the devastation of war which is produced by the distant, recording camera seems to extend beyond such divisions.

Issues of men and women indirectly provide one sort of focus for the more general themes of *Paisà*. But Italy itself, and the encounters between various others brought together by war on Italian soil and the encounters between different Italys carry this film to greatness. Through the use of women, men, children and a series of invaders, whether allies or enemies, set in a changing landscape, Rossellini made visible the Italy of regional differences which has become such a central consideration in contemporary thought. The results of war and its ending, the reality of life and death, in the present and in the future, are represented in this film, and women assume their place in these universals.

In the Rossellini films starring Anna Magnani (see Chapter 9) that follow *Paisà* the focus is individualizing and internal, a focus which is further developed in *Stromboli* where the woman and the island are its centre. In *Stromboli*, Karin (Ingrid Bergman), an educated woman, meets a southerner in a refugee camp and marries him to escape, returning with him to his island home. There, overshadowed by the volcano of the title, the different worlds of the two, husband and wife, of the islanders and the foreigner are shot by Rossellini with enormous sympathy, particularly for the woman. Karin's incomprehension and isolation, her difference, is contrasted with her fisherman husband, the other women and almost everyone else on the island. But beyond this, Rossellini raises the very real possibility that, for someone who comes from outside, the life of *Stromboli* is unrecognizable. Until the quasi-religious experience of Karin's encounter with nature on the slopes of the volcano, the barren landscape and the values of its inhabitants are filmed as irremediably other to the woman, while recognizable and real to the camera. This study of difference and its parameters is registered through the joint attention to Karin's point of view and the recording of the dimensions of the island and the life of its inhabitants.

The film is organized round a cultural commonplace, namely the primitiveness of the south as seen through the eyes of an outsider, a Lithuanian (though it could equally have been a northern Italian). The national repertoire of associations made available and explored here was continued in *Viaggio in Italia/Voyage to Italy* (1953), another examination of the alienated couple. As in this later film, it is the south, through its status as other, an otherness most powerfully evoked through the volcano itself, that produces a catharsis for Karin. Speaking of *Stromboli*, Rossellini (1973: 76) describes the Bergman character as 'brutalised by war, turned ruthless'. Elsewhere he says, 'The only hope for Karin is to have a human attitude towards something, at least once', and, again:

> A woman has undergone the trials of the war, she comes out of it bruised and hardened, no longer knowing what a human feeling is. The important thing was to find out if this woman could still cry, and the film stops there, when the first tears begin to flow. (Rossellini, quoted in Brunette, 1987: 126)

Rossellini's films in these years contain a strong sense of a personal trajectory, but their filmic interest, combined with his intense engagement with these women, resulted in a personal vision rendered general through its resort to a nationally inflected image repertoire. The films with Anna Magnani and with Ingrid Bergman concern him, them and a particular approach to film-making. Textually this lends itself to the presence of a woman whose selfhood is not in doubt, produced through Rossellini's mastery of cinematic codes. While it may be true that some of the aspects allied with femininity in these films work within obvious stereotypes, most notably in their capacity for an emotionalism absent in the men, this acts less to reduce the women to figures of inauthenticity than to capture an incomprehension and a lack on the part of the male characters. In an emotionality whose melodrama resonates not only with the south but with a more diffused sense of Italy, the excess offered by the characters played by Magnani and Bergman is not easily dismissable, precisely because it is confirmed, acknowledged and validated through the *mise-en-scène*.

Riso amaro (1948)

De Santis offers a very different reading from Rossellini of the place of women and femininity in the new Italy, one whose stirring portrayal of 'the people' in the female labour force of the rice workers also identifies a particular class group. In the 1946–51 period the number of women active in the labour force fell by 41 per cent, while the decline for men was 13 per cent, and, by 1951, women made up a quarter of the workforce. They continued, however, to be employed in seasonal labour, a practice that conceals high levels of under-employment. *Riso amaro* focuses on the rice workers of the Po valley. The women workers and the rice fields themselves are the main protagonists in a story organized around the competition between two women for a man. Walter (Vittorio Gassman) leaves his girlfriend, Francesca (Doris Dowling), for Silvana (Silvana Mangano) who, although one of the official workers, is continually set apart from them in the film by her actions. Her own desires have set her apart, but this is sustained through the camera work, which, rather than filming her working with the others, continually isolates her; she is to be looked at, but, even more, she is *seeking* to be looked at. Silvana is consumed by the pleasures of popular culture and of all things American, and these divert her from the workers' common struggle. Walter uses her to help him steal the rice harvest which would deprive the women of payment for their labour. In a subsidiary plot he has also misled her into believing a necklace he has given her is valuable. When Silvana discovers his deception she kills him and jumps to her death. Francesca, who has become a scab worker in the rice harvest with Silvana's ex-boyfriend, Marco, saves the rice crop; the rice workers then throw a handful of their hard-earned rice on Silvana's coffin, a moving gesture of solidarity after their betrayal.

A 1948 review of *Riso amaro* in the Communist newspaper, *l'Unità*, asserted that 'It is in the healthy men and women – mothers, wives, husbands, sons, who fight for their daily bread that truth appears the richest.' In the combination of elements that De Santis utilizes, the film produces a similar kind of emotional rhetoric, through its own deployment of the melodrama which was often condemned as the opposite of realism. Speaking of the film in 1948, De Santis himself said, 'I like to immerse myself in the tradition, express the current aspirations of the people through its tradition; besides, all of us from time to time happen to rediscover the Italian tradition of melodrama' (quoted in Aldgate, 1990: 37–8).

But *Riso amaro* also draws upon American popular cultural forms, intertwining them with the Italian in the life and landscape of the rice fields. The camera lingers over the massed bodies of the women workers, up to their knees in water, or lying on their dormitory beds, all the time individualizing the sexiness of one particular body, that of Silvana. De Santis thus produces a bodily eroticism that gathers together collective solidarity and individualized sexuality in a narrative of love, sex, money and crime, themes of the American cinema, represented in a *mise-en-scène* dominated by the landscape of the Po. In one particularly impressive sequence the women, forbidden to talk while they work, sing of the competition for labour between the official workers and the scabs. At the same time, another competition is being enacted between Silvana, who has taken to the bosses' cart to distribute the plants, and is displayed there, apart from and above her fellow workers, and Francesca, working with the others, who, through Silvana's incitement, becomes the first focus of attack. A fight then extends to all the women, before they finally make common cause against the bosses. In this sequence, as in many in this film, a proliferation of women's bodies is used diversely, in pursuit of different textual strategies. The individualized body, that of Silvana, is glamorized and produced as spectacle on the model of the Hollywood star. Martini and Melani (1978: 308) describe her thus: 'a worker or a peasant as beautiful, sensual, and perverse as Silvana Mangano is closer to a fantasy image of the harem than an actual, real character'. She is contrasted with the massed bodies of the workers, working and fighting. But if one emotional Italian connotation is collective solidarity, inscribed through the iconographical tradition of the heroic workers of socialist realism, this collective solidarity is also eroticized and spectacularized, with more than a nod in the direction of Busby Berkeley.

The female body, then, above all inscribed in the landscape, whether individualized or en masse, provides the visual centre of the film. Women as workers may be central to De Santis's account of the new Italy, but these are workers whose appeal derives from the transposition of the Hollywood musical to the northern rice fields, its conventions Italianized through the national associations which draw on the long traditions mentioned earlier. *Riso amaro* reiterates the placing of the human figure, especially in female form, in a succession of landscapes throughout Italian cinema both before and since (Grignaffini, 1988). It produces the working woman as sex and as body, its emphasis on sexuality and class both incorporated into an imaging whose national dimensions are expressed, in particular, through the landscape. For De Santis, as for Rossellini, this equivalence is one constituted narratively and symbolically through the female body, one basis for the constitution of Italian identity through the reorganization of Hollywoood genres and conventions.

Cronaca di un amore (1950)

The long take and the use of deep focus used by Rossellini and De Santis are techniques that draw attention to the setting. A focus on the setting and the long take is even more crucial in Antonioni's first feature-length film, *Cronaca di un amore*. Antonioni refers to the Hollywood genres of *film noir* and the police procedural as a framework through which to examine the power of the past to erupt into the present. But in his case, it is especially through the film's reversal and inversion of genre expectations that the Hollywood associations are exploited to produce an entirely different film form. He also inverts the emphases of neo-realism: this film contains no aspirations to a better life, no sentimental recording of its characters and no discourse of the people. Antonioni records the lives of the rich, and the lives of his protagonists, Paola (Lucia Bosè) and her husband, are distinguished by a pointlessness and an emptiness. The film's chronology parallels that of Italy: Paola met her husband in March 1943, and married him two months later. Their marriage occurs at the same time as the fall of Mussolini, and proceeds through the period of liberation and reconstruction. By 1950, the year of the film's setting and making, both a personal and a societal bleakness and failure are implied and made equivalent.

In *Cronaca* a woman from the opposite end of the class spectrum to the rice workers of De Santis becomes the focus. Two ex-lovers, Paola and Guido (Massimo Girotti – also the star of *Ossessione*), have become lovers again in the wake of a reopened inquiry into an old death, that of Guido's ex-girlfriend. The ex-lovers, while not directly responsible for it, did not prevent it. Paola's husband's jealousy about her past had prompted him to have her followed, and this led to their meeting again. In the tradition of the *noir* heroines with whom she has affinities, Paola proposes killing her rich husband; and her lover agrees. But again, the event they have wished for occurs without their intervention. Having obtained the evidence of their affair, the husband dies of a heart attack at the wheel, just as he approaches the exact place where they had planned that Guido would kill him. Legally innocent but emotionally guilty, Guido recognizes their relationship cannot be sustained, and he leaves for the station. She awaits the arrival of the police.

Paola is beautiful, elusive, opaque, untouchable, discontented and rich. As both rich and beautiful, she is often the focus of the look of Guido, her husband, most of the other characters and the viewer. From her first appearance, in a series of photographs thrown down by the private detective for his assistant, and for the camera, and from the first verbal description of her given by her old teacher, voice and look suffused with sexual overtones, which are insistently silenced by his companion's indication of another's presence, Paola's beauty and sexuality are identified as the commodity she has, and has sold – they are the currency of her power. But money is just as fundamental and the two are counterposed in *Cronaca*, as one becomes the condition of the other. She remains in the loveless marriage to the rich Milanese engineer, Enrico, rejecting any idea of living with the impoverished Guido. When Guido confesses he has no money, to stay in Milan or anywhere, she, until then oblivious to his circumstances – a commentary in itself upon her love – is shot from below, towering above him, the main gate of the park forming a barrier between them. But, unlike the Hollywood heroines, and like Guido, Paola too, is prey to terror and a persecutory guilt which, in panic, she seeks unsuccessfully, to displace onto him. The lovers' incapacity to escape their culpability in both the past and present dooms them and equalizes them. Although it is given to the man to articulate their conflicts and leave, while Paola remains to face the police, the ending implicates them both.

In *Cronaca* an overtly modernist preoccupation with cinema and with the difficulty of relations between men and women testifies to one important strand in Italian film-making beyond the years most directly affected by war, and the need to find ways of representing its results: 'For better or for worse, reality has been normalised once again, it seems to me more interesting to examine what remains in the characters of their past experiences' (Antonioni, quoted in Bondanella, 1991: 108).

Conclusion

This chapter has focused upon a selection of films which are cinematic classics, but which were not typical of the vast majority of films of these years. As part of a self-conscious approach to cinema, they use film for the exploration of contemporary themes and preoccupations, both Italian and personal. Their representation of femininity is various, but does not seem to be harnessed to any wider project, with the possible exception of *Riso amaro*. As cultural products of their time, however, they both participated in, and contributed to, the circulation of images available for audiences' appropriation. They advanced different understandings of femininity and extended the array of possible ways of representing women in Italian cinema from that time on. In so doing, they drew upon national cultural histories, both visual and discursive, in mapping out their accounts of a country marked by more than twenty years of oppression plus the physical and psychological results of war.

Their relation to the immediate period of post-war reconstruction also positions them as embodiments of a different possible future. As part of both a national heritage of ways of thinking about and representing the woman and a cultural project seeking new societal alternatives, they represent the beginnings of something different, even when the presentation and evolution of the characters occurs through their confinement in what may seem standard female roles and attributes. This was anyway the case for the majority of cultural initiatives of the time, even, and sometimes especially, those concerned with the emancipation of women. Given such constraints, these films advance a cinematic discourse which, through its combination of image, sound, narrative, the landscape and the body, interrogates the condition of modern life. Films of this kind indicated an intervention that contributed non-mainstream accounts through their invention and circulation.

Female identity increasingly assumed a sexualized and eroticized bodily signification in many, especially popular, Italian films of the 1950s. These developments sought both to displace and to accommodate stereotypes inherited from Catholicism and fascism, but also from communism, and from Italian mores in general. Perhaps it could be said that the range of different understandings of masculinity and femininity and their ascription to individual men and women characteristic of modernity were more widely represented by the end of the decade than they had been in the films of their predecessors, neo-realist or not. The films described here extended that search for meaning in 'a country that has emerged from an important and grave adventure' (Antonioni, in Bondanella, 1991: 108).

Filmography

I bambini ci guardano (Vittorio De Sica, 1942)
Cronaca di un amore (Michelangelo Antonioni, 1950)
Ladri di biciclette (Vittorio De Sica, 1948)
Ossessione (Luchino Visconti, 1942)
Paisà (Roberto Rossellini, 1946)
Quattro passi fra le nuvole (Alessandro Blasetti, 1942)
Riso amaro (Giuseppe De Santis, 1947)
Stromboli, terra di dio (Roberto Rossellini, 1949)

Anna Magnani in *Roma, città aperta/Rome, Open City* (1945, Italy, Roberto Rossellini)
Source: BFI Stills, Posters and Designs

CHAPTER NINE

Woman of Rome: Anna Magnani

MARY P. WOOD

The figure of the actress, Anna Magnani, is the embodiment of a paradox. She was at one and the same time hailed by critics as an 'anti-diva', the antithesis of the famous film star, and enjoyed such enormous popularity that she was universally known as 'Nannarella' by her adoring public. My aim in this essay is to consider the persona of Anna Magnani in the context of the immediate post-war period, the period in which she became established as a great cinema star, rather than theatre star which she had been for many years. In doing so, it may also be fruitful to consider the sort of narratives which this persona enabled, and their significance.

An intriguing aspect of the continuing popularity of the Magnani persona is its survival in the prosperous, postmodern 1990s, a very different time from the political and cultural situation of post-war Italy. A recent Dolce & Gabbana advertising campaign featured a nineteen-year-old Brazilian model wearing a bra and corset under a tweed coat. Running hard, with her hands clutching her hair, and an expression of anguish on her face, her pose echoes that of Anna Magnani in Rossellini's great neo-realist film of 1945, *Roma, città aperta/Rome, Open City*. The advertisement excited a great deal of attention in Italy and is interesting in its attempts both to define an ideal of Italian femininity and to determine the enduring appeal of the persona of Magnani (*La Repubblica*, 3 October 1996: 25). The 1990s public relations team wanted an image of softness yet strength, and they typified Magnani as exuberant, carnal, Mediterranean, extrovert – and erotic. This tame simulacrum with which they chose to represent her indicates a continuing problem with figures of powerful women in Italian culture.

The situation in Italy in the immediate post-war period was one of economic collapse and political turmoil. At the risk of being schematic, we should remember that Italy had had a fascist regime from 1922. Between 1922 and 1943 the country underwent a profound transformation into a modern, mass culture; and the fascists used the press, sport and cinema to build a sense of national identity, as opposed to regional identity. Fascist films have been typified as mainly 'white telephone' dramas, in that many of them were set in drawing rooms, and concerned the lives of the wealthy middle classes. Other films glorified the lives of strong heroes, echoing the cult of the leader embodied in Mussolini himself; the female equivalent being the 'joyful girls with healthy minds and healthy bodies' (Liehm, 1984: 22). However, this is not the whole picture. For example, it is not true that Italian films before neo-realism lacked realism, or that they ignored the working classes. Because the fascist authorities never managed to exert total control over the theatre or cinema, films more or less endorsed fascist ideology, and particularly the role of women as bearers of the next generation, as breeders, wives and mothers. I will limit myself here to saying that there were many continuities, not least of personnel, between cinema before and after the Liberation. In the context of this study, one of the problems thrown up by the continuity of attitudes, particularly patriarchal attitudes, in the post-war period was the difficulty of representing the changed role of women who had had to assume greater autonomy as breadwinners and defenders of the family in the long final stages of the war, and in its aftermath.

The invasion of Italy by the Allied armies started in Sicily in 1943. The fascist government moved north, creating the Republic of Salò. Rome fell in 1944 and fighting continued as the Allies advanced slowly northwards. This long period of invasion allowed Italy to come out of the war with more favourable terms, because of the assistance given to the Allies by anti-fascist groups of a wide variety of political persuasions. The left-wing generally had enormous prestige in 1945, but was too fragmented to be able to prevent conservative forces, supported by the occupation forces, from re-establishing themselves in positions of power in the period of reconstruction. Part of the problem was the weakness of the left in terms of developing cultural forms which reflected in some way the aspirations of ordinary people as life regained a certain equilibrium and prosperity increased (Forgacs, 1990: 100–5).

Anna Magnani was part of these historical, political and cultural processes and changes. Born in Rome in 1908, her theatrical career started in 1926. From 1930 onwards she moved from company to company gaining experience in variety, melodrama and comedy, building her reputation and getting ever more favourable notices; and in the early 1940s she appeared in many satirical reviews in Rome (Hochkofler, 1984: 21–34). Although the theatre work brought her fame and popularity, her cinema career was less successful. Magnani made about seventeen films before *Roma, città aperta*. At the time of her first film role, in 1934, she was not at all a fashionable cinematic type, projecting a strong personality and an unconventional beauty. In spite of marrying the film director Goffredo Alessandrini in the late 1930s, her film parts are all those of the supporting actress. By the end of the war she had become stereotyped in her screen career – the variety singer, the woman with a past, the gangster's girlfriend.

Significantly, however, she appeared in two films in the early 1940s set in working-class Rome, drawing together actors from the dialect theatre. Without doubt it is precisely *because* her film career thus far associated her with supporting roles, of outsiders or women of the people, and her theatre work had developed the necessary emotional range and the technique with which to convey it, that her moment came at the time of social and political change.

In examining the moment of transition in 1945, we can see that the stars changed because the stories changed. Film-makers of whatever political opinion or intellectual formation aimed both to distance themselves from the rhetoric of fascism and to constitute post-war cinema as critical of and different from what had gone before. The writings of Antonio Gramsci, which were published from 1947 onwards, found an immediate response among intellectuals, not least because they identified an important role for the cultural critic in making sense of a historical period, exploring and explaining the complexities of individual, class and national identities (Nowell-Smith, 1990: 169). Gramsci's idea that an exploration of a moment of social and political change involves a rethinking of the composition and history of those groups which have previously been denied power had a contemporary appeal. In this respect the Magnani persona – working class, mature, maternal, emotional – provides a suitable emblem of the experiences and aspirations of the working and lower middle classes. That persona had been honed in art forms associated with popular culture, 'constructed as the culture of the dominated classes in antithesis to "artistic culture"' (Forgacs, 1984: 92), and it could therefore be utilized as a site through which to gain access to a different world-view and as a locus typifying the surrounding conflict.

The immediate post-war period was a time of ferment when new social, cultural and political relationships were being rehearsed. Crucial political issues, such as the form that Italian post-war democracy might take, the role (if any) of the monarchy and the agenda of the Communist Party, were being debated, negotiated and put into practice. Most histories of neo-realist cinema of the 1940s and 1950s concentrate on the political background in purely masculine terms, reducing the role of female stars and characters to essences. However, when we look at aspects of the roles Magnani played in the immediate post-war period, we become aware that her persona strongly resists identification with characteristics regarded as essentially feminine, and that the incoherences inherent in the roles she played stem from uncertainties about the life the working and lower middle classes, particularly women, should aspire to in peacetime.

Magnani was thirty-seven years old when *Roma* was released in 1945. Rossellini had started to film his story of the Resistance four months after the Germans left Rome. There is a consequent feeling of immediacy. The film was shot in real locations, since the studios had been looted by the retreating Germans and Cinecittà (the state film studio complex built by Mussolini) was being used as a refugee camp. This is not the Rome of Mussolini; the dictator invoked Italy's glorious Roman past in order to glorify his own regime and, to that end, put his stamp upon his capital. Mussolini's Rome is monumental, powerful, mythic, celebrating the power, energy and genius of the Romans, and therefore the Italians. Rossellini's Rome, on the other hand, is that of ordinary people opposing or accommodating to the reality of fascism and occupation.

Magnani plays Pina, a woman of the people, a widow with a young son who is expecting a child by her fiancé Francesco, a printer who does clandestine work for the Resistance. Pina and Francesco are about to marry. The dialogue explains much of Pina's character to us. Francesco, is a communist and an unbeliever, who has already established a good relationship with Pina's son, Marcello. When Francesco hides Manfredi, the Resistance leader, in his apartment across the hall, the two lovers have only the stairs where they can be alone together to express their hopes for the future. Besides being a good story, with a well-constructed script, *Roma* functions at a deeper level, and much has been made of Rossellini's symbolic depiction of the alliance of catholics and communists to oppose the evil of Nazism (Brunette, 1996: 37; Bondanella, 1993: 50; Marcus, 1986: 33–53). As in all good melodramas, Pina has her opposite, Manfredi's girlfriend Marina, who betrays him for drugs and a fur coat. This dichotomy also indicates a fissure, an area of disruption and danger in patriarchal culture which allows us to see power relations, and to ask questions.

Magnani can be seen as a stereotype of the good working-class woman who is prepared to fight for her family and a better world. Brunette (1996: 50) suggests that it is Rossellini's larger-than-life male characters who initiate the action, female characters being usually seen as acted upon. Manfredi's presence in the block of flats provokes a raid by the Germans and the fascist police. As Pina comforts a neighbour, she spots Francesco being carried off by the fascists and launches herself after him. She fights off various Germans who try to stop her, and is shot as she runs after the truck. The cutting, camera work and Magnani's performance contribute to the emotional impact of this sequence. We are in no doubt of Pina's contempt for the Germans, or of the intensity of her feelings for Francesco. Roundups of men for forced labour in factories in Italy and Germany became increasingly common in the period before the Liberation and women would have had to actively mobilize a variety of social and personal resources in order to survive. Just as Rome stands for Italy as a whole, Pina and Francesco together are emblematic of the moral and ethical strength of the people. However, Pina's attempt at initiating action, albeit for good womanly reasons, fails – she dies, falling in a heap in the road, her skirt lifting to reveal suspenders and laddered stockings. On the point of death she is, therefore, objectified, made powerless, and at the same time eroticized.

There were examples of films in which the female characters were portrayed as more or less equals in the struggle – a number of partisan-financed films for example[1] – but *Roma* is not one of them. An interesting tension exists between the narrative drive of the dialogue, which presents Pina as inferior to Francesco by virtue of her class, education and gender, and the story events and Magnani's actual performance. Pina is represented as mature, active, earthy, strong, defiant: she is a mother. She may be poorly educated, but projects considerable native intelligence and honesty. She is, as Marcus (1986: 39) points out, also an activist who organizes the local women. The portrayal of Pina as the instigator of the women's raid on the baker's shop also evokes a form of female protest which had become a feature of the fascist period (Colarizi, 1996: 145), but which was played down politically and was certainly never represented on celluloid. The invasion exacerbated problems of food distribution, mobility and employment, and it is significant that when Rossellini wanted to typify female protest against the deprivations of fascism, it is embodied in the looting of a food shop. Pina's action is emblematic of the sense of injustice, of the harshness of life for ordinary people, of what women are constrained to do in order to feed their families. Rossellini's film attempts to suggest a commonality of purpose for the Italian people: namely, the need to provide for a new generation, the children seen walking back into the city in the final shots of the film.

In this respect *Roma* reflects the explosion of optimism in Italy when the end of conflict was in sight. Nonetheless, in the film the social hierarchies (Sorlin, 1991: 57) remain firmly in place, as does the gender hierarchy. Pina is not represented as refined. Her accent is working class and her emotionality is represented as an integral and essential part of her. It is this forceful emotional and ethical integrity which is so interesting and which, perhaps, offers us additional explanations as to why Magnani was sought after not only by populist film directors but also by Fellini, Rossellini and Visconti. Her appeal was both visceral and intellectual. Moreover, Magnani's emotionality is not inconsistent with realism, because the emotional depth of characterization inherent in melodrama enables the film-maker to probe beneath the surface of events and thereby to indicate, however unconsciously, inconsistencies and incoherence. In effect, women such as Pina will have to struggle with attempts to limit their role both in class and in patriarchal terms in the post-war period of reconstruction.

After this film Magnani seemed to slip back into more stereotypical roles, although the stories were set in a recognizable post-war turmoil – problems of returning home and re-establishing life and relationships, stories of the resistance, of the black market. In *Abbasso la miseria!/Down with Poverty!* (Gennaro Righelli, 1946) she plays the discontented Nannina, married to an honest man who adopts an orphan and refuses to get rich in black-market deals; she comes round to his way of thinking in the end when her husband's black-marketeer friend is arrested. In Max Neufeld's *Un uomo ritorna/A Man Returns* (1946) she is a widow trying to take revenge on the people who had her son arrested during the war; she joins up with the hero who has returned from prisoner-of-war camp to find his family destroyed, and they set off to build a new life together. In Alberto Lattuada's *Il bandito/The Bandit* (1946) she plays a central figure in a band of robbers who transfers her affections from the old to the new leader; and in Carmine Gallone's 1948 *Davanti a lui tremava tutta Roma/All Rome Trembled before Him* she is a singer whose jealousy almost betrays a Resistance group led by her fiancé. Magnani's emotionality is metonymic of the sufferings of women in the period of post-war chaos and the general desire for something different. Again, there is tension between emotional engagement with the strength and force of Magnani's performances and her portrayal of women who are subordinate to men, either as wives, gangsters' molls or because they lack judgement.

A flavour of this tension can be seen in Gennaro Righelli's 1946 film, *Abbasso la ricchezza!/Down with Riches!* Magnani plays another woman of the people, Gioconda, a widow who ran a vegetable stall in Trastevere, a working-class quarter of Rome, and who has earned millions trafficking in the black market. Magnani conveys the vulgarity, ambition and self-deception of the new rich. Gioconda and her sister now occupy a different world, living in a splendid villa and enjoying their wealth. They're going to be middle class! The sequence where Gioconda travels back to her stall by horse-drawn carriage lasts long enough for us to appreciate the jealous calls that issue from the windows and balconies of her female former neighbours, and her pleasure in the experience as she lolls back dressed in furs and an excessive hat crowned by two large white birds. The subtleties suggested by Magnani's performance resonate wider than just the drama of the rise and fall of an opportunistic woman. Critics of the time saw Gioconda as a negative character. Magnani's performance renders her understandable and sympathetic, because she portrays her as energetic, active, honest, kind (she supports her sister and a variety of hangers-on) and fun-loving (we see her jitterbugging, and singing at the piano). At the end of the film she loses all her money, having been duped and cheated by aristocrats and middle class speculators. Only the intervention of the Count (Vittorio De Sica) prevents her from being sent to prison for possession of a stolen ring, and she returns (hatless) to her market stall – a metaphor for class conflict and resolution.

Magnani's next film was Luigi Zampa's *L'onorevole Angelina/Angelina MP*, released in 1947. Here she plays the central character, Angelina, who lives in slum housing in Pietralata on the fringes of Rome with her policeman husband and five children. Circumstances propel her into taking the lead in fighting for better living conditions for her community. Zampa uses montage sequences to illustrate the process of her politicization and to show what is at stake. Shots of newspaper presses rolling with Angelina's story cue her appreciation of the power of the press. Collective action is indicated in scenes that depict Angelina in the midst of a crowd of women serving pasta. Shots of dry taps are followed by close-ups of the feet of women marching off to protest: the tap runs. A mob of women lie down in front of the bus: they get a bus stop. Feet march in the rain to the Assistance Office: they get a nursery for children. These sequences conclude with close-ups of Angelina looking at children.

Magnani herself claimed that the roles of Angelina and Gioconda were written for her, and that she thoroughly enjoyed playing 'lovely, authentic characters. I never said I wanted to act great tragedy queens. I want characters I and the public can believe in. Well-constructed characters, . . . authentic and true to life' (Faldini and Fofi, 1979: 125). Again, Angelina is a complex character, having to juggle her role of wife and mother with that of community leader. She is aggressive, raucous, vital, energetic, tender and compassionate, and her performance was praised for its authenticity. But what happens in the story? Angelina's politicization leads to family conflict; her son threatens to go to the bad; Pasquà, her husband, bemoans the lack of home comforts; again, she is duped by the upper classes represented by the landlord. And when her community urge her to be their deputy in the national parliament, she declines, saying that she will leave that to those who are more articulate. She goes back to her place, as wife and mother, although still politically active. Patriarchy has established its rule once again and, metaphorically, the working class has given in to its political masters. The longed-for reforms (Ginsborg, 1990: 82) will not take place in this period.

The underlying concerns of *L'onorevole Angelina* undoubtedly reflect worries about women taking power. In 1946 women had the vote for the first time in Italian history and, in the first free general elections for over twenty years, took part in the decision between monarchy and republic and the election of representatives to the Constituent Assembly (Ginsborg, 1990: 98). The wider political struggle, which resulted in Christian Democrat success in the April 1948 elections, was also reflected in the Italian film industry.

Christian Democrat politicians and appointees to state bodies opposed neo-realist films on the grounds that they presented a bad image of Italy abroad. Minister Giulio Andreotti's dubbing tax of 1947 swelled the funds available to producers in the shape of state loans, but the bureaucratic mechanisms by which access to these funds was gained constituted an additional form of censorship (Quaglietti, 1980: 76–7). And Andreotti called for 'fewer rags, more legs'![2] Although neo-realist films were initially popular at the box office, the fastest-growing production sector was that of the so-called 'average film', modestly budgeted and making a reasonable profit. These included the old popular genres, such as comedy and melodrama.

Magnani's career reflects this development and, in box-office terms, is quite uneven between 1945 and 1950. Films by 'good' directors, for which Magnani won awards, often made less money than more standard melodramatic or comic fare. In the films released in 1948 it is also clear that her persona is becoming more problematic. The outsider figure becomes overtly that of a prostitute in

Michael Waszinsky's *Lo sconosciuto di San Marino/The Unknown Man of San Marino*. In Mario Camerini's *Molti sogni per le strade/Many Dreams along the Way*) she is again an emotional wife/mother fighting to keep her family honest in the face of poverty and unemployment. The only successful relationship in this film is that between Linda and her son, Romoletto, who has never seen a chicken or the sea, and who represents what she is struggling for. Mario Mattòli's remake of *Assunta Spina* has Magnani as a turn-of-the-century Neapolitan who sacrifices herself sexually to ensure better prison treatment for her lover. In these films she is not an ordinary woman and there are interesting parallels with the transgressive female roles in French and German cinema (Signoret in *Dédée d'Anvers*, Knef in *Die Sünderin*).

Visconti's 1951 film, *Bellissima*, is certainly a film which made very little money, and in which Magnani plays a woman who transgresses the boundaries allotted to women of the time. In it she plays Maddalena Cecconi, a married, working-class nurse. She is obsessed with getting her plain little daughter, Maria, into the films and we see what success would mean as she sacrifices her time and money buying costumes and arranging acting and dancing lessons. This is all too much for Maria, who spends the entire screen test crying her eyes out. Eventually, Maddalena is so insulted and mortified at the film people's howls of laughter at the sight of her weeping daughter that she begins to realize the unattainability of her dreams. At the end of the film we watch as the men from Cinecittà come to offer Maria the prize of one million lire; Maddalena refuses with enormous dignity and sorrow.

Bellissima is a complex and entertaining film in which the Marxist Visconti employs the popular, melodramatic form to tell a story about the aspirations of those excluded from economic and political power. That these aspirations are represented by the meretricious world of the cinema, the world of illusion, allows connections to be made with the elusive prospect of prosperity promised by the ruling classes, while still effectively excluding ordinary people from the decision-making process. Again, Magnani's performance is so forceful, and her emotional and ethical integrity so marked, that she demands reflection on Maddalena's life – and, metonymically, on the lives of all working-class women. Again, she embodies a fissure in the conventional representation of self-sacrificing, catholic motherhood, in that she is both Madonna and sexualized. Far from being a submissive Madonna, she is fierce, quarrelsome and vulgar. She slops around her building in her petticoat and when she dresses up, it is in a low-necked suit. All of her desires for a better life are projected onto her daughter. In the final scenes Maddalena retreats into the domestic sphere, the bedroom. She seems to abdicate her feminine power, but the final images of her husband, Spartaco, massaging her feet as she lies on the bed in her petticoat seem to leave her dangerous sexual power undiminished. The emotional force of Magnani's performance is at odds with the narrative drive to contain her character and, according to Mitchell (1989: 13), it is this oscillation between portrayals of sexual independence and the affirmation of the eternal Christian family beliefs fundamental to a conventional patriarchal view of Italian womanhood which produces the sense of danger and 'the seductive enigma of her appeal'.

Magnani's persona in this period expresses areas of danger and incoherence in post-war life. As Piero Meldini (1989: 124) has pointed out, neo-realist films tended towards stereotypical depictions of the working classes, as epitomized by Antonio's dirty, baggy suit and bare flat in *Ladri di biciclette* (Vittorio De Sica, 1948), and these stereotypes tended to persist even through the 1940s and the period of reconstruction. Maddalena and Spartaco's home is a two-room flat with bare, damp walls and no luxuries, yet both are working. We are meant to despise Gioconda's showy dresses and hats, and to reject the world of the rich, the criminal and the meretricious, but, in doing so, no channel is afforded for the legitimate aspirations of the poor to leave that condition. The jewels and feathers, furs and silks which Magnani wears in films like Lattuada's *Il bandito* and Righelli's *Abbasso la ricchezza!* could be enjoyed because they had been acquired by a woman of the people, even if the circumstances of their acquisition were represented as somewhat equivocal.

One can argue that the so-called 'pink neo-realism' of the 1950s carried social melodramas forward in an emasculated form. These films have convoluted plots, rehearsing with emotion roles available to ordinary women, but inevitably concluding with the heroine accepting her lot with resignation. The persona of Magnani does not fit with these roles of suffering acceptance. Nor does it fit with new comedy vehicles depicting spirited younger women finding their niche in modern Italian society. As Spinazzola (1974: 125) suggests, that niche was the traditional one of marriage and motherhood. The working-class origins and speech patterns of these plump, sensual girls was emphasized as if this class environment provided a space in which new, freer social interactions could safely be rehearsed. Magnani is very different from the Gina Lollobrigida of *Pane, amore e fantasia/Bread, Love and Dreams* (Luigi Comencini, 1953), from Sophia Loren or the sex bombs of 1950s comedy. When we examine the personae of stars such as Lollobrigida, Loren and starlets like Marisa Allasio, the subtle irony of Magnani's portrayal of her characters becomes evident. Lollobrigida and Loren represented an innocent sensuality, free from any suggestion of vice or transgression, and their performances emphasized both their physical attributes (plump breasts, stomachs and hips) and their 'southernness'. These stars epitomize physically the class which has left poverty behind, and as long as it knows its place can enjoy the fat of the land. As Spinazzola (1974: 131) suggests, they can look forward to a future 'rich in electrical appliances, furniture on the never never, and a lovely Fiat 600'.

Rossellini's film *L'amore/Love* (1948) is symptomatic of the difficulty of being Anna Magnani throughout this period. It was as if the stories through which

Italian society tried to rehearse and explore change, and the aspirations of women, and of men and women excluded from power, could not contain her persona. Film narratives of the 1940s and 1950s failed to integrate successfully a strong, emotional, active, female character.

Throughout the post-war period, Magnani is most commonly represented as a mother; she rehearses roles in which she plays women fighting for their rights, or for the family's rights, or for a fair deal for the national family. These are women taking power – a profoundly threatening phenomenon in post-war Italy. The only ways that a Magnani character could be integrated were either in a narrative in which she was a social outsider, and usually killed off at the end (even by an exploding volcano in William Dieterle's 1949 film, *Volcano*), or in a film in which her persona was identified ontologically with Magnani herself, so that she either actually or metaphorically played herself, displaying her acting technique in terms of emotional range. *L'amore*, Visconti's 'Anna Magnani' episode in *Siamo donne/We Are Women* (1953) or Jean Renoir's *The Golden Coach* (1953) are all examples. In artistic and human terms, she was trapped, so much so that in 1954 she went to Hollywood, and only Pasolini's 1962 *Mamma Roma* indicates what she could have been.

In the context of the immediate post-war period, her emblematic role in films such as *L'onorevole Angelina* suggests that the persona of Anna Magnani continues to resonate, because the reality behind these post-war stories remains, to a large extent, unresolved. Her final narrative containment is indicative not only of the sexual but also the class politics of the period. Contemporary Italy is a prosperous, modern, industrial society, but Italian culture still appears to find problems with representing a strong female figure who is active and erotic, as well as maternal.That Italians still feel it important to attempt to reconcile these conflicting drives can be deduced not only from continuing critical and journalistic reappraisals of her work but also from the persistence of the affectionate nickname her public gave her, 'Nannarella'. Magnani's fiery, gutsy, intensely feminine persona represented, and represents, a disruption – something which cannot be contained within conventional storylines of patriarchal discourse – which draws attention, as Gramsci says, to the social condition of women and the working class. That is why she is emblematic for the post-war period, and remains such a fascinating figure in Italian cinema.

Notes

1. It is interesting that the National Association of Italian Partisans (ANPI) felt the need to put their hard-earned cash into presenting their own version of wartime resistance in such films as Giuseppe De Santis's *Caccia tragica/Tragic Hunt* (1947), Aldo Vergano's *Il sole sorge ancora/The Sun Rises Again* (1946)

and Carlo Lizzani's *Achtung, banditi!* (1951). All had bad distribution deals and failed to make money. An additional contributing factor to their failure lay, perhaps, in the fact that in their good/evil narrative oppositions, capitalist consumption was firmly presented as bad.

2. In 1949 the 'Andreotti Law' was passed, establishing government control over the financing and censorship of film. This is the same Giulio Andreotti, the former Prime Minister, who was convicted of involvement in Mafia corruption.

Filmography

Abbasso la miseria! (Gennaro Righelli, 1946)
Abbasso la ricchezza! (Gennaro Righelli, 1946)
L'amore (Roberto Rossellini, 1948)
Assunta Spina (Mario Mattòli, 1948)
Il bandito (Alberto Lattuada, 1946)
Bellissima (Luchino Visconti, 1951)
Davanti a lui tremava tutta Roma (Carmine Gallone, 1948)
Mamma Roma (Pier Paolo Pasolini, 1962)
Molti sogni per le strade (Mario Camerini, 1948)
L'onorevole Angelina (Luigi Zampa, 1947)
Roma, città aperta (Roberto Rossellini, 1945)
Lo sconosciuto di San Marino (Michael Waszinsky, 1948)
Siamo donne (Luchino Visconti, 1953)
Un uomo ritorno (Max Neufeld, 1946)

Spain

Aurora Bautista in *Agustina de Aragón* (1950, Spain, Juan de Orduña)
Source: Filmoteca Española, Madrid

CHAPTER TEN

Feminizing the Nation: Women, Subordination and Subversion in Post-Civil War Spanish Cinema

JO LABANYI

Introduction

Late-1940s Spanish cinema presents a major paradox, for this is a period of dictatorship characterized by the most retrograde patriarchal values and at the same time the period when female stars dominated the screen more than at any other time in the nation's film history. It is necessary to ask how this foregrounding of the feminine may have served the interests of the Franco regime, and at the same time how these female stars may have generated meanings that went beyond, or against, dominant ideology. Crucial here is the slippage between popular and populist conceptions of culture, both of which in different ways aim to incorporate the lower classes into the nation. The Spanish Republic of 1931–6 had promoted a national-popular cinema on Gramscian lines, using popular cultural forms such as melodrama and folklore (often combined) to give self-expression to marginalized sectors of the population. Early Francoism exploited the same cultural forms, with the popular again figured by the cinematic heroine, as part of a populist project for securing the lower classes' allegiance to a hierarchical model of society, conceived as a rejection of modernity. In Republican cinema, too, women had been the bearers of an ideological critique of modernity, in the form of capitalist exploitation. But the theme of the fallen woman who falls victim to the wicked city, frequent in Republican cinema, disappears in late 1940s film for two main reasons: strict censorship, increasingly under Catholic control; and the Franco regime's definitive break with the radical, anti-capitalist strand of fascism in favour of a more retrograde exaltation of the national past. The result is curiously positive for the representation of women: female victims disappear from the screen, which instead is filled with strong heroines who provide role models not only for women but also for wayward or ineffectual males.

Although Spain's post-Civil War period began in 1939, with the fall of the Republic to Franco's Nationalist troops after three years of conflict, the period 1945–51 was still dominated by the need for national reconstruction and yet can be seen as a discrete interval in its own right. It was not until 1951 that the Communist Party pulled out the last of its guerrilla cadres, finally bringing military action to an end. And the 'years of hunger', as they were called, continued through to the early 1950s, when the United Nations' boycott of Spain was lifted (1950), the first US wheat loans were forthcoming (1951), rationing came to an end (1952) and US military and economic aid arrived (1954). Although Spain did not fight in the Second World War, it was significantly affected by the fascist defeat: from 1942, when the tide turned in the Allies' favour, the Franco regime started to disengage from its fascist militaristic trappings. With Allied victory in 1945, the regime removed the Spanish fascist party, Falange Española, from key government positions, ended the obligatory fascist salute at public meetings, promulgated some semblance of a Constitution and took censorship and propaganda away from direct Falangist control, handing them to the Catholic-dominated Ministry of Education. The period 1945–51 is thus marked by continued economic hardship, but also by a new stress on national reconciliation (at the level of propaganda, at least), as the abandonment of fascist militaristic values allowed the beginnings of an attempt to reconstruct civilian society, albeit within a totalitarian model.

This new stress on national reconciliation is directly responsible for the woman-centred emphasis of late 1940s Spanish cinema. The spate of war films that appeared in the immediate post-Civil War period – exalting fascist warrior virility, constantly seen as threatened by women – ceased in 1942. From now on, and particularly after 1945, Spanish cinema concentrated on the world of romance, home and family, in a depoliticizing strategy that encouraged men as well as women to identify with the private sphere. As in contemporaneous Hollywood *film noir*, which was strongly influential on Spanish cinematic production from 1946, this served as a way of helping men negotiate the transition from the 'tough guy' of wartime to the 'family man' of peacetime. But in early Francoist Spain, where dictatorship denied citizens active participation in the public sphere, the need to encourage men to identify with the private was particularly urgent. Indeed, as we shall see, the corollary of the strong woman of late 1940s Spanish cinema is the 'feminine' man. The fact that, in so many films, the heroine provides lessons for men is crucial, for it means that male spectators are invited not just to desire her fetishized female figure but to internalize it. The extreme specularization of the heroine characteristic of most late-1940s Spanish movies thus serves as a strategy not so much of objectification as of identification, on the part of male as well as female viewers.

The year 1951 marked the end of this focus on the family and the feminine, as the development of an oppositional cinema led to a new stress on the political, with plot lines consequently focused on the male. The trigger for this new oppositional cinema was twofold: the initial stirrings of internal unrest from 1951, and above all the first showing in Spain in that year of Italian neo-realist cinema. This emergent oppositional cinema was also an attempt to create a new art cinema, breaking with the studio system that governed Spanish film production in the 1940s. The results were again negative for women, since this meant a rejection of the female stars around whom the studio system was organized. And above all, the attempt from 1951 to create an auteurist cinema signified a rejection of the notion that film was a popular medium, produced and marketed by the newly expanding culture industries and aimed at the masses. Male-dominated 1950s oppositional cinema never reached beyond an intellectual elite, by definition predominantly male, whereas the woman-centred cinema of the late 1940s (both that produced in Spain and Hollywood imports) was massively popular with Spanish audiences. Indeed, in the late 1940s Spain had more cinemas per capita than any other country in Europe (Carr, quoted in Kinder, 1993: 19).

Cinema audiences during the late 1940s were predominantly female and lower class: that is, made up of the two social groups who most suffered the effects of Francoist repression. This was, of course, especially true for matinée performances, where the few men in the audience tended to be ex-Republicans, denied identity papers and unable to find work. The lower classes flocked to the cinema as the only available cheap form of entertainment in a period of deprivation and repression, and also, simply, to keep warm. The medium's popularity with popular audiences, and especially with women, means that one must be careful about assuming that early Francoist film production was a straightforward reflection of the regime's ideology. I hope in a future project to attempt an oral history of cinema spectatorship in 1940s Spain; for the time being, the only evidence available is memoirs and individual testimonies (with heavy censorship, film magazines of the period cannot be taken as indicative of public opinion; indeed, the main film magazine *Primer Plano* was Falangist-owned). My analysis of audience response in this essay is thus tentative, based on a reading of the multiple possibilities for identification offered by the films themselves. I am aware of the risk here of reading retrospectively into late 1940s Spanish cinema values and concepts derived from contemporary feminist film theory. Nevertheless, the fact that the audiences were primarily lower class and predominantly female suggests that the films are likely to have enabled at least some scope for positive identifications.

In practice, late 1940s film production is hugely varied, and even those films that are an explicit mouthpiece for National-Catholic values allow contrary readings. Indeed, the existence of strict censorship – whose prime target was the representation of the female body – inculcated in contemporary audiences the habit of reading against the grain (Labanyi, in Graham and Labanyi, 1995:

207–14). Although the state exerted a high degree of control over the film industry, through economic protectionism as well as censorship, production companies were privately owned and many directors had previously worked under the Republic or had even made propaganda films for the Republican government or Communist Party during the Civil War. The best-known art directors and cameramen were Central European Jewish refugees from Nazism, who arrived in Spain under the Republic but continued to work throughout the 1940s. The director most identified with the regime through his production of a series of patriotic epics in the late 1940s, Juan de Orduña, was known (though it could not be stated publicly) to be homosexual. What we have, then, is a complex negotiation of cultural meanings in which dominant values compete on screen with other readings articulated not through plot or dialogue but through performance style or *mise-en-scène*. The female stars of the period, whose bodies dominate the screen, were central to this process.

Spanish film critics and directors, while nostalgically looking back to a period when Spanish films were massively popular, have generally dismissed late 1940s Spanish cinema as escapist and frivolous; by implication, a cinema made for women. The only contemporary Spanish director to have engaged with national cinema of this period is Almodóvar, whose camp melodramatic excess combines with a focus on women in order to question gender roles. Many of the female stars of the late 1940s have been reclaimed in contemporary Spain as gay icons, and at the time were popular with gay as well as female audiences (Moix, 1992). While it would be a mistake to ignore the repressive political context of Spanish film production in the late 1940s, it is also important to recognize the ways in which, through their female stars, they offered their audiences possibilities of identification that worked against their surface message. In this essay I should like to explore the responses these films may have allowed contemporary audiences. What most interests me is the ways in which plot structures which seem designed to elicit a particular response from male viewers offer scope for different readings by female spectators.

My generic subdivision into folkloric musicals, war and missionary films, historical epics, costume drama and *film noir* is not intended to give a comprehensive survey of film output of the period, but isolates those genres where the representation of women is especially interesting. Comedy, largely conformist in gender terms, is excluded, except where it overlaps with *film noir* in the cinema of Edgar Neville. It should be noted at the outset that all the generic categories discussed can largely be subsumed under melodrama, commonly regarded as the 'woman's film'. The only exceptions are the war and missionary films – though, as we shall see, the former fuse war story and romance, and the latter allow a melodramatic reading.

Female stars

Through the studio system the female stars of the period were tied to specific cinematic genres, associating them with particular plots, costumes and acting styles – to the extent that, when they appeared in a different genre, they created a disturbance. Before discussing the dominant genres of the period, it is useful to survey the main female stars whose image was marketed via film magazines, as well as by film posters which gave their name more prominence than that of the director (it was also normal for the female star's name to appear on screen before the film's title). Film magazines explicitly drew parallels between Spanish stars and those of Hollywood, juxtaposing reportage on both and alternating them on the cover picture; despite patriotic emphasis on the construction of a national cinema, Hollywood female stars predominated. Articles and cover pictures featuring male actors were relatively rare, and they were not invested with the same aura of glamour; there is a noticeable contrast here with the early 1940s, when the vogue for war films exalting warrior values had offered considerable scope for the glamorization of masculinity.

Indeed, one of the notable features of late 1940s Spanish cinema is the low-profile, if not wooden, acting of most of the male leads, projecting either an image of man as passive and inept, or as the 'strong, silent type' incapable of voicing emotion. In almost all the films of the period, the heroine serves, for male as well as female audiences, as a projection of emotions which only woman is licensed to speak: many plot structures hinge on the heroine teaching the hero the value of emotion – that is, converting him to feminine values. In all these films women are the seducers and men the seduced, in a disavowal of male emotion and sexuality whose result is the projection on to women of a verbal and physical freedom and vitality that makes them the agents as well as the objects of desire. Laura Mulvey's (1989) theory of the gaze as a masculine objectification of woman is not adequate for reading these strong female images; a better model is provided by Kaja Silverman's (1992: 153) insistence that 'power can invade spectacle, and disinvest from the [masculine] gaze – that spectacle, in other words, can function phallically'.

If on the one hand such strong female images represent the traditional Catholic notion of woman as sexual temptress, and construct her as not fully socialized (i.e. repressed), on the other they endow her with an agency and sexuality lacking in bourgeois constructions of femininity. This has important consequences for the female stars of the period, who are thus constructed as mobile and articulate, particularly in the huge number of costume dramas where their free body movements are facilitated by their full skirts and (apart from nineteenth-century bourgeois heroines) gathered peasant-style blouses, contrasting with the heroes' tight jackets and hose. While one senses that the female stars' embodiment of energy and sexuality was intended as a release for the repressed emotions of male spectators, the result for female spectators is intense identification with female figures whose freedom of action and expression contrasts violently with the restrictions imposed on women by early Francoist legislation – under which married women could not work, reside away from the marital home or hold a passport or bank account without their husbands' permission.

The glamour associated with such active, expressive female stars may have been escapist, but it also kept alive the belief that things could be otherwise. Indeed, the popularity of Hollywood movies in late-1940s Spain owed itself at least partly to the fact that the affluent domestic lifestyles portrayed on the screen showed female spectators in the 'years of hunger' that somewhere there existed alternatives to their own deprivation. Indeed, at a time of international political and economic boycott, and state enforcement of economic and cultural autarky, cinema was virtually the only link with the outside world. The popularity of Hollywood female stars helped construct the outside world in the popular imaginary as a feminine space; the mimicry of their costumes and performance styles by Spanish female stars also constituted an important transgression of cultural autarky.

The frothy, frivolous female stars of early Francoist bourgeois comedy and the Mary Magdalene figures of early Francoist melodrama, both reflecting the misogyny of a period dominated by military values, by and large disappear after 1945. From that date even heroines sentenced by the plot to self-sacrificial renunciation are played by actresses who endow the roles with a stoic strength of purpose: for example, the regal Juanita Reina (a folkloric singer specializing in costume dramas) and Maruchi Fresno (star of several historical epics). Particularly notable is the swashbuckling gusto of Aurora Bautista, the thick-eyebrowed, powerfully energetic star of various costume dramas directed by Orduña, in which she ranges from the role of leader in battle (*Agustina de Aragón*, 1950)[1] to wronged queen (*Locura de amor*/*Love's Madness*, 1948) and heartless adulteress (*Pequeñeces*/*Trivial Matters*, 1950). In all of these films her unrelenting physical mobility and powerful voice projection dominate the screen, creating an impression of emotional power tempered, even in her rendition of madness in *Locura de amor*, by a controlling intelligence. The equally intelligent, but more controlled, performances of Ana Mariscal are discussed in Chapter 11. Intelligence is also the hallmark of the acting style of Conchita Montes, Vassar graduate and creative writer, who starred in many of her writer-director husband Edgar Neville's film comedies of the late 1940s: her performances delightfully mix elegant refinement with witty repartee in a subtly subversive way that allows her to run rings round her various male leads without ever losing her cool. Neville's loving treatment of her onscreen is a rare example of a male director conveying his admiration for an intelligent woman, while also endowing her with a sense of fun.

Other female stars were more traditionally associated with emotional excess. The nervous fragility of Amparo Rivelles particularly suited her to the role of tragic heroine of nineteenth-century costume dramas, in which she brilliantly conveys the pent-up hysteria of bourgeois femininity. Her star persona's conventional equation of femininity with destructive (and self-destructive) emotional excess nevertheless gave her a subversive quality, as her female roles precariously balanced self-sacrificial devotion with attraction to dangerous love objects: a star image elaborated via media gossip about her unconventional love life, which in the 1950s led her to leave Spain for the Mexican film industry. The most shocking as well as most lionized star of the late 1940s was Lola Flores: the devastatingly sexy singing and dancing star of many folkloric musicals, whose stormy affair with her married acting partner Manolo Caracol (allegedly linked to the clandestine Communist Party) clinched her screen persona as irresistible, flamboyant seductress who overcomes all obstacles to get her man, and ensured her massive popularity with lower-class audiences, who no doubt delighted in the havoc she persistently wreaks on polite society in her films. Earthy and excessive, her main quality is nevertheless a capacity for quick-witted repartee, constructing woman as agent through language as well as the body. However, from around 1948, as the folkloric musical genre became increasingly Hollywood-inspired and glitzy, it attracted new stars who were more saccharine than gutsy: for example, Carmen Sevilla with her immaculate hairdo, toothpaste-advert smile and sanitized little-girl sexuality. Significantly, her performances cast her more as dancer than singer: the folkloric heroine becomes a body without a voice, style without content.

It is also worth briefly mentioning here two bit-part actresses whose specialisms encapsulate contrary attitudes to women in 1940s Spain: Camino Garrigó, who appears in countless films as devoted old servant or dotty granny (the latter undermining the image of woman as stability conveyed by the former); and Julia Lajos, a kind of Hattie Jacques figure[2] who combines female silliness with a huge capacity for fun. Her cameo performance in Neville's romp *Domingo de carnaval/Carnival Sunday* (1946), in the scene where she and Conchita Montes get drunk together, is a rare example in 1940s cinema anywhere of two women having a great time on their own.

Folkloric musicals

Although created under the Republic, when its female stars were more popular with Spanish audiences than those of Hollywood, the folkloric musical genre reached its height, in terms of number of films produced, in the late 1940s and very early 1950s. The fact that the genre was a cinematic legacy of the Republic no doubt contributed to its popularity with lower-class audiences. Under the

Republic, the genre had been used to expose social injustice. But under early Francoism it was renegotiated to figure the incorporation of the lower classes into a unified nation, overcoming class conflict through the marriage of lower-class heroine to higher-class male. After 1939, the genre also acquired a racial slant, with its lower-class heroines, in those films set in Spain, exclusively cast as gypsies (not always the case in Republican folkloric musicals, where class is the dominant factor), and their higher-class suitors as rural landowners (under the Republic they were more often artists or professionals, figuring modernity). Thus, in early Francoist cinema, the cross-class romance represented the domestication of 'unsettled' elements of the population (through the landless gypsy heroine's marriage to the landowner), as well as the idealization of a pre-modern feudal rural order (the female singing star frequently performs to a natural backdrop).

Indeed, the mixing of races turns the romance plot into a miscegenation narrative, constructing a model of national unification on colonial lines – with the heroine figuring the 'natives' who need to be 'civilized'. A few early Francoist folkloric musicals were set in Spanish Morocco, the Philippines and Cuba: the last two, Antonio Román's *Los últimos de Filipinas/Last Stand in the Philippines* and José Luis Sáenz de Heredia's *Bambú*, were made in 1945 as swansongs to Spanish Nationalist dreams of imperial resurgence, dashed by Allied victory in the Second World War. Throughout the 1940s, a large proportion of folkloric musicals took the form of costume dramas set in the mid-nineteenth century, at a time when the modern nation first got under way: in these films, the heroine (again, always a gypsy) usually falls for an army officer, representing the central state.

In all these folkloric musicals, audience sympathies are with the lower-class heroine, ostensibly encouraging lower-class spectators to identify with her assimilation into a vertically ordered society. But the counter-productive result is that audiences identify with her class values, which indeed she requires her higher-class suitor to accept before she will agree to marriage. It is not difficult for lower-class spectators to read these films as an apology for popular cultural values – embodied by the female star through whose eyes events are always narrated. These films' melodramatic plots, concentrating on the lower-class heroine's sufferings (usually rewarded with love and riches, though some films end with her noble renunciation of the love of a man 'destined' to remain her superior), could slide into a masochistic glorification of female suffering. But even this could offer emotional compensation for women who, in the post-Civil War period, took the brunt of material deprivation, many of them forced into the role of breadwinner with their husbands killed, absent or unemployed as a result of the war or subsequent repression (it is estimated that, after the war, half a million families were left without a male breadwinner).

However, the female heroines of the folkloric musical are also carnivalesque trickster figures, who outsmart the socially superior male with their native wit and energy, presented as superior to his bookish education, stiffness and inability to voice emotion. The emotional and physical expressiveness of the female star's singing and dancing, while on the one hand representing a retrograde attack on education and intellectualism (so promoted by the Republic), at the same time makes her infinitely more human and likeable than her male higher-class suitor, to the extent that their final union is usually bathetic. Indeed, the heroine's final abandonment of folkloric for bourgeois dress constructs her incorporation into society via marriage as a loss of bodily freedom, undercutting the 'happy end'. In several films, the lower-class heroine exacts revenge on her higher-class suitor, forcing him into a union on her terms: as in *Filigrana* (Luis Marquina, 1948), where the star Conchita Piquer (who first made her name in silent film in the 1920s), having become a successful singer and millionaire's widow, buys up the mansion of her erstwhile aristocratic seducer and throws him out in the street, forcing him to come slinking back to her in humiliation. Even in those films where the heroine renounces her higher-class suitor's love, aware of her social inferiority, she does so in order to maintain her independence, recognizing that this will be lost if she marries a social superior: as in Orduña's *La Lola se va a los puertos/Lola Goes Back to the Sea* (1947, starring Juanita Reina), allowing its 1993 feminist remake by the woman director Josefina Molina.

The fact that these folkloric musicals are mostly about female protagonists who are professional performers also allows them to be read as a demonstration of the notion that gender identity is performed rather than inborn, undermining the essentialist gender rhetoric of early Francoism. The heroines of these films move freely between their two stock locations: wild natural environments (mountain crags, caves) and the *café cantante* or cabaret. Even in those musicals where the female protagonist 'spontaneously' bursts into song, it is because she is a 'born performer', suggesting that 'natural femininity' (particularly in the case of the lower classes who have to rely on masquerade and mimicry to manipulate their superiors) consists precisely in a capacity for performance. This concept is extended to male subaltern protagonists in Luis Lucía's camp romps of the late 1940s and early 1950s, sometimes tipping explicitly into self-reflexive pastiche, which pit the heroine against a lower-class male singing star (bandit or bullfighter) feminized by being endowed with the vocal expressiveness and physical litheness normally reserved for the female protagonist. This gender reversal is notable in *La duquesa de Benamejí* (1949) where Jorge Mistral as a singing bandit wins the love of Amparo Rivelles as duchess, the latter conveniently killed to avoid the unthinkable marriage of female aristocrat to male social inferior.

In the course of the 1950s, the folkloric genre was increasingly urbanized and masculinized with new male singing leads, whose triumph as performers within the story signals a new awareness of the need to offer conflict-free models of social mobility to an increasingly discontented male workforce. The result is that woman's presence in the plot becomes reduced to that of prize for the socially aspiring hero. It has now become thinkable for a lower-class male to marry the higher-class female, but the result is disempowerment for women.

War and missionary films

If the folkloric musical represented the recycling for new political ends of a pre-war genre, the return in the late 1940s to the war film meant a reworking of the explicitly fascist war movies of the immediate post-Civil War period, abandoned in 1942 as the regime started to disengage from its militarist rhetoric. These later war films are very different, stressing national reconciliation through the incorporation of the male-dominated war story into a woman-centred romance plot. The feminine values of romance are thus presented as the antidote to the divisive values of war, associated with masculinity. These later war films were, significantly, directed by former Republicans. The ex-communist Carlos Serrano de Osma's *Rostro al mar/Looking Out to Sea* (1951) – extraordinarily, given Francoist censorship – depicts the plight of a woman left to give birth alone as her communist husband escapes to France at the end of the war. The film ends with her rejecting her portly Nationalist suitor for the much sexier communist when he returns, having escaped from a German concentration camp. As in several other films of the period, the Nationalist suitor's love for the heroine is mediated via his love for her little daughter, on the one hand constructing him as the good father, but on the other implying that his patriarchal brand of masculinity is the flipside of an inability to express sexual attraction to women, requiring it to be displaced on to a safely asexual little girl. Like Serrano de Osma's other films, *Rostro al mar* draws on the visual conventions of *film noir*, but here contrasting 'safe' and 'dangerous' models of masculine, rather than feminine, sexuality: the association of the dangerous sexuality of the Republican hero with darkness, and of the safe sexuality of the Nationalist suitor with light, produces a negative 'flat' reading of the latter (in a reversal of Hollywood *noir* found in several 1940s Spanish films).

The other major war film pleading for national reconciliation is *¡El santuario no se rinde!/The Sanctuary Will Not Surrender!* (1949), by the former Republican Arturo Ruiz-Castillo, who in the early 1930s had worked with Lorca's travelling theatre. Here, extraordinarily for a war film, the story is narrated by a female voice-over, as the Nationalist heroine remembers her wartime love affair with a Republican who defected to the Nationalists out of love for her. The values of romance triumph over those of war, not only through their narration by a female voice-over but also because the male military hero lets private emotion dictate his public allegiance: significantly he was played by Alfredo Mayo, fascist warrior star of the war films of the early 1940s, including the notorious *Raza/Race* (José Luis Sáenz de Heredia, 1941) scripted under a pseudonym by Franco himself. The film's heroine is depicted as active and emancipated, smoking, wearing jodhpurs on first appearance, working as a nurse and organizing the refugees in the Sanctuary besieged by the Republicans, talking to men (including her lover) as an equal, and exhibiting no inhibitions about physical contact with the other sex. Her nostalgia for the war, despite its deprivations, implies a critical comment on the loss under Francoism of the mutual respect between political enemies, and between men and women, that is shown to have existed in wartime.

The late 1940s and early 1950s also produced a crop of missionary films, set in colonial locations and in Madrid's shantytowns, as the Church gained political ascendancy with the Falange's downgrading after 1945. During this period the Church, in addition to exercising control of censorship, also invested financially in the film industry. Although women were marginal to these missionary films (in one film set in Madrid's slums, all the slum children being proselytized are male), femininity was central: the priest represents the 'maternal' man able to express emotion, contrasting with the fascist emphasis on 'virile' body-control. The *mise-en-scène* constructs the jungle or shanty-town locations as a 'heart of darkness', which at the same time is the projection of a feminine unconscious which the priest heroes – in colonial scenarios dressed in white – 'master' not by repudiating but by internalizing it. The male missionary's incorporation of the maternal nurturing role constitutes an alternative Catholic misogyny to the fascist misogyny characteristic of many early 1940s films, for it makes women redundant to the narrative. The father–son relation (literal or figurative) is in all cases central, allowing the construction of a feminized, domestic model of masculinity while maintaining hierarchical structures. Indeed, these films' concentration on the repressed emotions involved in the father–son relationship allows them to be seen as a form of 'masculine' melodrama, feminizing the male while preserving male dominance. In the early 1950s the missionary genre was further feminized with a short-lived vogue for films about nuns (with Lucía again at his camp best), improbably starring the female singing stars of the folkloric musical, which at this time was conversely starting to be taken over by male stars: in both cases, the result was a return to stereotypical gender roles.

Historical epics

The complex generic transactions between war film and romance were also reworked from 1944 to 1951 in a succession of big-budget historical epics, which from 1948 were mostly produced by the pro-regime production company Cifesa (Evans, in Graham and Labanyi, 1995: 215–22) under the direction of Orduña. Orduña's speciality was the meticulous re-creation in his *mise-en-scènes* of late nineteenth-century historical paintings, themselves originally part of a nation formation project. In this way, Orduña's historical films recycle a ready-made repertoire of visual clichés, largely neo-classical in origin and grounded in a pre-existing gender symbolism. It is this genre which, more than any other, came to typify the period, being mercilessly parodied in several 1950s neo-realist oppositional films. These big-budget productions launched many of Cifesa's female stars, whose glamorous period costumes, together with the lavishly detailed sets, created a vision of the national past imagined via Hollywood as much as via any national pictorial tradition. Although these films are a branch of costume drama, they have a specificity that requires them to be discussed under a separate heading.

The political project in these historical epics was the insistence on a 'glorious' national past, not just as compensation for present penury, but as a way of reinforcing the need for national unification in the present. In all cases, the resistance to foreign power and the capacity to mediate internal conflict are represented by the female protagonist, either a queen or a Joan of Arc figure inspiring men to fight. On a surface level, the heroines act as mouthpieces for the regime's rhetoric of national reconciliation and hostility to foreign influence; in this sense, the image of woman that is mobilized is entirely retrograde. But for this symbolization to work, the female star has to be cast as a dominant player in the political sphere; and at this level, the heroines of these films provide some strikingly unconventional role models for Spanish women, contrasting markedly with their real-life lack of status under Francoist legislation.

In a few films, the female protagonist's public prominence is undercut by the melodramatic excess of the performance style, verging on hysteria and reinforcing the traditional notion that women, being bound up in the world of private emotion, are incapable of an impartial sense of justice. The casting of Amparo Rivelles, whose star image was based on her roles in nineteenth-century domestic melodramas, as the Catholic Queen Isabel in *Alba de América/American Dawn* (1951), a ghastly biopic of Columbus, and as the widowed leader of the sixteenth-century Comuneros' Revolt in *La leona de Castilla/The Lioness of Castile* (1951), is disastrous both for the political message and for the representation of gender. Her pouting tantrums and fragile beauty undermine her authority as historical leader, suggesting that women are unfit for political leadership. *Locura de amor* (1948) is the only one of these historical epics where the female star does not play a political leader: as Queen Joan the Mad, driven to insanity by her Habsburg husband's infidelities, Aurora Bautista's forceful performance engages the audience's sympathies for woman's traditional role as long-suffering victim in what, despite the lavish sets, is more of a domestic melodrama than an epic. Nevertheless, her refusal to relinquish the throne contrasts favourably with her foppish husband's (Fernando Rey) neglect of affairs of state for serial adultery. In both these films, the grandiose palace or castle sets dwarf or trap the heroines in a succession of stone corridors and vaulted interiors.

Running through these historical epics is the theme of women forced into political prominence because the men are effeminate, concerned only with private pleasure. Although the heroine's political activism is overtly a message to men that they must not shirk their patriotic duties, in practice this places woman in the position of role model for men, as an embodiment of 'true masculinity'. This would have provided female spectators with huge gratifications, at a time when, despite the legal refusal of any public role for women, they were in practice forced into the public sphere via the black market and in many cases prostitution, in order to secure the basic necessities for their families (Graham, in Graham and Labanyi, 1995: 182–95). These films could thus be read by female spectators as a recognition of the public competence demonstrated in their daily lives but denied by officialdom, and no doubt by the majority of men. Indeed, one suspects that identification with these competent historical heroines must have served for some women as a form of psychological revenge on men for their present disempowerment. Additionally, the fact that the national past was represented as allowing women a public role denied in the present is likely have reminded some female spectators that Franco's victory in the Civil War meant the end of the legal gains (suffrage, divorce) won by women under the Republic. And the fact that most of these films showed women as military leaders in war could not help but remind female audiences of the public role many of them had played in the Civil War, whether as soldiers (on the Republican side, up to May 1937) or nurses at the front, or as factory or relief workers behind the lines. Many of these films are set in the Middle Ages during periods of civil war, directly functioning as an allegory of the Civil War recently ended. But if the heroines in these films act as traditional mediators, they do so by taking the reins (figuratively and literally) at court and on the battlefield.

The active, leading roles played by these historical heroines – all but two of these epics have female protagonists – have no equivalent in the male-dominated Hollywood epic film. These female leads not only rally the men and fire the canon (as in Aurora Bautista's aggressive rendering of Agustina de Aragón) but also fight and win duels and jousting tournaments (*Doña María la Brava* [Luis Marquina, 1947]), and ride victoriously into battle (*Reina santa/Holy Queen* [Rafael Gil, 1946]; *Catalina de Inglaterra/Catherine of Aragon* [Arturo Ruiz-Castillo, 1951]). Even when shot in palace or castle interiors, the effect is not so much of entrapment as of authority, as they repeatedly mount the sweeping staircases ahead of the men and move freely between interior and exterior locations. On the one hand, this female activism is presented as a sacrifice of the private (love) which, it is implied, is woman's 'normal' sphere: Doña María la Brava, forced by widowhood into occupying a male role, refuses to surrender in love or war; Agustina de Aragón ditches her fiancé when she discovers that he has collaborated with the French and loses her new guerrilla-fighter lover in battle. But at the same time, these films show women, contrary to gender stereotypes, to be better than the men at putting the political before the personal: both Agustina's fiancé and her later lover (the film's male lead) state that their political decisions are motivated by love for her, while she repeatedly takes political decisions on patriotic grounds knowing they threaten the lives of the men she loves.

It is tempting to see these historical epics as a rare case of the war film as woman's movie. But their exaltation of female military prowess is undercut by a contrary discourse of male anxiety. Apart from the explicit message that these heroines are forced by male effeminacy or absence into a public role that is 'against nature', their political interventions, intended to heal discord, sometimes backfire (as in *Reina santa* and *La leona de Castilla*). The male anxiety is particularly marked in *Agustina de Aragón*, where the depiction of the heroine's wartime heroics is contained within a narrative frame depicting her in later life, restored to matronly modesty, going down on her knees before one of the nastiest patriarchal tyrants in Spanish history, King Ferdinand VII, to receive the medal that declares her a symbol of the nation. In this scene, her figure is eclipsed by the majestic palace scenario as she is definitively 'fixed' in the role of national monument. The schizophrenic split between wartime and peacetime views of Agustina was reproduced on the poster for the film where demure domesticity appears at the top and phallic aggression below. Male viewers may have found this peacetime 'castration' of her wartime prowess reassuring, but it was the image of her firing the phallic cannon that passed into the popular imaginary through its reproduction in children's storybooks and on postage stamps, calendars and brand labels.

Costume drama

The historical epic's insistence on affairs of state sets it aside from the more conventional costume dramas, in the form of family melodramas, that also proliferated throughout this period in Spain, as they did elsewhere. These domestic costume dramas, in keeping with their concentration on the private, tend to be set in the nineteenth century: that is, the period responsible for constructing and 'normalizing' the bourgeois notion of the nuclear family as a private 'feminine' zone cut off from the masculine world of public affairs. Although Freud was banned in 1940s Spain, this concentration on the nuclear family invites Oedipal readings, particularly given the patriarchal emphasis of Francoist society.[3] As in Hollywood family melodrama of the 1940s, such readings expose the repressive workings of the family structures which these films simultaneously uphold.

An exception which proves the rule is Lucía's *La princesa de los Ursinos* (1947), an engaging historical romp set in the eighteenth century before the consolidation of the bourgeois doctrine of separate spheres. The film's heroine

(Ana Mariscal) is a supremely intelligent, Machiavellian French political intriguer at the Spanish court, physically mobile throughout and shot largely in sunlit exteriors. Gender norms are, however, restored in the course of the narrative, as she succumbs to the charms of the Spanish hero, who seduces her with his singing, teaching her the value of love. Nevertheless, the fact that she is taught this by the male lead produces a gender reversal. His final death in battle, while restoring him to masculine valour, rescues her from the risk of domestication by marriage, to the female spectator's almost inevitable relief.

The popularity of these costume dramas no doubt lay in their message that the personal sphere is what matters, contradicting the historical epic's advocacy of the sacrifice of the personal to the political. This may be an escapist message, but under a totalitarian regime, which attempts to subsume the personal in the political, the construction of a private space can be a minor act of resistance. In general, the exaltation of private feminine values in late 1940s costume drama seems to have served male interests, placing women 'where they belonged'. But the emphasis on women's entrapment, and often hysteria, could be read against the grain by female spectators as an exposure of the mechanisms by which female desire is repressed: the visual encoding of such repression in the heavy, dark, affluent interiors and costumes specifically marks it as the product of bourgeois domesticity. Even though most of these costume dramas end conventionally with wayward female behaviour punished (with death, or by the death of a son, always leading to last-minute repentance/redemption), the intense close-ups produce empathy with her in transgression and in punishment. For female audiences struggling with the harsh material realities of 'the years of hunger', this glorification of suffering, while not conducive to rebellion, must at least have fuelled a sense of the injustice of women's lot.

The most subversive costume dramas of the period were adaptations of nineteenth-century classics by novelists known to have been conservatives: a ploy for getting scripts past the censors. The flagrantly immoral *Pequeñeces*, with Aurora Bautista as compulsive adulteress, was based on a novel by a Jesuit: her volte-face repentance at the end is not able to counter the relish with which, throughout the film, she disposes of men at her whim. The film which most incurred the wrath of the Church was *La fe/Faith* (Rafael Gil, 1947), based on a novel by the frequently filmed Alarcón, which, although awarded top prize by the Falangist-controlled Actors' Union, was banned by the Catholic Primate of Spain for its depiction of a hysterical girl's (Amparo Rivelles) attempt to seduce a priest. At the end she is crushed to death by a train, dying in the priest's arms as he grants her absolution.

The sense that women have to die to procure men's salvation runs through almost all these costume dramas. In *Mariona Rebull* (José Luis Sáenz de Heredia, 1947), based on a contemporary novel, the wife's death with her lover in an anarchist terrorist attack – in a box at the opera, signalling the enclosure and artificiality of her bourgeois role – teaches the capitalist hero that, in sacrificing his life to the work ethic, he has neglected the private sphere and destroyed his own happiness. Another costume drama that teaches its hero the value of the family is Serrano de Osma's *La sirena negra/The Black Siren* (1947), based on a novel by the nineteenth-century feminist Emilia Pardo Bazán. The film eliminates any feminist potential in its representation of its decadent hero's obsession with a dying woman: an obsession from which he is finally liberated by the accidental death of her young daughter whom he has taken in, freeing him to propose to his long-suffering bourgeois fiancée in a final outdoors scene, contrasting with the previous dark interiors that project not so much female entrapment as a male fear of the feminine. Again, this fear is mediated by the displacement of his attentions on to her little girl; in the original novel, the child was a boy, which creates very different gender implications.

The most disturbing of these costume dramas is Lucía's *De mujer a mujer/Woman to Woman* (1950), brilliantly acted by Rivelles and Mariscal as, respectively, the wife who, unable to have more children, goes mad after her husband inadvertently causes her little girl's death and her nurse, who gets involved with the husband during his wife's internment in a mental asylum. (For Mariscal's performance in this film, see Chapter 11 by Núria Triana-Toribio.) The husband becomes irrelevant in this drama about the strong emotional bonds that exist between two women, overcoming their enmity and the threat to the family unit. When the wife regains her sanity, the film ends with the mistress self-sacrificially gassing herself (particularly shocking, since press mention of suicide was banned at the time) and giving her illegitimate baby girl by the husband to the wife. The conventional narrative of a woman's self-sacrifice to redeem the hero is here twisted to become her self-sacrifice for the sake of another woman, as the title implies. Although the wife is thereby safely restored to the role of bourgeois mother, the film effectively writes the husband – left speechless for much of the film – out of the script, reduced to the instrumental role of fathering daughters by both women.

Film noir

The most complex representation of gender occurs in melodramas made under the influence of *film noir*. German Expressionism, which provided the visual basis of Hollywood *noir*, had been imported into Spain directly via the various Central European Jewish cameramen who had fled Nazism for Republican Spain in the mid-1930s, before the better-known exodus to Hollywood, and who continued working under Franco; the most outstanding of these was Heinrich Gaertner, naturalized as Enrique Guerner, who became 1940s Spain's major art director. Hollywood *film noir* was known in Spain from at least

1944, two years before its discovery in France. The investigative structure, paranoia and gloom of *film noir* are evident in many 1940s Spanish films. Such features lent themselves well to the climate of hardship and political persecution, and Expressionist distorted angles and chiaroscuro were used effectively by several directors to undermine, in otherwise apolitical films, the moral certainties and Manichean rhetoric characteristic of Nationalist ideology.

The impossibility of exposing police corruption under dictatorship led to the transposition of *noir* techniques on to the family melodrama, 'privatizing' the investigative structure and thus intensifying the inquiry into the enigma of woman that is central to the genre. As in Hollywood melodrama, the investigation of femininity is the pretext for an exploration of anxieties about masculinity. We have already seen how the need for men to negotiate the transition from wartime to peacetime models of masculinity was crucial but especially problematic in late 1940s Spain, given male political disempowerment. Spanish male difficulties in accepting a domestic role perhaps account for significant departures from the Hollywood *noir* association of light with the nurturing woman and dark with the dangerous sexual temptress. One also senses a desire by directors to use the visual codes of *film noir* to undermine the surface narrative privileging of domesticity over sexual attraction, required by the censors. If in Serrano de Osma's *Rostro al mar* light is, through the Nationalist suitor, associated with an unappealing male domesticity based on a denial of sexuality, in other films it is domesticity that is depicted via typically *noir* dark *mise-en-scènes*.

In *Abel Sánchez* (1946), by Serrano de Osma, who specialized in and theorized the use of *noir* techniques (Labanyi, 1995), the investigation of the paranoid male protagonist's murder of his debonair alter ego, who unlike himself is successful with women, dramatizes anxieties about masculinity in a particularly graphic way, for the two men are clearly projections of a split male psyche. Here, the seductress (whom his alter ego steals from him and marries) is blonde, while the redemptive woman (whom the protagonist marries out of desperation) is dark. This produces a complex scenario whereby the light associated with the seductress signifies a negative superficiality (the film cites Wilde's adage that woman is a sphinx without an enigma), while the redemptive family home is, through the use of shadows and distorted camera angles, constructed as a *noir* hell. The light/dark contrast thus figures two differently negative images of femininity.

In Neville's *La vida en un hilo/Life in the Balance* (1945), *noir* visual conventions are also used to construct a negative picture of bourgeois marriage, in this case unambiguously (albeit unconventionally, given early Francoist moral repressiveness) contrasted with sexual freedom and pleasure. Conchita Montes, on the train back to Madrid after the funeral of her boorish provincial husband, meets up with a comic figure, Julia Lajos, and between them they construct a fictional past in which, instead of accepting her future husband's offer to escort her home, she goes off with another man, a bohemian artist, who offers her risk but also fun. As the women step off the train in Madrid, Montes finds herself next to the hero of the fantasy life she never had, and this time grasps the opportunity. While the film supposes that women find satisfaction via a man, its rejection of bourgeois values for pleasure is striking, even if female pleasure is defined in conventional terms: the bohemian hero's climactic gesture is to sell his El Greco to buy Montes a mink coat. Reversing the usual gender scenario of *film noir*, in which the hero's anxieties about his masculinity are expressed through his investigation of negative and positive models of femininity, we have here two women's investigation of negative and positive models of masculinity, in which they explore, not anxieties about their own sexuality, but female pleasure. The result is a reworking of *film noir* for the purposes of comedy rather than tragedy.

In other films by Neville, a cosmopolitan aristocrat who had worked in Hollywood in the early 1930s, *film noir* conventions are used simply as a light-hearted, if visually brilliant, exercise in pastiche. However, in his 1947 adaptation of Carmen Laforet's contemporary novel *Nada/Nothingness*, set in post-Civil War Barcelona, he applies *noir* narrative conventions and visual techniques to the investigation of the family with devastating consequences. Here the investigator is a female student Andrea (played again by the cool, lucid Conchita Montes), who uncovers the nightmarish relationships beneath the respectable surface of the bourgeois home shared by her grandmother, aunt and two uncles Román and Juan, plus Juan's wife Gloria. The film is a melodramatic exploration of perverse forms of masculinity: the major example, Román, who throws himself down a typically *noir* stairwell at the end, is played in an inspired piece of casting by Fosco Giachetti, known for his earlier heroic military roles in Italian fascist cinema. The atmosphere of hysteria throughout the sequences in the family home is reinforced by brilliant use of shadows, suggesting split personalities, and of low-angle shots that make the ceiling weigh down on the characters' heads. This repressive bourgeois domesticity is contrasted visually with the light, outdoor scenes at the university, representing for Andrea the possibility of a freer lifestyle. If the male characters are alternately hysterical and brutal, the film stresses women's strength through the contrary figures of the lower-class Gloria, who secretly supports the family through her gambling activities in Barcelona's red–light district, and Andrea's wealthy student friend Ena, who uses her seductive charms to get her revenge on Román for having seduced her mother, in an act of mother–daughter solidarity. Both the dark Gloria and the blonde Ena are split good/evil female personalities, but in the sense that evil masks good. Given this vindication of the ostensibly wicked woman, it is not surprising that the film had 30 minutes cut by the censor.

Conclusion

I have called this essay 'Feminizing the nation' because of the crucial role played by late-1940s Spanish cinema in helping men make the transition from the military values of wartime and of early 1940s fascist propaganda to a 'privatized' domestic model of masculinity appropriate to peacetime under dictatorial rule. My hypothesis has been that this was achieved not only through the representation of masculinity but also by inviting male spectators to identify with the female images onscreen. No doubt, given the fetishization of the female stars, this involved an ambivalent disavowal (denial/affirmation) of the feminine on the part of male spectators. In the case of female spectators, identification with these female stars must have produced a different kind of split response, in that – if my hypothesis is correct – they were identifying with images of their own sex whose function was largely to work out behavioural norms for men: whether by embodying the masculine role (as in the majority of historical epics), by offering a feminized model of national reconciliation (as in the folkloric musical and war film) or by investigating masculinity (as in *film noir*). (The missionary film is a curious anomaly, since it allowed female spectators cross-gender identifications through its male heroes' embodiment of femininity.) Only in costume drama does one feel that the representation of women was aimed at women. It seems no coincidence that this genre is, overall, the most conservative in gender terms. The genres (historical epic, folkloric musical, war film, *film noir*) which allow female spectators to identify with a heroine whose function is to work out a problem of masculinity allow more leeway for non-standard identifications. And the fact that, contrary to Hollywood, Spanish *film noir* tends to involve the investigation by a woman of contrasting models of masculinity allows it to explore the 'enigma' of femininity, not as perceived by the male hero, but as dramatized by the investigator heroine's own desires and fears. While Spanish cinema of the late 1940s certainly did function as a tool for consolidating the Francoist New State (and has been unthinkingly dismissed by critics for that reason), the strong roles given to so many of its heroines seem likely to have allowed its predominantly female audiences scope for negotiating their own private gender identities in ways that could escape the constraints of both dominant ideology and material reality.

Notes

1. I have not translated film titles when they consist only of the female protagonist's name.
2. I owe this observation to my research student Steven Marsh and his work on 1940s and 1950s Spanish film comedy.
3. Marsha Kinder (1993: 136–275), discussing Spanish film of later decades, insists on the political implications of its Oedipal structures.

Filmography

These films can be viewed at the Filmoteca Española, Madrid, whose staff I wish to thank for their continued help over the years.

Abel Sánchez (Carlos Serrano de Osma, 1946)
Agustina de Aragón (Juan de Orduña, 1950)
Alba de América (Juan de Orduña, 1951)
Bambú (José Luis Sáenz de Heredia, 1946)
Catalina de Inglaterra (Arturo Ruiz-Castillo, 1946)
De mujer a mujer (Luis Lucía, 1950)
Domingo de carnaval (Edgar Neville, 1946)
Doña María La Brava (Luis Marquina, 1947)
La duquesa de Benamejí (Luis Lucía, 1949)
La fe (Rafael Gil, 1947)
Filigrana (Luis Marquina, 1948)
La leona de Castilla (Juan de Orduña, 1951)
Locura de amor (Juan de Orduña, 1945)
La Lola se va a los puertos (Juan de Orduña, 1947)
Mariona Rebull (José Luis Sáenz de Heredia, 1947)
Nada (Edgar Neville, 1947)
Pequeñeces (Juan de Orduña, 1950)
La princesa de los Ursinos (Luis Lucía, 1947)
Raza (José Luis Sáenz de Heredia, 1941)
Reina santa (Rafael Gil, 1946)
Rostro al mar (Carlos Serrano de Osma, 1951)
¡El Santuario no se rinde! (Arturo Ruiz-Castillo, 1949)
La sirena negra (Carlos Serrano de Osma, 1947)
Los últimos de Filipinas (Antonio Román, 1945)
La vida en un hilo (Edgar Neville, 1945)

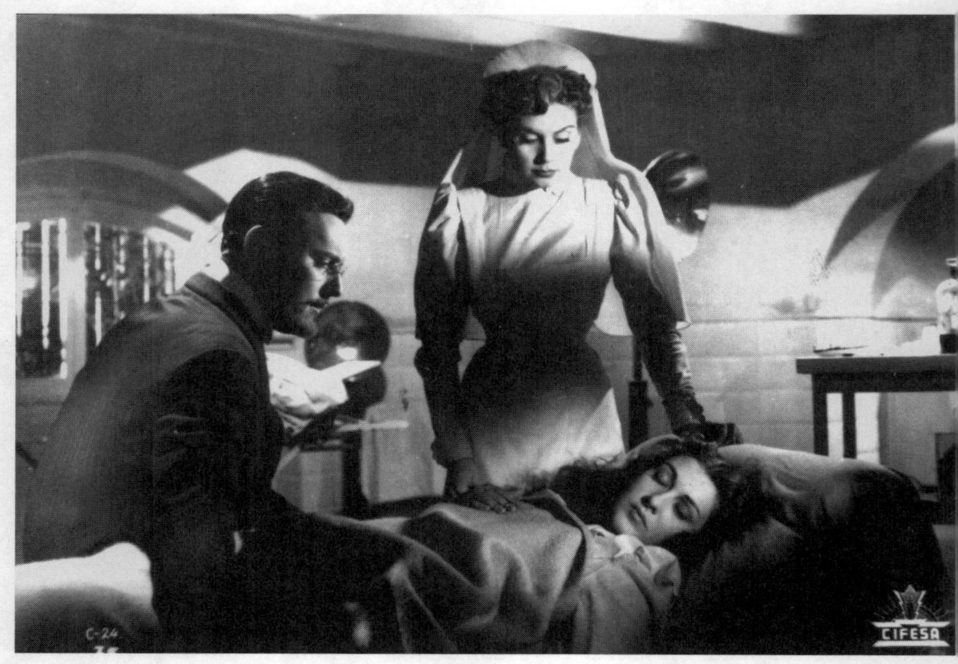

Ana Mariscal (nurse), Manolo Fàbreges and Amparo Rivelles in *De mujer a mujer/From Woman to Woman* (1950, Spain, Luis Lucia)
Source: CIFESA
Reproduced courtesy of Mr Javier

CHAPTER ELEVEN

Ana Mariscal: Franco's Disavowed Star

NÚRIA TRIANA-TORIBIO

The remembrance of a country's past is always problematic. If this country has a past under a right-wing repressive regime it is inevitable that many legacies are also repressed. Ana Mariscal represents a repressed memory of the Spanish cinema from 1945 to 1951. Although the work of cultural forgetting has almost erased her, she just keeps coming back. The reasons for both the repression and the return are many, as will become apparent in studying her status as an icon of this period. Principally, she is the female star most closely associated with Franco and the years immediately after the Civil War, since she starred in one of Spain's most controversial films: the notorious *Raza/Race* (1941). The film was scripted by Franco under the pseudonym Javier de Andrade and was officially commissioned to be directed by José Luis Sáenz de Heredia, whose ideological credentials were impeccable, since not only was he a loyal *franquista* but also the first cousin of the founder of Spain's fascist party, Falange, José Antonio Primo de Rivera. Although *Raza* falls outside the period I am looking at, it is such a crucial stepping-stone in Mariscal's career that it is necessary at least to sketch out its plot. The story involves the Churruca family, made up of a devoted mother and heroic naval-officer father and four offspring: a daughter and three sons. The two 'good' sons become a priest (Jaime) and a military man (Franco's alter ego and protagonist José), and the 'bad' one, Pedro, pursues a career in politics. After suffering the death of their father in the humiliating defeat at the hands of the US Navy in 1898, the Churrucas then watch as their beloved Spain plummets into further disaster with the coming of the Republic, which put power into the hands of left-wing politicians such as Pedro. This prompts José and other prominent military leaders to stage a coup and rescue Spain from communism. The bulk of the film portrays the Civil War from the point of view of Franco and includes memorable sequences such as those in which José is captured and shot by the *rojos* (Reds) and refuses to be blindfolded on facing death. Immediately afterwards his body is claimed by his girlfriend Marisol and we discover that José is (miraculously) still alive and ready to carry on the fight.

Franco chose a matinee idol, Alfredo Mayo, to play his alter ego; and to play José's fiancée Marisol he chose Ana Mariscal (*Diario 16*, Madrid, 7 January 1981). Apparently Franco had been very impressed by her in *El último húsar/The Last Hussar* (Luis Marquina, 1940), a costume drama in an operetta-style setting in which she made her debut. The consequences for Mariscal were as beneficial at the time as they were detrimental once conditions changed. At the time, this role 'made her face fashionable and opened endless doors for her in the [acting] profession' (Berthier, 1996: 75). However, her involvement in *Raza* would mean that at the time of her death in 1995, as Francoism was seen as a regrettable epoch, newspapers published respectful, but mostly distancing, obituaries. In them it was said that she embodied the ideal woman, an example of femininity of the historical epics and the costume melodrama of the 1940s and early 1950s, but the obituaries also emphasized that these were the modes of 'other times' with headlines such as: 'From Other Times' (*Diario 16*, Madrid, 28 March 1995: 31) or 'Goodbye to Franco's Cinema Muse' (*El Mundo*, Madrid, 28 March 1995: 85).

We can start our survey of Mariscal with a look at her background. In 1923, Ana Mariscal (Ana María Rodríguez) was born in Madrid into a middle-class family with some connections with the stage. Her republican father, a furniture merchant, was for a short period the owner of a small theatre, the Salón Arniches. However, the business did not prosper and he closed it down. Her elder brother, Luis, would soon become an actor. In 1935, as a member of a theatre group with her brother, she met Federico García Lorca, who admired her voice and offered her a role in *Así pasen cinco años/Five Years from Now*, but rehearsals ended with the outbreak of the Civil War. After the war, while she was applying to study mathematics at university, Mariscal was chosen for a role in *El último húsar*, which was being shot in the Cinecittà studios in Rome. In 1941, she attained fame throughout Spain in *Raza* and her career took off. From that moment on she combined acting in cinema and theatre. From 1945 she embarked on several ventures: she founded her own theatre company, playing the role of Don Juan Tenorio in the eponymous play by José Zorrilla, and causing a scandal in the world of letters in Spain for 'daring' to play a male part (and the seducer-male, at that). In the same year she was awarded the first of several awards for acting by the Spanish Association of Film Writers. From then on, she featured in productions of plays by Tennessee Williams, Thornton Wilder and Jean Cocteau among others. In the 1940s she appeared in more than twenty films of the commercial cinema, but her most memorable film roles in *La princesa de los Ursinos/The Princess of the Ursinos* (Luis Lucía, 1947) or *Un hombre va por el camino/A Man in the Road* (Manuel Mur Oti, 1949), belong to the later 1940s. She started the following decade as the co-protagonist in *De mujer a mujer/From Woman to Woman* (Luis Lucía, 1950) with another star of the same period: Amparo Rivelles, for which she received yet more acting awards. She went on performing with great success for screen and stage alike, and in 1952 co-founded with her future husband, the cameraman Valentín Javier, a film company, Bosco Films, which would produce her own as well as other directors' films. Her first film as director, *Segundo López, aventurero urbano/Segundo López, Urban Adventurer*, was made that year. She toured Spain giving public lectures and taught film acting at the Spanish Official Film School and the University of Valladolid. She directed her last film in 1968. Her acting and lecturing career, on the other hand, carried on until the late 1980s.

Some of the achievements in her curriculum vitae, especially after 1945, are particularly outstanding for a woman in any period of Spain's history, let alone the years that concern us here. However, it is often the case that as critics are trying to write the history of Spanish cinema they often deny the existence of Ana Mariscal. This denial points to the embarrassment we feel as a nation about Francoism (especially before an opposition developed), which translates itself into the neglect of a period of history that most current film scholars consider did not produce worthwhile work, 'since cinema had been farmed out among the victors in the war. The Church took charge of its [cinema] morality; the state unions got its administration, racketeers and the rich the chance to make a buck' (Hopewell, 1986: 37). This is a common reaction to popular cinema made under an oppressive regime. In the 1970s German critics and film directors were making the same type of comments about their 'abused cinema' (popular cinema) under Nazism, and it was the falsehood and manipulation of reality in Italian cinema of the fascist period that sparked the neo-realist movement in the 1940s. A similar type of abhorrence motivates the general emphasis on either a wider recovery of the popular cinema of pre-Franco or the concentration on oppositional or proto-oppositional cinema that pervades the historiographical work being undertaken in Spanish academic and popular film criticism (Torres, 1989; Gubern *et al.*, 1995).

The 'disappearance of Mariscal' is symptomatic of this phenomenon. Certainly, from the evidence of the historiographical studies of Spanish cinema, it seems that of all her roles (she appeared in fifty-seven films) the only one that stuck in the critics' minds is that of Marisol in *Raza*. If we add to her relation with this 'film *maldito*' the fact that she never tried to disassociate herself from it or from any other film she made in the 1940s and 1950s, it becomes clearer why many film critics would prefer not to delve further. Obviously the fear of being seen to 'celebrate' a *franquista* prevents Spanish critics from seeking the whole picture of Mariscal's career. Another factor contributing to her neglect is that most of the new historiographers do not give enough space or weight in their agenda to the influence of gender in the film industry. Even works of recovery which are intended to make up for past under-researched areas neglect gender when they set out their programmes for a new historiography (Gubern *et al.*, 1995: 20).

Mariscal's times

The role that Mariscal has in explaining the reconstruction of a national identity after the Civil War belies this critical neglect. It is undeniable that she poses special problems, that she seems unrecuperable for democracy or for the regime for reasons that we will see later. This is why I feel she is emblematic of the post-Civil War years. As a star, more than any other of her period, she embodied the contradictory demands that the regime was making on Spanish women of the time, and represented the fragmented images of femininity that were circulating then: ideas either imposed from above or those that reflected popular culture.

In order to study such reconstruction through Mariscal I shall concentrate on her career and public persona after 1945; although her work actually spans the two different periods of post-Civil War cinema outlined by Jo Labanyi in Chapter 10, I will focus on Mariscal's roles during the late 1940s. It was argued there how, after the defeat of fascism in the Second World War, and needing American and Western European allies, Franco's regime had to bring to the fore the religious component of their 'rebellion' and stress Catholic family values, partly restoring women and qualities seen as feminine to a place of centrality, even if the *Machista* attitudes of an earlier period were to impinge in these representations. Matching this evolution, as Labanyi argues, popular cinema underwent a valorization of the feminine from 1944.

To these circumstances we have to add the regime's intention to make women the transmitters of Christian and Francoist values: lest the next generation should forget Spain's imperial and Catholic past. It meant that a whole infrastucture of cultural dissemination was put into place to address and educate them to give the right message. This machinery made women conscious of their importance within families and society (Graham, 1995), a role held by many women, on both sides, whose husbands were dead or in prison and who had become heads of their families. A cinema to match this situation became the 'eternalizer' (Evans, 1995: 215) of such myths: genres like the historical epic (fully-fledged melodramas disguised under a historical cloak), costume melodrama and folkloric film made use of strong female protagonists.

This is particularly interesting, because certainly in the public arena strong women were suppressed, as feminine qualities were encouraged (especially passivity) and women lost their voice and were treated as legal minors. School texts were written in which most historical women originally characterized by masculine qualities (strength, independence, determination, rebelliousness) were stripped of them and given feminine ones. Policies to remove women from the workplace and consign them to the home, where their main duty would be to 'provide babies for the patria' (Graham, 1995: 187), were soon enforced.

Women were being pushed in different directions by the regime, which created an atmosphere that was highly receptive to melodrama. As Elsaesser (1987) and others have observed, melodrama arises precisely in changing times, times of conflict between the private and the public. Moreover, it becomes an effective way to 'legitimize' a new system in the aftermath of a 'revolution', pointing out the 'good' and the 'evil' as well as the 'location, expression and imposition of basic ethical and psychic truths' in a language that everyone can understand (Brooks, 1985: 15).

The protagonists of these mid-1940s melodramas were haughty and proud female characters, dramatizing both repression and the return of the repressed, their strong features perfect for such tasks. Amparo Rivelles, Concha Piquer, Aurora Bautista and Ana Mariscal (among others) were the pillars of the star system in Spain. Obviously, they were valued in their own country for similar reasons as in other cultures: star systems provide role models and vicarious pleasure in identification and imitation. Most of these women were praised particularly for their melodramatic qualities: excess, externalization of mental states, embodiment of ethical forces – playing 'mad women' was their *forte* and the attribute for which most are remembered. Besides this 'excess' inherent in the melodramatic roles, few other references appear in current historiography and very little work has been done to individualize them and the types of femininity they were made to embody. The stars of the period have been diminished by the critics as being more 'archetypes' than 'individuals' who later had to fight their screen images to succeed (Galán, 1979: 43), rather than as repositories of dreams of agency and glamour, especially to women viewers.[1] Mariscal presented, within melodramatic acting, a distinctive style: her looks and star presence conjured up Greer Garson (Galán, 1979: 42) rather than, for example, Jennifer Jones, with whom Evans (1995: 220) associates Bautista. In contrast to these 'strong' females (Bautista, Piquer and Rivelles), Mariscal 'contributed a face both hard and soft' (Galán, 1979: 42): as opposed to the more pronounced darker eyebrows and hair that framed the faces of Rivelles and Bautista, Mariscal often was given lighter hair colouring (*Vidas cruzadas/Lives That Cross Paths* (Luis Marquina, 1942); *De mujer a mujer; Un hombre va por el camino*).

Mariscal's voice

In order to assess how Mariscal's star persona embodies (albeit ambiguously) the social roles of women during this period, it is crucial to acknowledge the 'composite structure' of the category of star. Christine Gledhill (1991b: 214) points out that several components must be addressed for achieving an understanding of how the star works:

> The components I am concerned with here include the 'real person', the 'characters' or 'roles' played by the star in films and the star's persona,

> which exists independently of the real person or film character, combining elements of each in a public 'presence'.

To take these in turn, the 'real person', the real Mariscal, was a traditionalist and staunch Catholic who could live contentedly under Francoism and who believed throughout her life that feminism is wrong, 'because feminism is trying to put women on a level with men and I think that is stupid' (*Revista Citybank*, February 1986, p. 29). Yet some characteristics of the 'real person' would confront head on the role of passivity and silence ascribed to women. In the culture of a regime that wanted to render women silent, two salient features of Mariscal were her voice and her eloquence. The number of references to her voice in press reviews, interviews and articles (both during Francoism and after) is staggering; it even features in the headlines of some. In 1983, her active career in cinema over, people would still turn round in the street when they recognized her voice (*Interviú*, 15 February 1983, p. 18).

However, this voice is also a site of struggle. Her clear and discrete pronunciation, her 'elevated' diction, represent sheer authority for many. As critic Galán (1979: 42) would put it: 'Ana Mariscal, popular in the 1940s for representing pompously a pompous cinema, for being the spokeswoman of so many empty phrases, so much history tampered with, so much regime intervention, so much concealment of truth'. Moreover, we know that Franco himself liked her voice enough to want it for Marisol: the model fiancée. And yet it was this same voice that had captivated García Lorca enough to induce him to offer her a role, as we saw earlier. The quality of her voice also raises interesting contradictions. It presents both 'traditionally' masculine *and* feminine characteristics, such as 'strength and emotion': 'A deep voice with a slight emotional quiver' (*Interviú*, 15 February 1983, p. 18). During her appearance on stage as Don Juan in November 1945 it became clear that some men were deeply threatened by this feminine *and* masculine quality. For instance, a reputed intellectual of the regime, Eugenio D'Ors (1945), preferred to believe that Mariscal was 'masculinizing' her voice for her role: 'Our actress's voice, on wanting to adopt some of the tones of the opposite sex becomes, in fact, so unpleasant that it keeps the listener constantly on edge.' She took offence and answered back, protesting that this was precisely the quality of her voice. The critic published an apology in the main Madrid newspaper *Arriba* (Eugenio D'Ors, 1945).

Another feature of her voice, which made it attractive for potential ideological use by a regime intent on defending the unity of Spain, was the lack of any regional accent. Many 1940s actors (even those who had not been born in Castile) developed a type of Spanish received pronunciation, recognizable as 'castellano de Castilla' but without the inflection of any of the Castilian provinces in particular, nor of the other national groups and regions. Hers was one of these pronunciations: she pointed out in an interview that, although she was born in Madrid, it had always been difficult for people to trace her origins. (Servera, 1991) However, as she declared, much of the rhythm of her declamation was due to a long stay on the island of Mallorca during the Civil War: Mallorcans speak Spanish as a second language and this affects the speed and carefulness of their pronunciation. This presence of Catalan identity clashes with the idea of a unified national identity that the regime was trying to achieve through speech: in effect, she speaks Spanish like someone whose first language is not Spanish.

This element of the 'real life' (in Gledhill's sense of the word) impinges on the 'star', as it affects how we read her in her roles. As we saw above, a process of selective memory led contemporary critics to recall Mariscal as Marisol. As a consequence she tends to be wrongly remembered as acting out the type of femininity preferred by the victors in the Civil War (the Catholic Church, the high-ranking military men, the landowning class and the conservative bourgeoisie); a femininity in which the voices of women were less important than their beauty and presence. Remembering her as one of these silent upper-class mannequin beauties has the added effect of giving pre-eminence to a rather mute and unrepresentative image of Mariscal. Because most critics have not seen beyond *Raza* this is the image that persists of her. Actually, in the films she made from 1945 to 1951, the mere presence of the very vocal Mariscal worked against the image of the 'silent beauty' that was desired from women.

Directors seem to have sought both aspects in the roles in which she was cast: the silent beauty and the eloquent, self-assertive woman. It is true that in many of her roles, at the beginning of the diegesis she is constructed as untouchable, dignified and silent: the perfect upper-class heroine. As the aristocratic socialite of *Vidas cruzadas* she is talked about admiringly by other characters before she actually appears, and when she does it is in a scene which combines long-medium and close-up shots of her laughing on a boat, conjuring up a figurehead rather than a real person. Yet, at the end of the film when she is willing to 'give her virtue away' to save her brother, her highly articulate justification is far from incongruous with her character. She was cast again as an upper-class heroine (albeit a bourgeoise rather than an aristocrat) in *El gran galeoto/The Great Lie* (Rafael Gil, 1951), a film about an ex-actress, married to a much older man, who, suspected of committing adultery with her husband's godson, is slandered by their acquaintances. Her initial appearance is as the actress who, sensing the absence of an admirer, forgets her lines; but the same pattern arises: virtue, which she symbolizes, will proclaim itself triumphant in the end through a spoken defence. This eloquence is not demanded by the genre. While aspiring to total articulation of the moral positionings of the characters, melodrama usually 'in climactic moments and in extreme situations, has recourse to non-verbal means of expressing its meanings' (Brooks, 1985: 56). Mariscal, in contrast, enunciates rather than gestures her virtue.

Another representation of femininity upon which Mariscal's voice would confer a very singular quality was that of the *vampiresa* (*femme fatale*). She was given so many of these roles at a very young age that she complained in an early fan booklet about her life:

> The director explained to me that I was going to play the second female character, a kind of vamp or femme fatale. I thought it excessive for my age. But it was a tempting offer . . . . My second film was [*La florista de la reina*]/*The Queen's Florist*. Here I also was given another little role as a vamp. This was no longer funny. Was I going to become a professional vamp? (Mariscal, 1943: 6, 11 [my translation])

The characters she played in these productions can be related to that of the silent-era vamp or its legatee in the 1940s American film noir, the *femme fatale*. *La princesa de los Ursinos* was a very popular costume drama loosely inspired by events in eighteenth-century Spanish political history. Mariscal plays Ana Maria de la Tremoille, princess of the Ursines. Sent to Spain to remind Philip V (grandson of Louis XIV of France) of his French origin and the allegiance owed to Versailles, the princess is depicted as a beautiful and intelligent French woman, 'so beautiful' – one character comments – 'that she deserves to be Spanish'. On her arrival in Spain the king organizes a ball in her honour. In the ball scene she is seen wearing the most elaborate dress: a velvet gown decorated with pearls. During this scene it becomes apparent that she is also constructed as treacherous and capable of ensnaring men. She displays a grace, beauty and elegance hitherto unknown in the Spanish royal palace – as another character comments – but to such characters' words we must also add visual reinforcement: she carries herself with arrogance and talks confidently to men, even asking one of them to accompany her to the garden. When later in her rooms the ambassador tries to woo her, exclaiming that 'nights like this are made for love', she responds rather garrulously, 'and for you to take a walk, my lord' (which, in Spanish as in English, can also mean 'to get lost').

Due to the specific characteristics of Spanish society and culture during the mid-1940s and early 1950s, some adjustments have to be made in order to fully understand these roles. We must read a lot into very priggishly played scenes like those described above. Church control on censorship ensured that the *femme fatale* would not make a full transition to the Spanish screens: the sexual allure fundamental to these characters in Hollywood cinema was eschewed in the earlier Spanish versions. What we get instead is a much tamer 'threat' or a female character whose mildly transgressive behaviour poses a disproportionate challenge. The Spanish *femme fatale* is not as fatal, but this does not mean that the outcome of her actions is not fatal to her. *Femmes fatales*, vamps and 'the other women' are representations of femininity that have their 'looked-at-ness' emphasized in their construction, not their speech. But again Mariscal plays eloquent women beyond the pale rather than speechless ones.

One of her most memorable roles is as 'the other woman' in *De mujer* (1950), where she retains this 'distant dignity' in combination with a position outside the domestic and matrimonial setting. The film tells the story of Isabel (Amparo Rivelles) and Luis (Eduardo Fajardo), a young, bourgeois, happily married couple with a small daughter, Isabelita. Luis buys the little girl a swing for her birthday, and while playing on it, the little girl falls and dies. Isabel is so affected that she loses her senses and is confined to an institution. As doctors say they cannot do much for her, a nurse, Emilia (Mariscal), takes care personally of Isabel and, because of her daily contact with the patient, becomes the bearer of news and consolation to Luis. She and Luis become lovers. Unable to cope with the guilt, Emilia leaves her job and is kept in a flat by her lover. From this relationship a daughter is born. Against all predictions, Isabel recovers her sanity and Luis is warned by the doctors that any sudden shock would plunge her into deeper depression, which could this time be incurable. Therefore, normality is restored as Luis abandons Emilia for his wife. Isabel, having found out about Emilia and the child, decides to visit them and confront Emilia with her anger. But the woman Isabel finds is remorseful and confirms that she has given Luis up for her, the lawful wife. After this meeting, Emilia opens the gas valves in her room. She is found close to death by the priest and the doctor, and her agony lasts long enough to allow her to entrust the baby to the couple and to be absolved of such a terrible sin.

Here, Mariscal embodies first a type of femininity of which both the State and the Church approved: caring and self-sacrificing; and later, displaying 'reprehensible' features and even entering terrain the depiction of which neither institution desired (giving up her virtue to co-habit with a married man, bearing him a child and, later, committing suicide). In both the dialogue and the *mise-en-scène* elements within *De mujer*, Mariscal is characterized by tensions and contradiction. The *mise-en-scène* helps by contrasting her presence in her white nurse's uniform (which includes a little halo-like head-dress) with the dark clothes worn by the doctors and Luis in the earlier scenes. Another scene is set in the reception room at the clinic which is decorated in dark oak furniture and sombre carpets. In this room, a devastated Luis, dressed in a dark suit listens as the terrible situation of his wife is explained to him by two men. Both interlocutors, a young and an old doctor, are dressed in dark colours. Emilia appears for the first time, entering the room silently and demurely dressed in blinding white. The contrast is so sharp it seems naively deliberate. Significantly, once her betrayal of Isabel has taken place and she becomes Luis's lover, she will be seen next in a severe black dress which, this time, is set against Isabel and her doctor's white gowns. Either way, the contrast singles her out as different and foreshadows a divergent character development, but more importantly she is seen to be both 'black and white'. The dialogue contributes decisively by making her utter comments that suggest she is capable of seeing things differently from other characters. For instance, during the nightshift as she watches over the sleeping patients, she observes how peaceful they look, and how, on witnessing such a scene, one could not be condemned for questioning whether these women have been put there simply for their relatives' convenience.

The diegesis places Emilia on the margins and when convenient disposes of her altogether. She is the person who should not be named or talked about: 'that woman', as the priest repeatedly says. Emilia suffers a similar fate to those 'real women' who did not conform to the images of femininity that the regime or the Church approved of, and who also were not named. However, when given a voice she is the character who takes control of the story, relating it to Isabel in the scene in which the two women meet and from which her active role is uncovered: 'It was I who asked him . . . who demanded.' Furthermore, her voice is heard over the final images, as, literally, she has the last word.

Richard Dyer (1979: 18) points out that 'although stars and films are commodities, their only "value" (i.e. what people *use* them *for*) resides in what meanings and affects they have. Stars/films sell meanings and affects.' Roles such as these must have had enormous value for Mariscal's female audiences, most of whom were put in the impossible situation of having to act as transmitters of the values of the Church and the State and yet remain silent, and most of whom, despite experiencing poverty along with their families, were discouraged from taking up jobs. Ultimately, Ana Mariscal exemplified in 'real life' and roles what it was like to have the ambition to take on more than the regime was willing to permit, and the ability to take a more extensive role and more control over one's life. As we saw, she surpassed the role that women were ascribed, by not only, as an actor, being a working woman from the 1940s onwards but also by taking on more 'jobs' as early as 1952: director, scriptwriter and producer.

Raza blinds us to the 'other' emblematic roles that Mariscal played during the 1945–51 period. If we neglect the study of figures such as Mariscal, we perpetuate the view that the 'strong' Civil War and pre-war women in the public sphere were totally obliterated and replaced by 'passive' women in the 1940s and 1950s, and that the 1970s generation of 'strong' women reclaiming access to that public sphere came from nothing. This is simply not the case, just as the characters of Mariscal demonstrate: between 1945 and 1951, some women found ways of making their voices heard and remembered even from their 'silent' roles.

Acknowledgements

Thanks to Valentín Javier, P. Evans, J. Higgins and, above all, to P. Buse.

Note

1. This gap is related first to the above-mentioned outright dismissal of Francoist texts, but is accentuated by the resistance that the study of melodrama still inspires in Spanish film criticism (unless it is in the form of contemporary appropriations), and also by the fact that star studies is a category which is only now starting to be researched.

Filmography

De mujer a mujer (Luis Lucía, 1950)
El gran galeoto (Rafael Gil, 1951)
Un hombre va por el camino (Manuel Mur Oti, 1949)
La princesa de los Ursinos (Luis Lucía, 1947)
Raza (José Luis Sáenz de Heredia, 1941)
El último húsar (Luis Marquina, 1940)

References

Addison, P. (1985) *Now the War Is Over: A Social History of Britain 1945–51*. London: British Broadcasting Corporation and Jonathan Cape.

Aldgate, T. (1990) *The Italian Neo-realist Cinema*. Units 8–9, Arts A, *Liberation and Reconstruction: Politics, Culture and Society in France and Italy.* Milton Keynes: The Open University

Améry, J. (1995) *Köpfe and Karrieren*. Zurich: Thomas Verlag.

Aprà, A. (1978) 'Rossellini oltre il neorealismo', in Micciche (1978), pp. 288–99.

Aprà, A. and Pistagnesi, P. (1978) 'The unknown Italian cinema', hand-out for the retrospective *Before Neo-Realism: Italian Cinema 1929–1944*, 5 October–21 December, Museum of Modern Art Department of Film, New York.

Aspinall, S. (1983) 'Woman, realism and reality in British films 1943–53', in J. Curran and V. Porter (eds), *British Cinema History*. London: Weidenfeld and Nicolson, pp. 272–93.

Aspinall, S. and Murphy, R. (eds) (1983) *Gainsborough Melodrama*. London: British Film Institute.

Audé, F. (1987) 'Micheline Presle: profession actrice', in *Films de femmes 1987*. Paris: AFIFF, pp. 74–6.

Bard, C. (ed.) (1999) *Histoire culturelle et politique de l'antiféminisme en France au XXe siècle*. Paris: Fayard.

Barr, C. (1977) *Ealing Studios*. London: Cameron and Tayleur.

Bazin, A. (1975) '*Boule de suif* de Christian-Jaque', in *Le Cinéma de l'occupation et de la résistance*. Paris: Union générale d'éditions, pp. 145–6.

Berthier, N. (1996) 'Ana Mariscal, directora de cine bajo el franquismo', in E. Larraz (ed.), 'Filmar en femenino', *Hispanística,* Vol. 20, no. 14, Centre d'Études et Recherches Hispaniques du XXe Siècle. Bourgogne: Université de Bourgogne, 73–86.

Bessen, U. (1989) 'Eine Frau fällt aus der Rolle. Hildegard Knef im deutschen Nachkriegsfilm', in *Trümmer und Träume – Nachkriegszeit und Fünfziger Jahre auf Zelluloid*. Bochum: Studien Verlag Dr N. Brockmeyer, pp. 203–26.

Beveridge, W. (1942) *Social Insurance and Allied Services*. London: HMSO.

Bondanella, P. (1991) *Italian Cinema from Neorealism to the Present*. New York: Continuum Publishing.

Bondanella, P. (1993) *The Films of Roberto Rossellini*. Cambridge: Cambridge University Press.

Brivati, B. and Jones, H. (eds) (1993) *What Difference Did the War Make?* Leicester : Leicester University Press.

Brooks, P. (1985) *The Melodramatic Imagination: Balzac, Henry James, Melodrama and the Mode of Excess*. New York: Columbia University Press.

Brossat, A. (1992) *Les Tondues, un carnaval moche*. Paris: Manya.

Brunette, P. (1987) *Roberto Rossellini*. New York: New York University Press.

Brunette, P. (1996) *Roberto Rossellini*. Berkeley and Los Angeles: University of California Press.

Bruno, G. and Nadotti, M. (eds) (1988) *Off Screen*. London: Routledge.

Bullivant, K. and Rice, J. (1995) 'Reconstruction and integration. The culture of West German stabilization', in Burns (1995), pp. 209–56.

Burch, N. and Sellier, G. (1996) *La Drôle de guerre des sexes du cinéma français 1930–1956*. Paris: Nathan.

Burns, R. (ed.) (1995) *German Cultural Studies*. Oxford: Oxford University Press.

Calder, A. (1969) *The People's War*. London: Jonathan Cape.

Cannella, M. (1966) 'Ideology and aesthetic hypotheses in the criticism of neo-realism', translated in *Screen,* Vol. 14, No. 4, Winter 1973/4, 5–57.

Carter, E. (1997a) 'Culture, history and national identity in the two Germanies since 1945', in Fulbrook (1997), pp. 432–53.

Carter, E. (1997b) *How German Is She? Postwar West German Reconstruction and the Consuming Woman*. Ann Arbor: University of Michigan Press.

Chaperon, S. (1999a) *'Haro sur le Deuxième Sexe'*, in Bard (1999), pp. 269–84.

Chaperon, S. (1999b) *Les Années Beauvoir*, Paris: Belin.

Colarizi, S. (1996) *Storia D'Italia* Vol. 4, *La seconda guerra mondiale e la Repubblica*. Milan: TEA.

Cook, P. (1996) *Fashioning the Nation: Costume and Identity in British Cinema*. London: British Film Institute.

Cook, P. (ed.) (1997) *Gainsborough Pictures*. London: Cassell.

Crew, D. F. (ed.) (1994) *Nazism and German Society 1933–1945*. London and New York: Routledge.

Crisp, C. (1996) 'What did wartime audiences want to watch?' Paper given at Rutgers University, New Jersey, October.

Deleuze, G. (1989), trans. 1991 Cinema 2, *The Time Image*. Minneapolis: University of Minnesota Press.

Denman, M. C. (1997) 'Visualizing the nation: madonnas and mourning mothers in postwar Germany', in Herminghouse and Mueller (1997), pp. 189–201.

Dietrich, D. R. and Shabad, P. C. (eds) (1989) *The Problem of Loss and Mourning: Psychoanalytical Perspectives*. Madison, CT: International Universities Press.

Doniol-Valcroze, J. (1954) 'Déshabillage d'une petite bourgeoise sentimentale', *Cahiers du Cinéma*, Vol. 6, No. 31 (January), 2–14.

Duchen, C. (1994) *Women's Rights and Women's Lives in France 1944–1968*. London: Routledge.

Ducout, F. (1978) *Séductrices du cinéma français 1936–1956*. Paris: Henri Veyrier.

Durgnat, R. (1970) *A Mirror for England: British Movies from Austerity to Affluence*. London: Faber.

Dyer, R. (1979) *Stars*. London: British Film Institute.

Dyer, R. (1980) 'Resistance through charisma: Rita Hayworth and *Gilda*', in Kaplan (1980), pp. 44–6.

Dyer, R. (1986) *Heavenly Bodies: Film Stars and Society*. London: British Film Institute/Macmillan.

Dyer, R. (1988) 'White', *Screen*, Vol. 29, No. 4, 44–66.

Dyer, R. and Vincendeau, G. (eds) (1992) *Popular European Cinema*. London: Routledge.

Elsaesser, T. (1987) 'Tales of sound and fury: observations on the family melodrama', in Gledhill (1987), pp. 43–69.

Evans, P. W. (1995) 'Cifesa: cinema and authoritarian aesthetics', in Graham and Labanyi (1995), pp. 215–22.

Faldini, F. and Fofi, G. (1979) *L'avventurosa storia del cinema italiano raccontata dai suoi protagonisti 1935–1959*. Milan: Feltrinelli Editore.

Fehrenbach, H. (1995a) *Cinema in Democratizing Germany: Reconstructing National Identity after Hitler*. Chapel Hill: University of North Carolina Press.

Fehrenbach, H. (1995b) '"Die Sünderin" or who killed the German man?: early postwar cinema and the betrayal of Fatherland' and 'The fight for the "Christian West": film control and the reconstruction of civil society', in Fehrenbach (1995a), pp. 92–117; 188–47.

Ferrero, A. (1978) 'La coscienza di se: ideologie e verità del neorealismo', in Micciche (1978), pp. 229–49.

Fishman, S. (1991) *We Will Wait: Wives of French Prisoners of War 1940–45*. London and New Haven: Yale University Press.

Forbes, J. (1997) 'Winning hearts and minds: the American cinema in France 1945–1949', *French Cultural Studies*, Vol. 8, Part 1, No. 23, 29–40.

Forgacs, D. (1984) 'National popular: genealogy of a concept', in *Formations of Nation and People*. London: Routledge and Kegan Paul, pp. 83–98.

Forgacs, D. (1990) 'The Italian Communist Party and culture', in Z. G. Baranski and R. Lumley (eds), *Culture and Conflict in Post-War Italy*. Basingstoke: Macmillan/University of Reading.

Freud, S. (1915) 'Repression', in *Standard Edition of the Complete Psychological Works of Sigmund Freud*, Vol. 24. London: Hogarth.

Fulbrook, M. (ed.) (1997) *German History since 1800*. London and New York: Edward Arnold.

Galán, D. (1979) 'Ana Mariscal, una mujer va por el camino', *Triunfo*, Vol. 25, August, 42.

Ginsborg, P. (1990) *A History of Contemporary Italy: Society and Politics, 1943–1988*. London: Penguin.

Gledhill, C. (ed.) (1987) *Home Is Where the Heart Is: Studies in Melodrama and the Woman's Film*. London: British Film Institute.

Gledhill, C. (ed.) (1991a) *Stardom: Industry of Desire*. London: Routledge.

Gledhill, C. (1991b) 'Signs of melodrama', in Gledhill (1991a), pp. 207–29.

Gledhill, C. (1996) '"An abundance of understatement": documentary, melodrama and romance', in Gledhill and Swanson (1996a), pp. 213–29.

Gledhill, C. and Swanson, G. (eds) (1996a) *Nationalising Femininity: Culture, Sexuality and British Cinema in the Second World War*. Manchester: Manchester University Press.

Gledhill, C. and Swanson, G. (1996b) 'Introduction', in Gledhill and Swanson (1996a), pp. 1–12.

Graham, H. (1995) 'Gender and the state: women in the 1940s', in Graham and Labanyi (1995), pp. 182–95.

Graham, H. and Labanyi, J. (1995) *Spanish Cultural Studies: An Introduction*. Oxford: Oxford University Press.

Gregor, U. (ed.) (1966) *Wie sie filmen*. Gütersloh: Mohn.

Grignaffini, G. (1988) 'Female identity and Italian cinema of the 1950s', in Bruno and Nadotti (1988), pp. 111–23.

Grignaffini, G. (1989) 'Lo stato dell'Unione', in A. Farassino (ed.), *Neorealismo: Cinema italiano 1945–1949*. Turin: EDT Edizioni.

Grossmann, A. (1991) 'Feminist debates about women and National Socialism', *Gender and History*, Vol. 3, No. 3, 350–8.

Grossmann, A. (1995) 'A question of silence: the rape of German women by occupation soldiers', *October*, Vol. 72, Spring, 43–63.

Gubern, R., Monterde, J. E., Pérez Perucha, J., Rimbau, E. and Torreiro, C. (eds) (1995) *Historia del cine español*. Madrid: Cátedra.

Gundle, S. (1996) 'Fame, fashion, and style: the Italian star system', in D. Forgacs and R. Lumley (eds), *Italian Cultural Studies: An Introduction*. Oxford: Oxford University Press, pp. 309–26.

Hansen, M. (1985) 'Dossier on *Heimat*', *New German Critique*, Vol. 36, Fall, 3–25.

Harper, S. (1994) *Picturing the Past: The Rise and Fall of the British Costume Film*. London: British Film Institute.

Harper, S. (1995) '*Madonna of the Seven Moons*: film in context', in *History Today*, Vol. 45.

Harper, S. (1996) 'From *Holiday Camp* to high camp: women in British feature films, 1945–1951', in A. Higson (ed.), *Dissolving Views: Key Writings on British Cinema*. London: Cassell, pp. 94–116.

Haste, C. (1992) *Rules of Desire: Sex in Britain, World War I to the Present*. London: Chatto and Windus.

Heinzelmeier, A. (1980) 'Hildegard Knef das Trümmer Mädchen', in A. Heinzelmeier, B. Schulz and K. Witte, *Die Unsterblichen des Kinos: Glanz und Mythos der Stars der 40er und 50er Jahre*. Frankfurt: Fischer Taschenbuch Verlag, pp. 113–19.

Hennessy, P. (1993) *Never Again Britain 1945–1951*. London: Vintage.

Herminghouse, P. and Mueller, M. (eds) (1997) *Gender and Germanness: Cultural Productions of Nation*. Providence, RI, and Oxford: Berghahn.

Hewitt, N. (ed.) (1989) *The Culture of Reconstruction: European Literature, Thought and Film, 1945–50*. Basingstoke and London: Macmillan.

Hickethier, K. and Zielinski, S. (eds) (1991) *Medien/Kultur*. Berlin: Volker Spiess.

Higson, A. (1994) *Waving the Flag: Constructing a National Cinema in Britain*. Oxford: Oxford University Press.

Hill, J. (1986) *Sex, Class and Realism: British Cinema 1956–63*. London: British Film Institute.

Hochkofler, M. (1984) *Anna Magnani*. Rome: Gremese Editori.

Hoffmann, H. and Schobert, W. (eds) (1989) *Zwischen Gestern und Morgen: Westdeutscher Nachkriegsfilm 1946–1962*. Frankfurt am Main: Deutsches Filmmuseum.

Hopewell, J. (1986) *Out of the Past: Spanish Cinema after Franco*. London: British Film Institute.

Jary, M. (1993) *Traumfabriken: Made in Germany – Die Geschichte des deutschen Nachkriegsfilms 1945–60*. Berlin: Edition Q.

Jaspers, K. (1946) *Die Schuldfrage*. Heidelberg: Verlag Lambert Schneider.

Kaplan, E. A. (ed.) (1980) *Women in Film Noir*. London: British Film Institute.

Kinder, M. (1993) *Blood Cinema: The Reconstruction of National Identity in Spain*. Berkeley: University of California Press.

Kirkham, P. (1995) 'Dress, dance, dreams and desire: fashion and fantasy in *Dance Hall*', *Journal of Design History*, Vol. 8, No. 3, 195–214.

Kirkham, P. (1996) 'Fashioning the feminine: dress appearance and femininity in wartime Britain', in Gledhill and Swanson (1996a), pp. 152–76.

Knef, H. (1970) *Der geschenkte Gaul*. Köln: Lingen Verlag (Special Edition).

Knef, H. (1989) 'Ein Rückblick aus der Gegenwart: Hildegard Knef über ihre frühen Nachkriegsfilme', in Bessen (1989), pp. 229–33.

Knight, D. and Still, J. (1995) *Women and Representation*. Nottingham: Women Teaching French – Occasional Papers 3, pp. 75–91.

Kolinsky, E. (1989) *Women in West Germany: Life, Work and Politics*. Oxford, New York and Munich: Berg.

Kolker, R. (1983) *The Altering Eye*. Oxford: Oxford University Press.

Kreimeier, K. (1989) 'Die Ökonomie der Gefühle. Aspekte des westdeutschen Nachkriegsfilms', in Hoffmann and Schobert (1989), pp. 8–32.

Kristeva, J. (1981) 'Women's time', translated by Alice Jardine and Harry Blake, *Signs: Journal of Women in Culture and Society,* Vol. 7, No. 1, 13–35.

Kuhn, A. (ed.) (1984) *Frauen in der deutschen Nachkriegszeit. Band 1: Frauenarbeit 1945–1949*. Düsseldorf: Schwann.

Kuhn, A. (1995) *Family Secrets: Acts of Memory and Imagination*. London: Verso.

Labanyi, J. (1995) 'Masculinity and the family in crisis: reading Unamuno through *film noir* (Serrano de Osma's 1946 adaptation of *Abel Sánchez*)', *Romance Studies,* Vol. 26, 7–21.

Laing, S. (1986) *Representations of Working-Class Life 1957–64*. London: Macmillan.

Landy, M. (1997) 'Melodrama and femininity in World War Two', in Murphy (1997), pp. 79–89.

Lauwick, H. (1950) '*Manèges*', *Noir et Blanc*, No. 259, 15 February.

Levy, B.-H. (1981) *L'idéologie française*. Paris: Grasset.

Lewis, J. (1992) *Women in Britain since 1945*. London: Blackwell.

Liehm, M. (1984) *Passion and Defiance: Film in Italy from 1942 to the Present*. Berkeley: University of California Press.

Lovell, A. (1997) 'The British cinema: the known cinema?', in Murphy (1997), pp. 235–43.

Marcus, M. (1986) *Italian Film in the Light of Neorealism*. Princeton, NJ: Princeton University Press.

Mariscal, A. (1943) *Mi vida*. Madrid: Ediciones Astros.

Martini, A. and Melani, M. (1978) 'De Santis', in Micciche (1978), pp. 307–17.

Mash, M. (1996) 'Stepping out or out of step? Austerity, affluence and femininity in two post-war films', in Gledhill and Swanson (1996a), pp. 257–63.

Meldini, P. (1989) 'L'abito e l'arredamento', in A. Farassino (ed.), *Neorealismo: Cinema italiano 1945–1949*. Turin: EDT Edizioni.

Micciche, L. (ed.) (1978) *Il neorealismo cinematografico italiano*. Venice: Marsilio Editori.

Mitchell, T. (1989) 'The construction and reception of Anna Magnani in Italy and the English-speaking world, 1945–1988', *Film Criticism,* Vol. 36, No. 1, 2–21.

Mitscherlich, A. and Mitscherlich, M. (1967) *Die Unfähigkeit zu Trauern*. Munich: Piper. In English translation (1975) as *The Inability to Mourn: Principles of Collective Behavior*, translated by B. C. Placzek. New York: Grove Press.

Mitscherlich-Nielsen, M. (1989) 'The inability to mourn today', in Dietrich and Shabad (1989), pp. 405–26.

Modleski, T. (1987) 'Time and desire in the woman's film', in Gledhill (1987), pp. 326–38.

Moix, T. (1993) *Suspiros de España: la copla y el cine de nuestro recuerdo.* Barcelona: Plaza and Janés.

Monterde, J. E. (1995) 'El cine de la autarquía (1939–1950)', in R. Gubern *et al.*, pp. 181–238.

Mulvey, L. (1989) *Visual and Other Pleasures*. London: Macmillan.

Murphy, R. (1992) *Realism and Tinsel: Cinema and Society in Britain 1939–49.* London: British Film Institute.

Murphy, R. (ed.) (1997) *The British Cinema Book*. London: British Film Institute.

Murray, B. (1991) 'Postwar discourse about the National Socialist past: are the murderers still among us?', in Hickethier and Zielinski (1991), pp. 255–74.

Myrdal, A. and Klein, V. (1956) *Women's Two Roles: Home and Work*. London: Routledge and Kegan Paul.

Nelson, G. K. (1969) *Spiritualism and Society*. London: Routledge and Kegan Paul.

Nowell-Smith, G. (1990) 'On history and the cinema', *Screen,* Vol. 31, No. 2, 160–71.

Nowell-Smith, G. (1996) 'After the war', in *The Oxford History of World Cinema*. Oxford: Oxford University Press, pp. 436–43.

Nowell-Smith, G. (1998) 'Introduction', in G. Nowell-Smith and S. Ricci (eds), *Hollywood and Europe: Economics, Culture, National Identity 1945–95.* London: British Film Institute, pp. 1–16.

Perkins, T. (1996) 'Two weddings and two funerals: the problem of the post-war woman', in Gledhill and Swanson (1996a), pp. 264–81.

Presle, M. (1994) *L'Arrière-mémoire: conversation avec Serge Toubiana*. Paris: Flammarion.

Priestley, J. B. (1948) 'Foreword', *The Neglected Child and His Family: Sub-Committee of the Women's Group on Public Welfare*. London: Geoffrey Cumberlege, Oxford University Press.

Prinzler, H. H. (1993) 'Chronik, 1895–1993', in W. Jacobsen, A. Kaes and H. H. Prinzler (eds), *Geschichte des deutschen Films*. Stuttgart: Verlag J. B. Metzler, pp. 519–58.

Quaglietti, L. (1980) *Storia economica politica del cinema italiano 1945–1980.* Rome: Editori Riuniti, Chapter 2.

Régent, R. (1946) *Cinéma de France sous l'occupation*. Paris: Éditions d'Aujourd'hui.

Rossellini, R. (1973) 'A discussion of neo-realism', Rossellini interviewed by Mario Verdone, reproduced in *Screen,* Vol. 14, No. 4, 69–78.

Rousso, R. (1987) *Le Syndrome de Vichy*. Paris: Seuil.

Rowbotham, S. (1977) *Hidden from History: 300 Years of Women's Oppression and the Fight against It*. London: Pluto Press.

Rowbotham, S. (1997) *A Century of Women: The History of Women in Britain and the United States*. London: Viking.

Sanders-Brahms, H. (1985) 'Hilde', in Bessen (1989), pp. 226–9.

Santner, E. (1990) *Stranded Objects: Mourning, Memory and Film in Postwar Germany*. Ithaca, NY, and London: Cornell University Press.

Scott, J. W. (1988) *Gender and the Politics of History*. New York: Columbia University Press.

Seeßlen, G. (1991) 'Die andere Frau: Hildegard Knef', *Epd Film*, No. 8, January.

Servera, I. (1991) 'Ana Mariscal', *Perlas y Cuevas*, No. 787, July, p. l.

Sheridan, D. (ed.) (1991) *Wartime Women: An Anthology of Women's Writing, Mass-Observation 1937–1945*. London: Mandarin Paperbacks.

Silverman, K. (1992) *Male Subjectivity at the Margins*. New York and London: Routledge.

Smart, C. (1996) 'Good wives and moral lives: marriage and divorce 1937–51', in Gledhill and Swanson (1996a), pp. 91–107.

Smith, H. L. (1996) *Britain in the Second World War: A Social History*. Manchester: Manchester University Press.

Sorlin, P. (1989) 'Tradition and social change in the French and Italian cinemas of the reconstruction', in Hewitt (1989), pp. 88–102.

Sorlin, P. (1991) *European Cinemas, European Societies 1939–1990*. London: Routledge.

Spinazzola, V. (1974) *Cinema e pubblico: lo spettacolo filmico in Italia 1945–1965*. Milan: Bompiani.

Street, S. (1997) *British National Cinema*. London: Routledge.

Summerfield, P. (1993) 'Approaches to women and social change in the Second World War', in B. Britavi and H. Jones (eds), *What Difference Did the War Make?* Leicester: Leicester University Press.

Summerfield, P. (1996) '"The girl that makes the thing that drills the hole that holds the spring . . .": discourses of women and work in the Second World War', in Gledhill and Swanson (1996a), pp. 35–52.

Tarr, C. (1995) 'Wilful women in Occupation Cinema', in D. Knight and J. Still (1995), pp. 75–91.

Thumim, J. (1992) *Celluloid Sisters*. London: Macmillan.

Thumim, J. (1996) 'The female audience: mobile women and married ladies', in Gledhill and Swanson (1996a), pp. 238–56.

Timmins, N. (1996) *The Five Giants: A Biography of the Welfare State*. London: Fontana Press.

Torres, A. M. (ed.) (1989) *Cine español (1896–1988)*. Madrid: Ministerio de Cultura.

Turner, B. and Rennell, T. (1995) *When Daddy Came Home: How Family Life Changed Forever in 1945*. London: Hutchinson.

Vincendeau, G. (ed.) (1995a) *Encyclopedia of European Cinema*. London: Cassell.

Vincendeau, G. (1995b) 'France', in Vincendeau (ed.) (1995a), pp. 155–8.

Vincendeau, G. (1998) 'Issues in European cinema', in J. Hill and P. Church Gibson (eds), *The Oxford Guide to Film Studies*. Oxford: Oxford University Press, pp. 440–8.

von Moltke, J. and Wulf, H.-J. (1997) 'Trümmer-Diva: Hildegard Knef', in T. Koebner (ed.), *Idole des deutschen Films*. Munich: edition text + kritik, pp. 304–16.

von Saldern, A. (1994) 'Victims or perpetrators? Controversies about the role of women in the Nazi state', in Crew (1994), pp. 141–65.

Wagstaff, C. (1989) 'The place of neorealism in Italian cinema from 1945 to 1954', in Hewitt (1989), pp. 67–87.

Webster, D. (1988) *Looka Yonder! The Imaginary America of Populist Culture*. London: Routledge.

Wilson, E. (1980) *Only Halfway to Paradise: Women in Postwar Britain 1945–1968*. London: Tavistock.

Further Reading

Adams Sitney, P. (1995) *Vital Crises in Italian Cinema*. Austin: University of Texas Press.

Aprà, A. and Ponzi, M. (1965) 'An interview with Roberto Rossellini', *Screen*, Vol. 14, No. 4, Winter, 112–26.

Bazin A. (1983) *Le Cinéma français de la Libération à la nouvelle vague*. Paris: Cahiers du Cinéma.

Bertin-Maghit, J-P. (1989) *Le Cinéma sous l'Occupation*. Paris: Olivier Orban.

Billard, P. (1995) *L'Age classique du cinéma français*. Paris: Flammarion.

Cavell, S. (1979) *The World Viewed*. London: Harvard University Press.

Clio, Histoire, Femmes et Sociétés, no. 1 (1995), 'Résistances et Libérations (France 1940–1945)'. Toulouse: Presses Universitaires du Mirail, pp. 187–94.

Costello, J. (1985) *Love, Sex and War: Changing Values 1939–45*. London: Collins.

Dalle Vacche, A. (1992) *The Body in the Mirror*. Princeton, NJ: Princeton University Press.

Daquin, L. (1980) *On ne tait pas ses silences*. Paris: Les Éditeurs Français Réunis.

Duchen, C. (1994) *Women's Rights and Women's Lives in France 1944–1968*. London: Routledge.

Flock, J. (1995) *Jacqueline Audry et l'inscription de la féminité dans le cinéma français de l'après-guerre*, Mémoire de maîtrise (MA thesis), Université de Paris III.

Hay, J. (1987) *Popular Film Culture in Fascist Italy*. Bloomington: Indiana University Press.

Hopewell, J. (1986) *Out of the Past: Spanish Cinema after Franco*. London: British Film Institute.

Koonz, C. (1988) *Mothers in the Fatherland: Women, the Family and Nazi Politics*. London: Methuen.

Labanyi, J. (1997) 'Race, gender and disavowal in Spanish cinema of the early Franco period: the missionary film and the folkloric musical', *Screen*, Vol. 38, No. 3, 215–31.

Lewin, C. (1986) *Le Retour des prisonniers de guerre*. Paris: Publications de la Sorbonne.

Lockwood, M. (1955) *Lucky Star*. London: Odhams.

Marcus, M. (1986) *Italian Film in the Light of Neorealism*. Princeton, NJ: Princeton University Press.

Moi, T. (1995) *Simone de Beauvoir: conflits d'une intellectuelle*. Paris: Diderot Éditeur.

Sellier, G. (1993) 'Le précédent des accords Blum-Byrnes', in *Le Monde diplomatique*, November, Paris, p. 15.

Sellier, G. (1994) 'L'après-guerre: contradictions d'un "auteur"', *La Pensée*, No. 300, Autumn, 19–32.

Siclier, J. (1957) *La Femme dans le cinéma français*. Paris: Éditions du Cerf.

Truffaut, F. (1987) *Le Plaisir des yeux*. Paris: Éditions des Cahiers du Cinéma.

Weeks, J. (1989) *Sex, Politics and Society*. London: Longman.

Index

Note: Page numbers for illustrations are shown in *italics*.